ALIAS AGNES

ALIAS AGNES

The NOTORIOUS TALE of A GILDED AGE SPY

ELIZABETH A. DeWOLFE

UNIVERSITY PRESS OF KENTUCKY

Published by The University Press of Kentucky

Scholarly publisher for the Commonwealth, serving Bellarmine University,
Berea College, Centre College of Kentucky, Eastern Kentucky University,
The Filson Historical Society, Georgetown College, Kentucky Historical Society,
Kentucky State University, Morehead State University, Murray State University,
Northern Kentucky University, Spalding University, Transylvania University,
University of Kentucky, University of Louisville, University of Pikeville, and
Western Kentucky University.

Editorial and Sales Offices: The University Press of Kentucky
663 South Limestone Street, Lexington, Kentucky 40508-4008
www.kentuckypress.com

Cataloging-in-Publication data available from the Library of Congress

ISBN 978-1-9859-0223-7 (hardcover)
ISBN 978-1-9859-0224-4 (paperback)
ISBN 978-1-9859-0226-8 (pdf)
ISBN 978-1-9859-0225-1 (epub)

Member of the Association
of University Presses

To Tony

CONTENTS

Contents

Illustrations follow page 130

AUTHOR'S NOTE

In my rendition of this notorious tale, scenes between Jane Tucker and Madeleine Pollard are drawn principally from *The Real Madeleine Pollard* and Jane's letters. Likewise, trial scenes from *Pollard v. Breckinridge* have been synthesized from newspapers and *The Celebrated Trial* (1894). Dialogue or other text appearing in quotation marks is drawn directly from a historical source such as a newspaper, book, letters, or other written material.

Where verbatim accounts were lacking, I adapted the available sources to re-create passages of indirect dialogue, without quotation marks, to capture the import of the moment. For ease in reading, I have silently corrected punctuation and obvious typographical or spelling errors. I have created no thoughts, words, or actions that do not have a referent or precedent in the historical record of this event or time period.

PROLOGUE

January 1894

In her parents' chilly dining room, Jane Tucker huddled under warm quilts, weary, spent, and unhappy. It was January in coastal Maine, and the train ride from Boston had seemed interminable, with bumps and sways rattling her aching teeth and burning backside. Her mother, Mollie, hovered, offering a Listerine rinse for Jane's sore mouth, sarsaparilla for her weakened blood, and Pond's Extract for the bleeding piles. "Pretty much all she has earned for the two last years has gone up in doctors' bills," Mollie wrote to Jane's sister, Mame, explaining her plans to give Jane a long rest under a mother's care while also anticipating that Jane, at twenty-eight, would forgo her city life and resume a quiet, domestic existence at home.[1]

Jane had enjoyed a dizzying array of opportunities in Boston as one of the young, single, white women who flooded cities seeking jobs during the tremendous economic growth of the Gilded Age. For young working women like Jane, cash wages offered a new, albeit limited, independence to spend their money and their time, unchaperoned, as they wished.

Jane thrived in this novel world of urban work. Yet she had to hustle to make ends meet. She settled in Boston in late 1887, determined to achieve financial security. She put her needlework skills—gained in study at a Maryland academy—to good use, working for a seamstress and then in a department store's custom dress department, embroidering fancy buttons for the clothing of the fashionable and well-heeled. She gave needlework lessons, took in private sewing, and spent evenings making yards of braid for milliners' elaborate hats. She took bit parts on Boston's stages to earn a few more dollars. She painted flowers on fine porcelain that would find its way to the parlors of the elite. But low wages made the lives of working women like Jane unsustainable. To minimize expenses, she raced all over Boston looking for good deals on rented rooms, food, and clothing, so busy that she signed letters to her family "Hastily, Jane."[2]

The new times demanded new proficiencies; savvy and strategic, Jane learned typing and stenography, tools that paved her way to office work—to one job instead of several and with better wages. But as single women like Jane flocked to cities, moralists scrutinized their new lives. Concern seemed to shadow every advance: financial independence and evenings out would place single women's morality at risk, overwork outside the home would lead to breakdown, higher education would make women unmarriageable, bicycles would damage women's health. Away from the watchful eyes of parents, young working women were said to be "adrift."[3]

Nonetheless, despite occasional illness, Jane had insisted in a letter to her mother that she needed to keep working, not just to pay the bills but also for her mental health. While Jane's brothers lived quiet lives pursuing conventional professions, the three Tucker sisters were doers: "It isn't in any of us to be quiet," Jane added, writing from Boston in December 1893.[4] While their mother saw daughter Patty's life as an author, Mame's work as an actor, and Jane's hustling about as dangerous and deadly, they saw this work as life-sustaining. For Jane, to return to the fold ill and in debt and to assume an unmarried daughter's family duties was a crushing defeat. But she found an escape by taking on a job few Victorian women could have ever imagined. Ironically, for success in her mission, Jane would need to exploit not only the modern freedoms and clerical skills embraced by young, urban women but also the traditional domestic aptitudes she'd hoped to leave behind.

While Jane lay comfortably ensconced on a daybed, thirty-year-old Madeleine Pollard slept on an unforgiving mattress in an iron-framed bed at a home for "fallen women," the House of Mercy in Washington, DC. Like Jane, Madeleine had recently suffered a reversal of fortune, and like Jane, she was not content in her assigned place in life. A former favorite of the Washington social scene, she was now a social pariah, the plaintiff in a trial that would soon be the talk of the nation. In August 1893, she had sued her lover for breach of promise when he failed to marry her. That her lover was a married, five-term US congressman almost thirty years her senior made Madeleine the focus of daily newspaper coverage: Was she the victim of a cruel man's lie or a calculating vixen? By January 1894, instead of attending fancy teas and delightful soirees with Washington's social elite, Madeleine hid from paparazzi and the prurient public. She endured grueling meetings with her attorneys each day and taught basic writing to the House of Mercy residents in her dull nights. Her society friends had abandoned her, her mother disowned her, and her fellow House of Mercy teachers turned cold shoulders to this unwelcome temporary resident. She needed a friend.

———

Madeleine Pollard called out to me at a rare book show in a New Hampshire hockey rink, and once I learned the faint traces of her story, I could not let her go. I had stumbled on a "salesman's sample" of *The Celebrated Trial* (1894), a slim volume containing a smattering of nonconsecutive pages, distributed in hopes a customer would preorder the soon-to-be-printed complete book.[5] I skimmed the text—a congressman, a mistress, a broken promise of marriage. The notion of a scandal that filled the newspapers in the first half of 1894 but was all but forgotten today intrigued me; in its time, the story merited not one but, as I discovered that evening as I googled Madeleine's name, four books about what he said and she said in a Washington, DC, court in 1894.

In 1894, Madeleine Pollard was the most well-known woman in America. The six-week trial charging Kentucky congressman W. C. P. Breckinridge with breach of promise was covered daily in newspapers in every US state. Shortly after the trial ended, Madeleine disappeared from public commentary and the historical record. A century later, historians focused on the impact the trial had on Breckinridge's political life with nary a comment on Madeleine's life before or after the trial. I had to know what happened to her, and so I began my quest to flesh out Madeleine's life beyond the moniker *mistress*.[6]

As is the case with many stories in women's history, Madeleine's tale was buried within that of a man's, and thus my first step was to explore the Breckinridge Family Papers at the Library of Congress. As I traced her life from her youthful steps in Kentucky to college in Cincinnati to working in Washington, DC, I saw a young woman desperate for a life of music, literature, and travel, a woman searching for a path away from the expected fate of being a rural farmer's wife. But historical research has a way of derailing what you think you're studying. As I followed Madeleine's faint footsteps, I made a staggering discovery. Entwined with Madeleine's story was the equally compelling narrative of another woman, someone whom no previous historian had ever recognized: the "girl spy" Agnes Parker.[7]

At first, the hints were vague—letters to Congressman Breckinridge about his lawyer's plan to hire an "unprofessional."[8] But an unprofessional what? And for what purpose? Facts in the Breckinridge letters mirrored details in *The Real Madeleine Pollard*, a book written by Agnes Parker—an account of an undercover mission at the House of Mercy that purported to be true . . . or was it?[9] From the thin archival record, I pulled out every bit of information about Parker, comparing events in her book with comments in Breckinridge's and his lawyers' letters. I made timelines and maps of her movements. Over several weeks, I searched the census, city directories, and vital records; I peeled apart a tangle of aliases, hitting brick walls on Parker's real identity. And then my dogged persistence paid off, and Agnes revealed her real name in a note tucked within a letter to the congressman from his daughter.[10] Agnes was Jane Tucker, an unfortunately common name in the late nineteenth century, giving me dozens of Jane Tuckers to consider for the role of girl spy.

And then lightning struck twice, and in a folder of miscellaneous bills in the Breckinridge papers, I found Jane's invoice for her work on the congressman's behalf. The first expense recorded provided the clue I had been looking for: "Travelling Expenses: Maine to Washington."[11] Jane Tucker was from Maine, where I happen to live. My eyes went wide, and I knew I had found my next book project. Census and family history records helped identify the correct Maine Jane, Google informed me she had lived in what is now a historic house museum, and I was thrilled to learn from the website of the preservation organization maintaining the home that her papers survived in a Boston archive.

If you didn't know the backstory of the Breckinridge-Pollard trial of 1894, you would assume from Jane's letters to her family that she was simply a stenographer and typist, one of several working in the background of a huge trial. And indeed, the archivists caring for the Tucker family papers had no idea of Jane's covert operation. But with the trial backstory, and the confirming details in the Breckinridge papers and "Agnes Parker's" book, it was clear: Jane Armstrong Tucker worked as an undercover detective in the spring of 1894 in Washington, DC, tasked with becoming Madeleine's friend in order to learn her innermost secrets and pass them on to Breckinridge to use against her in court. Jane was very good at her job: her secret task remained hidden not only from her contemporaries in 1894 but also from the curators, archivists, and historians who followed in the decades after. I had uncovered a spy, and no one had written a word about her.[12]

Jane joins an intrepid group of nineteenth-century female spies and detectives, women who used their intelligence, intuition, bravery, and feminine culture to sneak behind enemy lines in the Civil War; to thwart embezzlers, counterfeiters, and assassins; and, in 1894, to pass along confidences shared among friends to the opposing party in a lawsuit. Women were especially valuable and well-suited to this role. The Pinkerton detective agency hired their first female operative, Kate Warne, in 1856. Warne, and the female Pinkertons who followed, could enter spaces men could not and could slyly interrogate—while drinking tea in parlors—the women connected to men under surveillance. That women were often overlooked and relegated to the background offered them ideal opportunities to observe, listen, and pass by unnoticed. And well-dressed women of (or presenting themselves to be) middle class were understood to be the moral bearers of American society, without artifice or any hidden agenda.[13]

Jane and Madeleine, while adversaries in the winter and spring of 1894, had much in common, and studying them in tandem gives us insight into the challenges presented not just because of gender but also of social class, geography, and education. Both were avid readers, and reading, particularly novels, sparked possibilities for crafting their lives.[14] Madeleine imagined a literary life like that of her role model, George Eliot; Jane imagined adventures beyond her home. Unsatisfied with a traditional domestic role, both exploited the limited public spaces women could enter in the last decades of the nineteenth century, blazing quiet pathways to a self-designed future that was dangled in front of some, but not all, women. Still, they were not alone in their quest for self-directed lives.

On the surface, the trial captures, and dissects, the story of a bright but poor Kentucky girl who had set her sights on a larger life stage. Yet the trial is also the story of Julia Churchill Blackburn, elite Southern grand dame who fiercely protected her family name—twice. It's the struggle of doctors Belle Buchanan, Kate Perry Kane, Mary Street Logan, Mary Parsons, and nurse Mary McKenzie to be recognized as legitimate health-care providers. It's the story of a typist whose intuition led her to take notes on suspicious letters, and it's the story of Sarah Gist, whose business of choice made her eyewitness to the foibles of privileged men. No less interesting are the stories of Louise Wing Breckinridge, the congressman's beleaguered wife; and Sister Dorothea, the House of Mercy matron whose biggest threat to her mission of redeeming lost girls came from within her own home. Embedded in their testimonies were remarkable stories of how these women made and marked their places in the world. And behind the scenes is Jane Tucker, who took on an extraordinary job in a terrible economy to, as Jane would later say, "grab the gold."

Jane's grabbing the gold was not greed; accepting a spy's mission was a calculated, pragmatic approach to getting out of debt and, perhaps, even getting a bit ahead. Wages granted a single woman the possibility of safe housing, material comforts, and decent, adequate food. An income offered mobility, not simply for recreation but to take advantage of better jobs or opportunities elsewhere. The gold permitted women to move beyond the watchful eyes of parents and beyond the demands of others; financial resources let a woman be her own person and dictate her own life. For Jane, the stakes of this job were high: her treasured independent life. And that life required money.

Similarly, Madeleine's quest for marriage to Breckinridge was not simply some romantic fantasy. Through marriage, Madeleine would receive protection, material comforts, and the financial support to enact her role as a congressman's wife. His status would be her status. No longer needing to work for wages, Madeleine's domain would be the home, and within, she would create and manage a space designed to highlight the Breckinridges' standing through material goods and social events. With a supportive husband, Madeleine could enjoy the life of study, literature, and travel she craved. In this trial, Madeleine's future hung in the balance: If she succeeded, her tarnished reputation would be made whole—a clean slate to begin again. If she lost, there was no removing the stain of *mistress*, and her fall from her position as a socialite would be rapid and permanent.

Madeleine and Jane illustrate the irony of the Gilded Age. The era celebrated geographic mobility and reinvention—trying one's luck in a new city, as Jane did in New York and then Washington, or taking on a new name and new backstory, as schoolgirl Mattie Valeria Pollard did when she became Madeleine Vivian Breckinridge Pollard, society protégé. Simultaneously, while praising the promise of America, those in the higher classes deeply feared the consequences of social movement; if all Americans could reinvent their lives, how could one tell the bona fide from the pretenders, impostors, and scam artists? Thus, a rigid social hierarchy scaffolded American society, keeping people in the places assigned by their gender, race, and class (among other complex attributes). Madeleine learned through etiquette and elaborate parlor rituals and Jane learned through paid labor how such structures regulated, tested, and authenticated every aspect of their existence. In Horatio Alger's 1868 bestselling novel *Ragged Dick*, the orphaned protagonist could exchange his rags for respectability as a clerk in a business office. At tale's end, Dick buys a nice suit, opens a bank account, and restyles himself Richard Hunter, but for Madeleine and other women, their best hope for a social boost was a good marriage. As Madeleine learned, it was not enough to change your middle name—your success depended on a good surname, and the way to move up was to marry a better one.

The breach-of-promise trial is a portrait of women at the end of the nineteenth century, reaching for opportunities that came to men as a matter of course—work, education, geographic mobility, the professions, even sexual freedoms. Simply put, these women wanted a piece of the American dream—not just the one of marriage and motherhood that many were offered and expected to want but the one with multiple possibilities offered to their brothers, fathers, and husbands. *Pollard v. Breckinridge* may not have come down through time as a trial of the century, but it was a trial of the moment, capturing the simmering sentiment that life's benefits weren't distributed equally. As America rushed headlong toward the turn of the century, the women of *Pollard v. Breckinridge* show us that although the world favored men, women found remarkable ways to navigate around barriers and expand their opportunities.

I

HASTILY, JANE

Jane Tucker elbowed her way across Copley Square, dodging horse-pulled wagons, electric streetcars, and a crush of bowler-hatted men and long-skirted women gathering dirt on their hems. The Museum of Fine Arts, enrobed in marble, rose behind her. Trinity Church held sway near the corner of Boylston Street and Huntington Avenue. Office buildings and spectacular homes surrounded the Boston square. But Jane's goal was not spiritual uplift or cultural growth. She sought her future, and the key to her goal—financial self-sufficiency—was stenography.

Born in 1866, Jane grew up in Wiscasset, Maine, climbing trees, shooting guns, riding fast horses, and making driftwood bonfires on the beach. Her ship captain father plied his trade along the Atlantic Seaboard and managed several other business interests. As newlyweds in 1857, Jane's parents enjoyed financial comfort. The captain, twenty-five years his wife's senior, had outfitted Castle Tucker, their Regency-style home, in one extravagant Boston shopping trip—but his far-flung businesses, as well as the growth of railroads, economic panics, the Civil War, and the shift from sail to steam, challenged seafarers and strained the family fortunes over the years. The captain's frequent travel pushed the patience of his young wife, Mollie, who was left at home to care for five children and the large house. As the Tucker clan grew and their financial resources shrank, Jane's parents' marriage became increasingly strained, and the home that was once a grand

I

castle became more of a burdensome prison, especially for Mollie Tucker.[1]

The dual cautionary tales of fragile finances and a strained marriage took hold in the Tucker girls, and Jane and her older sisters chose different routes. Martha "Patty" Tucker, at age seventeen, won a young authors' contest and used the award as a springboard for a writing life. Despite her parents' strong disapproval, Patty left Wiscasset for Boston, and then, still single, she moved to Denver, where she worked for the newspaper, married, and found financial and popular success as a novelist, author of short stories, and essayist supporting women's suffrage.[2]

Like Patty, Mary "Mame" Tucker also left home as a young, single woman and spent nearly twenty years as a professional actor. She toured the country with various traveling troupes, including a stint with Buffalo Bill Cody's Wild West shows in 1882 and 1883. She married a fellow actor, but the marriage collapsed when her husband took her hard-earned wages and abandoned her.

With her older siblings gone, Jane, the youngest Tucker child, unburdened her troubles, fears, and hopes to her "confidante"—her diary.[3] In 1881, at age fifteen, she offered her share of theatrics. She told her diary that she wished she were dead, one of many dramatic threats the teen shared on paper during this turbulent period. The next day, the storm passed, and the diary entries became mundane, but the calm did not last. A few days later, she was again up in arms, complaining that the "damned old fools" refused to let her attend a dance. Jane spewed her anger onto the pages: "How I hate life. What have I to look forward to? Nothing but being penned up as if I had not wit enough to take care of myself."[4]

When the family lived briefly in Boston, Jane was unhappy, bored, and impatient. Perhaps tired of the petulant teen's drama, her parents sent her to St. Joseph's Academy, a Maryland secondary school that Jane's mother had attended. At St. Joseph's, her curriculum mixed academic subjects with domestic arts. Jane studied French, modern history, geography, arithmetic, geometry, reading, and penmanship, as well as skills deemed essential to run a future middle-class home such as ornamental needlework, piano, domestic economy, and chemistry, the last of which was useful in the preparation of food before the availability of self-rising flour, fast-acting yeast, and prepackaged baking mixes.[5]

Despite her outbursts, her days were not all dark. She recounted youthful adventures with coded phrases and long penciled lines instead of words, a mystery message from the future spy, leaving the reader to wonder what she withheld when she wrote "*no more at present—*(ahem!)."[6] Jane imagined she had a future. As she searched for a passion, she contemplated having a life on the stage like Mame or becoming a famous author like Patty. To satisfy a writing assignment at St. Joseph's, she penned her autobiography in 1882, anticipating "a more interesting one if time permits [at] some future time," a promise on which she would make good.[7]

On the cusp of young womanhood, Jane resolved (repeatedly) to be more serious and good. She expected a future marriage. She declared herself skilled at flirting but had little success with young men and worried about becoming an old maid. In May 1881, she wondered "if I shall always see people go ahead of me and [I] have to stay in the background and have fellows drop me & take up other girls."[8] A few days later, she declared she was done flirting with boys.

Notwithstanding her apparent interest in young men, a home-bound, middle-class future did not appeal to Jane. She despised "damn housework," and one can imagine her foot-stomping when asked to perform a domestic task.[9] She would rather read than clean, and she read voraciously. Her favorites included George Eliot's *The Mill on the Floss*, several works by Hawthorne, and Dickens's *David Copperfield*. She read Sarah Orne Jewett and at least two authors of detective stories, Wilkie Collins and Anna Katherine Green, the latter called the "mother of detective fiction."[10] Around the age of fourteen, she read Louisa May Alcott's *Little Women*; she likely identified with Jo March, who longed for an adventure beyond the home and struggled with her fiery temper.[11]

In her sisters, Jane saw life paths taking her beyond the parlor walls and a future different from her mother's discontent in a large, aging house with an aged husband, in a marriage so estranged that she contemplated divorce and, at one point, checked herself into a mental health asylum. Mollie's frustrations challenged the myth of domestic happiness in hearth and home and reiterated the necessity of a woman providing for herself. But unlike Mollie, Jane and others of her generation had options. Marriage could be, and indeed was, delayed as many young women chose to enjoy a taste of self-reliance and independence before settling down to the domestic realm. The world was changing for Captain and Mollie Tucker too. The diaspora of their daughters to cities and careers underscored the distance between the senior Tuckers' nineteenth-century rural life and that of their urban, mobile daughters at the century's end. What their daughters experienced as gain, the parents experienced as loss.

By June 1887, her teen years behind her, Jane Tucker had found her own liberating path toward self-sustaining work in Boston. The dull city of her youth was now a beacon of exciting possibilities.

Age and urban living had not softened Jane's hard edge. She worked for a stingy seamstress on Boylston Street, the "darndest humbug [she] ever met." [12] Mrs. Paige had a disagreeable habit of taking credit for Jane's work, and "the old cat" was slow to pay Jane her wages of six dollars a week.[13] Yet, although Jane complained in every letter home, she conceded that she had mastered advanced needlework skills—skills she planned to take, along with Paige's customers, to her imagined future shop.

Jane was no Victorian porcelain doll, dressed and prettied up for someone to admire. She was tenacious and self-assertive. When Jane took her sewing skills to the fine embroidery room of the department store R. H. Stearns, she endured a cold reception as her new coworkers tried to "freeze" her out. She wrote, "I find you have to have lots of fight and push in you to get up in this world" and, once again seeing the pragmatic side of a challenging situation, added, "I'm getting lots of experience that will help me in whatever business I go into in life."[14]

By 1890, Jane Tucker had taken the first fateful step toward that future—she walked to Boston's Copley Square, dodging traffic and horse droppings, and enrolled in the Hickox School of Shorthand and Typewriting.

William E. Hickox taught the Pitman method of shorthand and trained typists exclusively on Remington typewriters, the latest skills and technology for the turn-of-the-century business. Shorthand provided an efficient system for recording spoken words using symbols for phonetic elements such as individual letters like *b* or *d* and for sounds such as *th*, *ch*, and *ng*, among others. A stenographer (one who wrote in shorthand) needed keen hearing, a strong focus, and close attention to detail, rendering into shorthand exactly what was said while it was uttered. Similar shorthand symbols varied only in the slant or thickness of a line, necessitating a consistent hand in taking down and then accurately reading back or putting the words into typewritten form.

Hickox's tuition was fifteen dollars a month plus an additional fee for paper. Textbooks were free. The typical course of study took six months.[15] By January 1891, Jane had been promoted to an advanced class, and her typewriting speed had increased. By spring, her investment had paid off; she found a job at a Boston fancy goods business, the Whitman Brothers.[16] While she earned a ten-dollar-a-week salary, Jane found she was relegated to copying orders and recording business expenses. She feared losing her hard-won typing and stenography skills, so she left.[17]

Jane next took an office position with the West End Street Railway Company, Boston's primary public transportation provider and the forerunner to today's Massachusetts Bay Transportation Authority (MBTA). West End managed a fleet of transportation options: horses pulled carriages and omnibuses, the new electric streetcars brought commuters from the suburbs to downtown Boston, and soon the West End Company would begin construction on the latest innovation in urban transportation, the subway—Boston's T.[18]

At the West End Street Railway's offices on Milk Street, Jane greeted aggrieved customers who came to complain about late trains, missed stops, or lost items. Etta Bailey, also a Hickox School graduate, proved a helpful mentor. The two quickly became friends, and Jane applied Etta's wise guidance. She practiced remaining calm, offering soothing words to the upset, and disarming the frustrated as she dutifully recorded their gripes. She held her own in the face of angry, empty threats.

Jane's position took her outside of the office when streetcars, horses, carriages, and pedestrians inevitably collided in the busy city. Jane documented the unfortunate accidents, recording in shorthand statements from victims and witnesses. The details could get quite gory. She had an unusual job, given the typically decorous nature of women's lives, particularly for a young woman raised in a middle-class home. But Jane relished her work.

From January 1891 to January 1892, Jane counted 10,607 accident reports, with 12 deaths since August alone. As she settled into the job, gruesome injuries failed to faze her. She joked with characteristic sarcasm in a letter home: "I suppose you have noticed by the papers that we've killed another man. It does make such a lot of work to have a death; if they would only be satisfied to get their legs or arms cut off, it would save me a lot of work."[19]

At age twenty-six, she had found her calling: stenography.

Jane loved her Boston life, but her conservative brother was less enamored with working women. Antipathy between the siblings grew, especially when brother Bill lectured Jane on what he imagined as her dissolute and dangerous life as a "lady of leisure."[20] When she ignored his advice, Bill turned to their mother, cataloging Jane's alleged deficiencies. Mollie, in turn, criticized Jane's work hours and busy social life, writing to her daughter that her activities would lead to "dissipation." Her daughter, she feared, was "morbidly restless and seeking excitement" and "on the go all the time."[21]

Mollie was not exactly wrong, but Jane was hardly living the life of gaiety her stick-in-the-mud brother believed. Bill worried about her reputation; her mother worried about Jane's health. Jane vehemently defended her life choices, noting that she saw Dr. Charles P. Thayer for a digestive disorder only twice a week, an improvement over her previous every-other-day schedule.[22] As for Bill's hand-wringing, she dismissed her brother, thinking him bitter because she could not, or would not, spare the money or time to visit his suburban Boston home more often, visits Jane endured but did not often enjoy, especially once young children were in his household.

Around May, exhausted by increasingly taxing work, Tucker left the West End Street Railway Company for a position with a downtown businessman, Mr. W. A. Boland. She earned the same pay but had fewer tasks, but after a few months, Jane once again thought she could do better elsewhere.[23]

In October 1892, she tried her luck in New York City, leaving the familiarity of Boston and moving farther from family. She quickly landed a job with the New York Life Insurance Company but left shortly after because her boss, described in a letter home, was the ugliest man she had ever encountered, "a regular fiend."[24] Jane then went to the Remington typewriting rooms, where she would be called on to provide businesses with stenography, typewriting, and other office services on a temporary basis.

Then, on a fateful day in November, Jane was sent to the luxurious Park Avenue Hotel to assist a prominent Lexington, Kentucky, businessman and attorney, Charles Stoll. Hotel staff gossiped about Stoll, sharing with Jane that he was a wealthy and prominent man. Jane impressed Stoll, and he offered her a permanent job as his private secretary.[25] She was delighted. Stoll and his associates had an office on Wall Street, where they managed railroad and other business interests. Snatching some stationery from the Park Avenue Hotel, she wrote to her mother. Stoll was "a real Southern gentleman, has lots of money & is the kindest nicest man to work for [that] I ever saw."[26]

Jane had landed a plum job. She worked five days a week from nine thirty to four thirty for fifteen dollars a week. She managed the office in his absence, opened his mail, answered correspondence, and attended to business matters. She added legal knowledge to her skill set when he took on a complicated law case. Jane's life in New York seemed "just too lovely to be true."[27]

Urban living agreed with Jane, and she relished her independence. A friend helped her get a clean and attractively kept room in a boardinghouse recommended by the YWCA. As Jane reassured her mother, the YWCA aided young women seeking work or housing and kept a register of appropriate living quarters: "So you know the house and people are okay."[28] Breakfast and dinner were included in Jane's six-dollar weekly rent.

Jane enjoyed what the city offered. Familiar with urban transportation systems, she explored the city. One trip took her to the end of the line at 155th Street near High Bridge, where a popular pastime was to stroll in the woods. She went to the circus, watched parades and fireworks, and walked along the busy harbor. She took evening promenades and enjoyed trips to Rockaway Beach in hot weather. She burnished her education, studying French at a Berlitz school. There were markets and restaurants to explore and friends' weddings to attend. She even encountered the famous, sharing an elevator with Grover Cleveland. Cleveland stood aside when they reached the lobby to let her exit first. When they simultaneously arrived at the nearby El station, she repaid the courtesy and held the swinging doors for him.[29]

The shaky economy rose and dipped, and Stoll's and Jane's fortunes rose and fell in tandem. In April 1893, Jane's luck ran out. Stoll called her into his office and handed her a bundle of glowing letters of recommendation: the Kentucky businessmen were closing their New York office. Stoll wrote, "I have found Miss Tucker to be a bright, energetic and competent young lady, and a valuable assistant as a stenographer, type-writer, and clerk, and cheerfully commend her to anyone needing such assistance." Stoll's associates were equally complimentary.[30]

Jane quickly found another position at a Wall Street insurance business but left by midsummer, beset by illness. She saw Dr. Thayer for treatment. She recovered and soon felt well enough to travel to the Chicago World's Fair—a once-in-a-lifetime opportunity and a rare chance for Jane to enjoy the fruits of her considerable labor. She wrote enthusiastic letters to her mother, marveling at the wonders of the fair and pleased to be getting her money's worth. "I wouldn't have missed it for anything," she said.[31]

Jane returned to Boston in the fall of 1893 and resumed her position at the West End Street Railway Company, negotiating a salary of eighteen dollars per week. Despite her raise, Jane's finances were stretched. The economic depression continued to grip the nation. National unemployment soared above 10 percent, and jobless rates reached as high as 35 percent in New York; she was lucky to have a job.[32] Her employer paid her monthly, but Jane was in debt with living expenses, medical bills, and her trip to the World's Fair. She cut costs, eliminating, among other things, her subscription to the *Ladies' Home Journal*: the recipes, domestic stories, and household hints were of little interest. Her seventy-seven-year-old father sent her a small check to tide her over between paychecks, but he admitted that he had difficulty paying the taxes. In a reversal of the usual roles, the wage-earning daughter advised her housebound father to avoid investing in the railroad and save his money for necessities.[33] Things were tight all over.

Then sadness settled on the Tucker family, ushered in with the falling leaves and the first cold winds of winter, and it brought with it a threat to Jane's hard-fought future. In November, between customer complaints of late trains and lost packages, Jane answered the telephone at the street railway office. Her brother-in-law, Will Stapleton, was calling from New York. Patty, he revealed, was in the city to have a cancerous uterine tumor removed. The operation was dangerous, and the chances of recovery were slim. Patty had been in pain for months and was desperate for relief. Jane had no idea her sister had been so ill. Dr. T. Gaillard Thomas, a nationally known gynecologist, performed the delicate surgery.[34] Patty survived the operation, but her heart gave out two days later. She was thirty-two.

Stapleton brought his wife's body to Maine, and the surviving Tucker women grieved. Jane wrote supportive letters to her mother, helping Mollie mourn the loss of a second child thirty years after the death of an infant, Matilda.[35]

In letters to Mame, Jane skipped platitudes of condolence. Middle-class social expectations demanded that one of the daughters manage the family household, leaving the bereaved parents space and time to grieve. The "family claim," the idea that one daughter would remain single and at home to care for aging parents, reached toward Jane, but she ducked.[36] Instead, she pressed Mame to return home to comfort Mollie and the captain.[37] Patty's death, Jane argued, could reunite the family. Her death would have meaning. Mame responded in kind, and back and forth they exchanged passively aggressive letters, part sob story, part self-defense, and part guilt trip.

All the while that she made appeals to Mame, Jane had been making plans. Her West End Street Railway Company friend Etta Bailey had an idea, and Jane jumped on board. The company had announced impending layoffs; when they lost their positions at year's end, she and Etta would go into business together, providing stenography and typing for lawyers.

A month after Patty's death, the Tucker sisters continued to argue over the siren call of a daughter's duty. Their exasperated mother jumped into the fray, writing to Mame not to come home if she was acting simply out of a sense of duty. "Darn duty," Jane grumbled. "I never felt it was your duty any more than mine."[38] When Mame conceded the war of words and agreed to give up her acting, Jane arranged to board at the Baileys' home on Hancock Street and begin work with Etta. The home was just behind the

State House and convenient to Boston's business and legal district. Lodging at the Baileys' would save two dollars a week on her room and board. Mrs. Bailey, a widow who took in boarders to make ends meet, provided delicious meals, and Jane looked forward to sharing a table with Etta and her sister, Tot.[39]

In the new year, 1894, Etta and Jane commenced their scheme. Jane typed documents taken in shorthand for Mr. Wright, a court reporter. Etta had lined up work to keep them busy until at least June. The steady work promised an equally steady income, which Jane hoped would settle her debts and cover her continuing medical bills. The benefits of self-employment were clear: "One good thing about this work [is] it could always give me the whole summer at home, and it's good to be so independent too as I am here."[40] But just as Jane set sail on this new course, Mame steered clear of Wiscasset, convinced that her parents pitied her and wanted to force a reform of her unhealthy habits. Mollie turned to Jane for support. Jane resisted, desperately wanting to make a go of her new business venture. A week later, however, she relented despite the enticements of her Boston plan, thus giving up a steady income, interesting work, friendly roommates, and her treasured independence and instead returning to the dreaded domestic fold.

It is unclear which provided the final straw: family pressure, guilty conscience, or exhaustion with the ongoing battle. Jane had a troublesome tooth filled and then headed north. With a heavy heart, she returned to Maine, snared by the family claim. She settled in on the daybed for a long, quiet winter with her grieving parents and Patty's typewriter. And then she received a most mysterious offer.

On January 16, 1894, a messenger delivered to Wiscasset, Maine, two telegrams and a letter to the bedridden Jane Tucker. More letters followed. Eight months after Charles Stoll had closed his New York City office and let Jane go, he desperately needed her help. Stoll knew Jane had the skills and stamina to meet the unusual demands of this new position, but he had to move fast. Stoll offered her six to eight weeks of steady work in the nation's capital. He could not share the nature of the task, but he promised that Jane could name her price. He needed her immediately.

Mollie worried. She imagined Washington as a paved-over swamp, and her daughter would surely catch malaria or typhoid fever in her run-down condition. And Jane hesitated too, at first declining Stoll's thoughtful gesture. She remained very grateful to her favorite employer—a man who appreciated and respected her hard work. He had occasionally treated her to lunch and once stopped work early to take Jane, the descendant of sea captains, to tour the SS City of Paris, the fastest transatlantic ship.[41] Nonetheless, Jane wrote, difficulties at this moment prevented her from saying yes. Her excuses did nothing to halt the daily onslaught of letters and telegrams. She tried again, unburdening herself of her challenges: her sister Patty's recent death, the loss of her latest job, her mounting debt, and her ongoing illness. She was too sad, too broke, and too ill to accept his job. Jane sounded like the homebound invalid she disdained. Stoll wouldn't hear of it. "Why, you of all persons," he wrote, "are the last to let a little sickness affect your spirits. . . . You have been exactly like the rest of us— knocked out by the infernal democratic administration. Of course you have not made money—who has?" He chided, "Brace up and throw that head back and defy sickness as you have survived the other troubles of life."[42]

The pep talk worked. Jane accepted the mystery job for fifteen dollars per week plus travel expenses, a decent salary for a single woman in 1894. Stoll advanced her fifty dollars. Washington, he wrote, "is just what you need—it is almost perfect [weather] and will probably be so from now on."[43] Jane could leave winter's snow, cold, and ice behind. She could leave her family and a daughter's duty. She could get back to work, earn money, and feel valued. Better to risk fever in Washington than be housebound in Wiscasset. Stoll sent another telegram: he had arranged to meet Jane in Boston, and he had something important to tell her.

2

My Dear Mr. Rodes

The setting sun had not cooled the sultry August day. Students and faculty of Cincinnati Wesleyan Female College stood on the portico, hoping to catch an evening breeze. Madeleine dressed in her room, selecting a dress appropriate for a concert. She set her hat atop her thick auburn hair, securing it with long hat pins. Madeleine had found her home at the college, thanks to the generosity of her benefactor, James Rodes. But Rodes had run out of money and told Madeleine her studies were over. Worse, he demanded they marry, as their deal had stipulated. In desperation, Madeleine wrote to a Lexington lawyer and rising politician she had encountered on a train. Today he visited; after a conversation in the school parlor, he suggested they attend a concert. He had not yet offered a solution to her dilemma with Rodes, but surely that would come this evening.

William Campbell Preston Breckinridge, a married man with five children, returned to the college just before 8:00 p.m., chauffeured in a rented carriage. He extended his hand as his young guest, thirty years his junior, approached the vehicle and stepped onto the white stone carriage block. Madeleine looked from the carriage to Breckinridge. "Are we going in a closed carriage [on] so warm an evening?"

"My throat," mumbled Breckinridge, "the night air is bad for my throat."

As her school friends watched, Madeleine reached for Breckinridge's guiding hand and stepped up and into the carriage.

The carriage door closed. Breckinridge sat next to Madeleine, now ensconced in a private world. Curtains shaded the windows. "Miss Pollard," he began, "my head aches in this summer heat." A concert would be too much. Perhaps they could take a drive? Madeleine's heart beat fast, and her breath came short. Vice President Martha McClellan Brown's weekly lectures to her female charges made such situations clear: a young, unmarried woman; a much older man who was not quite the family friend he had represented himself to be—this was how racy novels began. Still, in the privacy of the closed carriage, Madeleine could share her secrets. She could free herself from Rodes's marriage claim. A man of Breckinridge's standing would know what to do. "Yes, of course," agreed Madeleine, "a drive would be lovely." "Git up," called the driver to his horse, snapping the reins as he guided the carriage down the dark, quiet streets.[1]

Breckinridge deflected talk of Rodes's claim. He turned his attention to Madeleine: Tell me your hopes and dreams, he urged. A nervous Madeleine rattled on, relieved and excited to have an appreciative audience. She wanted to be an authoress, she said. She wanted to make a name for herself. And who serves as your model? he inquired. "George Eliot," Madeleine chose. Eliot, born Mary Ann Evans, had reinvented herself, taking on a male pen name to avoid critics' kneejerk assumptions about the merit of women's writing. Breckinridge admired Eliot, or so he claimed at the moment.[2]

The curtained windows remained closed despite the airless night. The carriage grew warmer; layers of clothing—shirtwaist and corset, skirt, and crinolines—pressed upon Madeleine, her face flushed. Breckinridge removed her hat, extracting the pins that had secured it to her head, his hand grazing her coiled hair. He rested the hat on the seat slowly and deliberately. He took Madeleine's hands in his own, stroking her smooth skin with his thumb. He released her hands, his dark eyes locked on her gray ones in the dim light of the carriage. Madeleine neither encouraged nor demurred, statue-still on the carriage seat. The carriage wheels turned, rattling over ruts and stones. Breckinridge drew the slender girl across his lap, swift and sure like summer heat lightning, a flash of passion. Madeleine's heart thumped in her chest. They sat inches apart, both immobile—frozen in desire or despair. Breckinridge closed the distance between them, pressing his married lips against hers. Taking liberties, the Victorians called it. The liberties, of course, were his—not hers—to take.

Madeleine cried out.

Two hours passed. The carriage returned to the college and pulled up along the wrought-iron fence. Students and teachers still mingled outside, the stars hazy in the humidity of the summer night. The horses panted and pawed at the dirt; the carriage doors remained closed. "But what of Rodes?" she asked. "We did not discuss my trouble."

"Tomorrow," Breckinridge promised. Madeleine replaced her hat, catching her hair between fabric and brass hatpin. Breckinridge opened the carriage door and stepped out into the night. He turned to assist Madeleine. As she exited the carriage, he pressed ten dollars into her hand. She tried to refuse. "There are a great many little things you need," he said, wrapping her fingers around the bill. She hurried past friends and faculty and retreated to her room. She told no one about the ride.[3]

———

A college education had long been Madeleine's dream. Her childhood in Crab Orchard, Kentucky, had been happy. A precocious little girl, "Mattie" was the darling of her father, on whose knee she learned Shakespeare and recited poetry. His sudden death in 1876 tore the family apart—two of her siblings remained with her mother, three children went to an orphanage, and thirteen-year-old Madeleine lived with a succession of aunts, first in Pittsburgh and then near Lexington. In these new circumstances, she had some access to educational opportunities but also witnessed her aunts' unending household labor and the financial struggles of her widowed mother, who lived nearby. Madeleine saw the uncertainty of a woman's fate. She wanted a different life of meaningful work, intellectual stimulations, and social advancement, so she devised a strategy to achieve her dreams: she would seek an education to prepare for that cultured life and if a good marriage presented itself, she was open to a union that could get her there.

In the 1880s, finding a seat in college became easier for women, but there was tuition to be paid and textbooks to buy. Madeleine had no funds of her own, and neither did her mother. The solution came in 1883 from bachelor James Rodes of Lexington, a family acquaintance.[4]

Rodes was a well-meaning man who farmed and tended the grounds of the local asylum. He was barely literate and twenty years Madeleine's senior. Some called him coarse, but he had saved some money and longed for a wife. Madeleine charmed Rodes with her charisma, knowledge, and ambition. Here, Rodes thought, was a woman who could raise him up. He offered her a deal: he would fund her education if, at its conclusion, she would marry him. Or, countered Madeleine, she would pay him back. The agreement was struck and captured in an informal contract. Madeleine's mother witnessed the signatures. No lawyers were involved.[5]

Rodes paid the fees for Madeleine to attend Notre Dame in the fall of 1883, a Catholic secondary school in Cincinnati, where his frequent visits and letters to Madeleine raised the nuns' suspicions that he was more than a guardian, as Madeleine had claimed. Embarrassed, she left the school, next entering Cincinnati Wesleyan Female College. Madeleine impressed Vice President Martha McClellan Brown at her admissions interview and enrolled in November 1883. She was delighted with the extensive library, the classes in Latin and rhetoric, Brown's daily lectures imparting the rules of etiquette and decorum, and the military exercises designed to improve a young woman's grace and carriage.

Madeleine's friends shared her love of learning, and they exchanged letters containing youthful attempts at poetry, their crushes, and predictions for their futures. Madeleine worked to build that future through pursuing her studies and consciously crafting her identity. Her voracious reading inspired her to replace her middle name, Valeria, with Vivian, a name she had read in a novel. Later, her friends responded to Madeleine's fanciful fan-girlish tales of meeting powerful men by renaming her Madeleine Vivian Joe Blackburn Bill Breckinridge Pollard, unwittingly capturing a salient aspect of her future.[6]

At Cincinnati Wesleyan, Madeleine won the annual school debate on the relative merit of words and deeds.[7] She championed the view that words took precedence. The *Cincinnati Enquirer* reported on the winner of the 1884 contest, "Miss Madeleine knows how to attract the popular ear, and, while her ideas did not seem particularly original, she had the tact to present them in a plausible light."[8] As she continued her studies, Madeleine quickly realized that the more she grew intellectually, the more significant became the gap between her and Rodes and the less she wanted to marry and be thrust into the kind of life from which education was supposed to free her.

Madeleine's expenses quickly drained Rodes's modest coffers. Their agreement had not guaranteed any specific length of time for her education, and at the end of the spring 1884 term, only her second semester of study, he told Madeleine her student days were over. It was time to marry.

Rodes pressed, and Madeleine panicked. She wrote to Breckinridge, begging him for help. In Cincinnati for business, he came to the college in early August 1884, and there ensued an afternoon conversation in the college's public parlor followed by the private ride in a closed carriage on a sultry summer night. Within a few days, the two became lovers. Madeleine left the college. By chance, circumstance, or calculation, Madeleine changed course, finding an amended path to the same dream: the marriage Breckinridge had promised would now get her there.

Three years had passed since that fateful evening carriage ride of August 1884. Breckinridge now served in the US House of Representatives and carried the reputation of a gifted silver-tongued orator. While he rose through the political ranks in Washington, Madeleine drifted. From Cincinnati Wesleyan she went to Lexington, at Breckinridge's behest, and enrolled at the Sayre School, but pregnancy in the spring of 1885 (endured alone and hidden in Cincinnati) derailed her education. She left her child, fathered by Breckinridge, at an orphanage and returned to Lexington, telling friends and family she had been on a lengthy trip. She reenrolled at the Sayre School, attending sporadically in 1885–1886. Madeleine worked briefly at the local paper, read and studied, and continued to spend time with James Rodes, who gave her money from his paycheck almost weekly. He remained smitten—one Christmas giving her a four-volume set of the works of Washington Irving, but Madeleine pushed off any talk of marriage and instead insisted she would repay him. She saw Breckinridge on his trips home from Washington, but his visits were few and increasingly far between. Madeleine's dreams drifted out of reach. If she was going to recapture her future, she knew the means of doing so were not to be found in Kentucky.[9]

Madeleine moved to Washington, DC, in October 1887, becoming one of the many young men and women who chased opportunity and flooded the capital in great numbers.

Madeleine found a city of broad streets paved in cobblestone and edged with granite blocks. Since the 1870s, the population had been growing dramatically, and by 1890, 230,392 people called Washington home.[10] Government offices multiplied, and the ever-increasing layers of bureaucracy called for legions of clerks, typists, stenographers, and other office assistants. Major public works projects had transformed Washington from a swampy collection of disconnected villages to a cosmopolitan center on the must-see list for visitors and tourists. Miles of brick sidewalks kept women's skirts from mud and dust. New sewers, water pipes, and gas mains had improved the standard of living, as well as the stench, of the city. Clean, sunlit boulevards were fronted by new homes, built in elaborate architectural styles with mansard roofs and bay windows. Green spaces featured statues of founding fathers and military heroes with carefully designed plantings. The wealthy clustered their elegant homes nearby. Monumental office buildings, gleaming white in the Washington sun, provided office space for the multitude of government workers.[11]

This workforce needed affordable accommodation. By the late 1880s, new apartment buildings dotted the city, where few had been a decade earlier. Lodging houses (a room but no meals) and boardinghouses (room and meals) abounded. Madeleine found a room in the boardinghouse of a Mrs. Hemingway, located at the corner of Thirteenth and F Streets, about ten blocks east of the Capitol. Breckinridge resumed regular visits, and the reunited couple created an alias—Mr. and Mrs. Charles Foster—to cover their affair. Hemingway might have turned a blind eye to the "Fosters'" dalliances, wise as she was to the ways of Washington politicos, but she could not ignore what very quickly would become visible to all: Madeleine was pregnant. To escape Hemingway's social judgment and public revelation of her state, Madeleine moved to St. Ann's Foundling Asylum, a Catholic-run home for unwed women. Breckinridge, foolish and selfish, continued his visits. The sisters, appalled at this moral failing, asked Madeleine to leave.[12] Madeleine's dream of a cosmopolitan life once again faded.

As autumn turned to winter and 1887 passed into 1888, Madeleine waited out her second pregnancy. Dr. Mary Parsons, a Washington physician, arranged for Madeleine to board with a Black nurse, Mary McKenzie, who called Madeleine "Lady Bird."[13] Breckinridge provided medical care and the funds to keep his lover out of public view but insisted she give up the child, which, she claimed, he fathered. Madeleine, ashamed and frustrated, hid in lonely silence. As far as her Kentucky relations knew,

Madeleine was working, too busy to write. And despite her ongoing and regular correspondence with her former benefactor, she failed to write Rodes during this period. Madeleine resumed her letter writing only after the birth and subsequent forfeiting of her child to an orphanage, apologizing to Rodes for her long silence with the excuse that she had nothing of interest to report.[14] As before, having had no choice but to perform the labor of pregnancy and childbirth, she had no child to show for her effort.

Madeleine found housing at the Academy of the Holy Cross, a convent and school on Massachusetts Avenue, and from 1888 to roughly 1890 she exchanged light teaching duties for her room and board. She worked and studied. Madeleine had learned how to type and set about doing what hundreds of other single, young women did in Washington—gaining a federal job. Women had worked in federal offices since the Civil War, when the Treasury Department turned to women to replace male clerks called to military service. Over the next thirty years, women claimed increasing numbers of office jobs. When Madeleine entered office work in the summer of 1888, nearly 64 percent of stenographers and typists were women.[15]

She wrote to James Rodes that these skills were in "constant demand here and I find I can make more money at them than at anything else."[16] For competent workers, there was abundant work, she assured Rodes, still dangling before him the potential for repaying his money. But government jobs required applicants to pass the civil service exam.

Madeleine took the examination in Washington in December 1888 and again in March 1889. The general exam tested knowledge of spelling, arithmetic, and the conventions of letter writing, penmanship, and copying texts, the rudimentary skills an entry-level office worker would need.[17] She scored 73.6 percent and 72.7 percent in two attempts, passable but not laudable, especially given the intense competition for federal positions.[18] Months passed without a job offer. But Madeleine had a patron.

Breckinridge's attempts to secure a position for Madeleine were initially unsuccessful. Although he appealed to Robert Porter, the superintendent of the census, recommending Madeleine, a woman of "literary taste and talent, and . . . unflagging industry," no offer came.[19]

A few months later, Madeleine secured a position as a laborer in the Department of Agriculture's botany division, handling general office work for $600 a year.[20] She worked for only a few months, losing her job due to an extended illness, leading her once again to Breckinridge.[21] Breckinridge leaned on the census office, reminding Porter that he owed his funding to the House Appropriations Committee on which Breckinridge served.[22] Porter hired Madeleine as a computer in February 1890 at an annual salary of $720.[23] She wrote James Rodes and told him the good news, promising, as she had since moving to Washington, that now she could pay him back.[24]

A federal job was good employment. Madeleine worked six days a week from 9:00 a.m. to 4:00 p.m., with a half-hour lunch break at noon, and received thirty paid vacation days plus holidays. Within four months, she was promoted to a copyist, with a salary increase to $900. Male clerks made more than female clerks and copyists, but this was one of the higher-paying positions for women in the period.[25] With a regular paycheck, Madeleine left the convent and rented a room in a boardinghouse at 1101 Thirteenth Street, NW. James Rodes faded from her life. When he died in June 1890, he was fifty-five years old, unmarried, and broke, having never received the funds Madeleine promised him.[26]

Madeleine's efforts at self-support through wage work continued until June 1891. The reasons she left the census office seem to have been twofold. First, the new Hollerith keypunch machine dramatically reduced the census tabulation time from the eight years it had taken to tabulate the 1880 census by hand to one year for the census of 1890.[27] But in addition, Madeleine's employment file records numerous absences, meticulously noted in an oversized, leather-bound volume. In just five months of work in 1891, she had been absent seventy-one days, including thirty sick days and twenty-eight days without pay.[28] With the census tabulation complete, there was little reason to keep her on. Her supervisor wrote to the interior secretary recommending dismissal "on account of necessary reduction of force."[29]

While office work may not have turned out to be Madeleine's métier, she was not lacking in other talents and was not at loose ends for long.

———————

Madeleine befriended her landlady, the worldly Mrs. Lizzie Fillette, in her new residence on Thirteenth Street. She charmed Fillette, who, having learned of Madeleine's Kentucky roots, introduced this sparkling young woman to a Bluegrass State acquaintance, Emily Churchill Zane, whom Fillette had recently met while on a European tour. Zane, in turn, introduced Madeleine to her sister, Julia Churchill Blackburn, the widow of Luke P. Blackburn, the former governor of Kentucky. Julia's brother-in-law, Joseph Blackburn, was Kentucky's senior senator, and Julia and Emily's brothers had donated the land on which the world-famous horse track Churchill Downs was built.[30] An astute Madeleine would have recognized her new friend's family lineage, social standing, and access to political power.

Blackburn, Fillette, and Zane invited Madeleine into their elegant homes, offered rides in their horse-drawn carriages, took her shopping for custom-tailored dresses, and included her as a guest at their private receptions. Although a generation older than Madeleine, the trio was charmed by this young woman who, all sources seemed to agree, was not conventionally pretty. Despite her plain appearance, she impressed those she met as striking, intriguing, and adept at social conversation.

Social calls were critical in Blackburn, Zane, and Fillette's world, and an elaborate round of visits occupied women's time. Madeleine learned the complicated etiquette that defined elite women's lives. Younger women called on older women, political newcomers called on established families, transitory Washingtonians called on the resident elite, and all supplicants hoped to be granted entrance to the parlors of the privileged.

As Washington grew and newcomers claimed privileges some of the old guard felt came only with years, etiquette became even more complex, and Madeleine was a quick study. These rituals served as gatekeepers to keep out the pretenders. The doyenne of social etiquette in Washington, Madeleine Vinton Dahlgren, published a popular etiquette guide to enforce standards and rein in what she perceived as the undignified behavior of the younger crowd. As *Etiquette of Social Life in Washington* went through several editions, Dahlgren noted, often with reluctance, new practices such as women who had taken on their husband's titles, calling themselves Mrs. Senator or Mrs. Admiral. She snidely opined, "Perhaps when a woman captures a President or other dignitary, she has won the right to claim the title, too."[31] A fervent antisuffragist, Dahlgren was no more impressed with women "who claim to be Miss Doctor and Mrs. Reverend on their own account!"[32] She would have been appalled when Madeleine added "Breckinridge" as a middle name and even more so when Madeleine replaced "Vivian" with "Vinton," perhaps in homage to the similarly named Dahlgren.

Madeleine Valeria/Vivian/Vinton Breckinridge Pollard had mastered enough social graces to impress Julia Blackburn and be included in the mandatory visiting rounds. Social visits featured a polite conversation on a narrow range of approved topics, garnished by sipping tea. The hostess herself did not serve the beverages; typically, that honor went to a young woman, perhaps a female relative coming of age or a protégé. At a reception at Blackburn's home, the *Washington Post* highlighted Madeleine's role as one of the "graceful helpers" pouring the tea and coffee alongside a "Miss Breckinridge," possibly the congressman's niece.[33]

By 1892, Madeleine had climbed further, having moved to the boardinghouse of Lucretia Maria Minear in fashionable Lafayette Square, just a block beyond the White House. Minear's residence sat between the private Cosmos Club—whose members represented the most distinguished men of literature, arts, and science—and the home of Senator James Donald Cameron, whose wife, Elizabeth, was an important figure in Gilded Age Washington. Madeleine had then found a place in the orbit of the Washington elite. She resided for six months in Cambridge, Massachusetts, where she studied and spent time with art and literary luminaries, including the sculptor Augustus St. Gaudens and authors William Dean Howells and Charles Dudley Warner. She visited Warner's home in Hartford, Connecticut, where she chatted with Yale professors, whom she found friendlier than those at Harvard.[34]

It's not precisely clear how Madeleine met Charles Dudley Warner. One of the most well-known men of the late nineteenth century and the editor of *Harper's Weekly*, Warner had spent several weeks in Washington in 1888 to research his novel *A Little Journey in the World*, the first of a trilogy on the perils of newfound wealth. The *Washington Post* linked Madeleine and Warner in an 1891 announcement of a London gathering to which they had both been invited.[35] Later, there would be ugly rumors about their relationship, but in the summer of 1892, Warner and Madeleine appeared to those who saw them at the Bread Loaf Inn in Ripton, Vermont, to be mentor and mentee.

The Bread Loaf Inn catered to the upper middle class, and summer guests included writers, scholars, and professors escaping hot, dirty cities for cool, clean Vermont air. The inn was a Victorian showplace high among the Green Mountains, just outside Middlebury. It boasted a music hall, a bowling alley, and a smoking lounge for the men; guests could stay in cottages or suites featuring fireplaces and private baths. Owner Joseph Battell wintered in Washington, DC, where he often sought a congenial young woman to invite as a summer guest at Bread Loaf. In 1892, he chose Madeleine.[36]

She arrived in Vermont in June and charmed her fellow guests. Later that summer, Mrs. H. L. Bridgeman reviewed her Bread Loaf experience in the *Brooklyn Standard Union*, singling out Madeleine as a hidden treasure she had discovered. The lithe, graceful Kentucky girl with the thoughtful, piquant face, Bridgeman observed, had the mental strength of a man yet retained a feminine sensibility. Bridgeman effused at length on Madeleine's literary successes, claiming that Madeleine had never had a manuscript refused and that, although her writing reputation was unknown then, the world would notice when Harper and Brothers published her forthcoming novel. She reported that Madeleine spoke several languages and had degrees from three or four colleges. Despite this account's apparent exaggerations (the source of which—Bridgeman or Madeleine?—is a fact lost to history), Madeleine's pensive gray eyes, Bridgeman concluded, held "many truths."[37]

They also held some secrets—including that she was the mistress of a married congressman and, in the capital, lived a double life, hobnobbing with the elite when she was not engaged with her lover at an assignation house, having lunch in a private room, or enduring multiple visits in a single day for what we might describe as a quickie.

During that summer, there was some talk among the regular Bread Loafers of her unprotected status—it was unusual for a single, young woman to arrive unchaperoned and take up residence alone in an inn. Professor H. B. Cornwall, a Princeton University chemist who spent the summer season at Bread Loaf, noted Madeleine's solitary arrival but reported that the other guests were not only civil to her, as etiquette demanded, but went beyond and were friendly.[38] The guests were impressed when Warner arrived for a one-week stay, spending much of his daylight hours with Madeleine. The pair went on picnics and joined Battell to take photographs after hiking the mountaintop.

Madeleine left the Bread Loaf Inn in early August. Some later accounts, published well after her secret life became public gossip, suggested that Battell had asked Madeleine to leave after she performed an overly flirtatious song at the inn's talent show.[39] Other accounts suggested she returned to Washington following the news of the death of Issa Desha Breckinridge. When Issa, Mrs.

William C. P. Breckinridge, died, Madeleine Pollard's path toward marriage was suddenly clear.

Congressman Breckinridge met Madeleine at the train station on her return from Bread Loaf. He took her on a carriage ride that would be as consequential—and, later, legally significant—as the one they shared on that sultry Cincinnati summer night in 1884. Breckinridge proposed marriage, and Madeleine accepted. But any joy she may have felt was tempered by his caution that they must follow decorum and wait for a year of mourning to pass before marrying, keeping the engagement secret in deference to his recently deceased wife and in consideration of his children, who did not yet know his plans. They celebrated the engagement at an Eighth Street assignation house, where one rented a room by the hour. What happened in the ensuing months would reveal much about the social, economic, political, and sexual structures that shaped women's options in the Gilded Age. It would also link Madeleine's fate to Jane Tucker's and Jane's future to Madeleine.

In Washington, DC, the social season began in January. Congress returned from its holiday recess, residents of northern climes migrated south for more temperate weather, and engravers printed towering stacks of calling cards. Leisure class women made endless afternoon calls to the parlors of the elite, and evenings brought dinners with glittering china and glamorous dresses, products of the labor of other women, like Jane Tucker, painting porcelain and sewing gowns in stuffy Boston workshops.

In January 1893, six months after the carriage ride proposal, Madeleine imagined this would be a season of congratulations. She would be the center of attention once Breckinridge announced their engagement. Yet the announcement did not come. Months had passed since Issa Breckinridge's death, and still the congressman evaded naming a wedding date. They bickered frequently, and their relationship remained at an impasse as Madeleine clamored to cement her claim and Breckinridge increasingly pulled away. What should have been a triumph devolved into a season of heartache, and Madeleine's hard-won foothold in Washington society became ever harder to maintain.

Madeleine had accepted a generous invitation to reside at the H Street home of Mrs. Eva Thomas, two blocks from Lafayette Square. Breckinridge visited Madeleine daily, sometimes twice during the daylight hours, and then came again in the evening. Thomas's servants took silent note. Neighbors noticed. People talked. Thomas blanched at the thought of her home being used for daily trysts. She confronted her houseguest, and Madeleine assured her host that Breckinridge's frequent visits were strictly respectable and that she and the congressman were secretly engaged. While Madeleine intended to put Thomas's mind at ease, her secret set tongues wagging. Thomas—eager to counter any murmurs about her home—shared the engagement news with Claude de la Roche Francis, a mutual friend and one fond of dissecting rumors over canapés and fine wine. Like smoke from a snuffed candle, whiffs of Madeleine's alleged impropriety drifted toward Julia Blackburn.

Rumors moved quickly from whispered suspicions to ugly accusations. Lizzie Fillette, who had helped launch Madeleine into Washington society, had seen and heard things too. Unsettled, she approached Julia Blackburn, revealing that when Madeleine had boarded in her home, she had entertained Charles Dudley Warner without permission and, even more troubling, without a chaperone.[40] Fillette reasoned there was only one kind of woman who would place herself in that unseemly situation. Madeleine was nothing more than an adventuress, Fillette argued, skilled at using famous men and society women to advance herself—a fatal charge. Fillette announced she was done with Madeleine Pollard, and to protect their reputations, she urged Blackburn to break with her too.

Madeleine knew she was the subject of gossip and speculation. Fearing for her reputation, which, once lost, could never be regained, Madeleine begged Breckinridge to intercede, to defend and claim her publicly as his fiancée. When he refused, she threatened suicide rather than face this social death. She cast off what she loved best, destroying her manuscripts and giving away her fashionable clothes. When Breckinridge still failed to be moved, she upped the ante: she told her fickle lover that if Fillette and Thomas's accusations spread, if Blackburn spurned her, she would not bear the disgrace alone. She would kill him too.

Breckinridge countered with an escape plan: Madeleine should leave Washington and continue her education in a new city, and he would provide funds; she could write a new life, and he could edit her out of his. She reluctantly agreed, but Breckinridge didn't know that although Madeleine agreed to leave Washington, she did not intend to leave him. She was but a marriage ceremony away from public respectability, and it was only a matter of time before circumstances would reveal the truth behind the rumors of her affair: she was pregnant by Breckinridge for a third time. And so, when Julia Blackburn pressed Madeleine on her behavior, demanding the truth of Thomas and Fillette's claims, Madeleine told her what she hoped would prove true, what would make her actions right before physical evidence made them wrong: she confided to Blackburn what she had already let slip to Thomas—that she and Breckinridge were secretly engaged.

Breckinridge learned of the pregnancy from Madeleine's doctor, but the revelation did nothing to change his position: she must leave.[41] Madeleine now refused; she had the upper hand, and she hounded her lover at the Capitol, in the street, and at his hotel, threatening to reveal him as the father of her unborn child until he, at last, agreed to announce the engagement. He had been backed into a corner. For all his male privilege, prestige, and power, his control of this situation—one he had created in that closed carriage in 1884—was revealed to be tenuous at best.

On Good Friday of 1893, therefore, Breckinridge and Madeleine presented themselves at the home of Julia Blackburn, where Madeleine would strong-arm Breckinridge into confirming their engagement. Blackburn, steaming over the rumors and the uninvited visit, initially refused to receive them.[42]

Blackburn could ruin Madeleine socially and destroy Breckinridge politically with one sharp statement at a social event or a snub at a tea. Her word was unimpeachable. But she had been forced into a corner: to avoid the humiliation of having befriended an adventuress or, worse, a profligate, she needed this engagement as much as Madeleine did. Relenting, Blackburn permitted Madeleine to enter. Then she scribbled a note and summoned the elevator boy: Breckinridge could come up. Madeleine intercepted him on the landing. With her gray eyes likely locked on his, she told him to tell Blackburn that they were engaged.

This was no social call. Blackburn served no pastries and made no offers of tea, and she kept them waiting again. As she entered the drawing room, the calculating congressman approached. Breckinridge confirmed their engagement and asked Blackburn to protect Madeleine's reputation by her "good influences." Blackburn stared at the unlikely couple and issued a stern warning: Madeleine must leave Washington, and they must not appear together until the wedding, or they would lose her support. It was the only way to wash away the questions Lizzie Fillette's rumors and Eva Thomas's worries had raised. This was not advice; it was a directive from a woman not unfamiliar with personal scandal and the weaknesses of men, and her reputation was on the same line as theirs.

In late April, while Madeleine prepared to leave Washington as instructed, she and Breckinridge held a weekend rendezvous at the Hoffman House in New York City.[43] Arriving separately after Breckinridge, Madeleine informed the hotel staff that she was his daughter and requested an adjoining room. She opened the connecting doors, expecting to find the congressman, but his room remained empty for two days. Madeleine was puzzled, worried, and angry.

When Breckinridge finally arrived, considerable conflict ensued. Breckinridge lied about his unexplained absence; he stepped out again for unspecified reasons, and Madeleine wandered the city in search of him. Madeleine searched his bags and found his pistol, and when he eventually returned, amid much yelling, sobbing, pleading, and pounding on the adjoining door, Madeleine threatened his life and her own; a busboy was called and dismissed. Breckinridge threatened to summon the police but ultimately thought the better of it.

Not surprisingly, word of the tempestuous assignation got back to Julia Blackburn, who threatened to withdraw her support unless Breckinridge could offer an explanation for their flagrant behavior, ignoring her mandate.[44] No explanation was offered.

Madeleine, having returned to Washington and continuing her preparations for waiting out her pregnancy in New York City, knew she had few options and little time. Adding to her worries, she soon discovered that Breckinridge was being seen frequently in the company of his distant cousin Louise Scott Wing, the widow of a diplomat. Recognizing the threat Louise posed for what it was, she stormed into one such meeting in which the two were dining at the Jefferson Place House, demanding to speak to Breckinridge privately.[45]

Outside as they walked, Madeleine, distraught and distracted, brandished a gun, not noticing Breckinridge had guided her to the office of the chief of police, Major William Moore. There, the congressman called for Madeleine's arrest and threatened to tell Moore the entire story of their affair, only desisting when Madeleine agreed to his terms. She must leave.

As they left the office, Breckinridge turned to Madeleine. He said he would not give her another dollar.[46] This affair was over.

Madeleine's vision of a successful marriage was being replaced by a nightmare of disgrace. She confided her feelings to Mrs. Thomas and Claude de la Roche Francis: she hated

Breckinridge—he was cruel; she loved him—he had been so kind. Madeleine rambled and cried and threatened suicide if the congressman failed to marry her. If trouble arose, she pleaded, eyes wide, please remain her friend.

The following days brought more tears and talk with the same pattern repeating: Madeleine pulled another gun, threats were made, and Breckinridge defused her anger with vague promises he had no intention of keeping. She demanded to know the meaning of his frequent appearances with Louise Wing. Breckinridge demurred, saying again that it was Madeleine he planned to marry. The pair renewed their appeal to Julia Blackburn for support—Breckinridge suggested Madeleine accompany Blackburn to the Chicago World's Fair—but Blackburn repeated her intention to withdraw her support. There would be no trip to Chicago.

That bridge burned, Madeleine made one last attempt at a foothold of legitimacy. Before leaving for New York, she insisted that she and Breckinridge make a statement before Major Moore, seeking an additional witness to Breckinridge's promise. They had agreed to tell Moore of her pregnancy, Breckinridge's paternity, and their firm plan to marry. At the police station, however, Breckinridge saw an opportunity to gain the upper hand and went off script, sharing the seamier details of their history. Breckinridge told Moore that they had been involved in a nine-year affair, begun in an assignation house within a day of their first acquaintance. Breckinridge added that Madeleine had had lovers before him; he had not, he insisted, seduced her. He was, after all, a gentleman.

Horrified, Madeleine predictably took out her pistol, but this time, she surrendered it to Moore as she demanded one last time that Breckinridge marry her. Within Moore's hearing, and likely simply to encourage Madeleine to board the next train to New York, Breckinridge pledged, "I will marry you the last day of the month if God don't interpose."[47] This was the last time Madeleine Pollard and William C. P. Breckinridge would be face to face until they met in court, ten months later.

The ensuing days would bring yet another chapter of their ill-fated relationship to a close. Breckinridge left Washington for Kentucky; Madeleine relocated to New York as promised, considering her future with Breckinridge as the train rolled north. She planned to take up painting on porcelain or dabble in watercolors and continue her studies in English literature. When the city became unbearable with summer heat, she imagined she would take a house elsewhere, perhaps in the Hudson River Valley. She envisioned the life of a fortunate, middle-class wife, not an exiled, pregnant mistress with an untrustworthy lover.

Just two days after she settled in, illness forced her to return to Washington as a dull ache grew to crippling cramps. She took refuge in Mrs. Thomas's home and called Dr. Tabor Johnson. Two months into her third pregnancy, Madeleine miscarried.[48]

Madeleine abandoned the New York City plan. Her sudden lack of pregnancy removed evidence of their sexual impropriety, and, with one year of mourning the late Mrs. Breckinridge nearing completion, the way was clear to the promised marriage and completing her quest for a respectable reputation and life in the leisure class. She no longer had to hide in a distant city. With the care of her physician, Madeleine recuperated in the capital and wrote Breckinridge daily.

In her letters and telegrams, Madeleine pressed for marriage, reminding Breckinridge of his previous promises to do so. Yet he continued to deflect and delay, offering her only stern directives.

He would not come to Washington, and he would not allow Madeleine to join him in Kentucky. Breckinridge implored her to let him do what was best.[49] Finished with asking for the marriage Breckinridge was unwilling to plan, she pulled a sheet of paper from her desk and picked up a pen. And in one straightforward sentence, Madeleine took matters into her own hands and did what was best for her.

3

A CONSIDERABLE SURPRISE

*The engagement of Representative W. C. P. Breckinridge
of Kentucky and Miss Madeline Pollard of this city is
announced.*

—WASHINGTON EVENING STAR, JUNE 23, 1893

The *Washington Evening Star* broke the news late on
June 23. The *Washington Post* and the *New York Times* followed.
The news spread east to west, telegraphed from paper to paper.
The *Frankfort Roundabout* emphasized Madeleine's Kentucky kin
and local roots. How proud Nannie Pollard must have been, vis-
iting old friends in Crab Orchard when the *Interior Journal* pub-
lished the report. Her daughter's education had paid off. Desha
Breckinridge read the announcement on June 24 in the *Cincinnati
Enquirer*. He tore it from the paper and sent it to his father in
Louisville.[1]

Breckinridge was shocked, furious at Madeleine's audacity.
He fired off a letter demanding an explanation. She replied to his
blistering note with calculated deference. To "My Dear Willie,"
she wrote that she felt it was only proper to make a definitive
public statement. She was sorry if she had erred. She explained to
her putative fiancé that she was leaving that day for The Farms,
near Charlottesville, Virginia, as a guest of the Blackburn family.
Indeed, she offered, she was confident that he and Mrs. Blackburn
would agree it was correct to continue under Blackburn's chap-
eronage during the formal engagement period. "I am your loving
Madeleine," she signed her note.[2]

Breckinridge replied with multiple directives: stay in Virginia, do not come to Lexington; being seen together would only end in scandal. He refused to acknowledge an engagement; he operated under the delusion that he was in control: "Do not make it impossible for me to do what is best," he wrote, signing his letter perfunctorily: "Yours, Wm. C. P. Breckinridge."[3] He did not clarify for whom his doing "what is best" would benefit most.

His children and close kin were foremost in Breckinridge's mind. He hurried to Lexington to speak to his family and offer an explanation. The historical record is silent on that difficult conversation. It is, however, clear that the congressman's constituents were talking. When a local acquaintance encountered Breckinridge and questioned him about the news, he strenuously denied the engagement. It was impossible, Breckinridge said, for any such relationship to exist with a woman like Pollard. The acquaintance told the local press of his encounter. The *Gazette* published Breckinridge's comments.[4]

In Louisville, the newspaper staff of the *Louisville Commercial* discussed a pervasive rumor. They had seen Madeleine's announcement, yet they knew that Breckinridge had made frequent trips to Louisville, and when he was in town, he always called on Louise Scott Wing. The editor smelled a story and dispatched a reporter to the home of Dr. Preston Scott, Louise's brother with whom she resided. Much to his surprise, the reporter found Breckinridge in the Scotts' parlor, just arrived from Lexington. The reporter bluffed: "From good authority," he said, he knew Breckinridge and Wing were engaged. What did the congressman have to say about that? And what of Miss Pollard? And why was Breckinridge in Louisville? Did Dr. Scott have a comment? Scott shifted uncomfortably, uncertain what he should reveal. Breckinridge interrupted the reporter and ended the interview, promising to stop by the newspaper office later that day.[5]

Accompanied by Scott, Breckinridge met with the *Commercial* reporters. Yes, he admitted, it was true. He had been calling on Louise Wing. With the consent of her brother, he had asked

Wing to be his wife. But, Breckinridge hastened to add, she had not yet agreed to his proposal, and he wasn't sure she would, he confessed.[6] Please, he asked, keep this out of the newspapers. Scott pushed further on behalf of his sister: there was no news yet to print; they are not yet engaged. As for Miss Pollard's announcement, Breckinridge explained as Preston Scott looked on, that was false. There had never been a possibility of marriage to Miss Pollard. And that they could print.

While Breckinridge in Louisville explained to a worried Louise Wing that Madeleine Pollard was a lovelorn young woman imagining a fantasy, Madeleine enjoyed the cool Virginia air at the Blackburns' summer residence. The publication of the formal announcement placed Madeleine back in Julia Blackburn's good graces, and she believed she had pinned Breckinridge down at last. In these first days of July, Madeleine shared her happy news, writing friends and family, including her former Lexington landlady, Mrs. Ketchum. She would soon marry, she announced, in case her correspondents had not seen the newspaper notice from a week ago. Following the wedding, the happy couple planned a trip to the World's Fair. Newspapers nationwide continued to print the Breckinridge-Pollard engagement.

On July 3, the Louisville paper published Breckinridge's denial of an engagement to Madeleine Pollard and kept Louise Wing out of the article as agreed. The Lexington papers reprinted the story; the *Brooklyn Eagle* repeated it, and the congressman's denial spread on and on.[7] In Virginia, a starry-eyed Madeleine read the Kentucky newspapers and learned that her gambit had failed.

Cutting Breckinridge's denial from the *Gazette,* she pasted the clipping at the top of a sheet of writing paper, throwing his own words back at him. Coldly addressing her lover as "Colonel Breckinridge," she insisted that his statement was utterly false. "You have gone back on a solemn promise," she accused and demanded a written statement countering the published denial. If he did not admit their marriage plans and provide the proof in writing by July 22, she would return to Washington and feel at perfect liberty to publish the fact of their engagement and potentially much more. While her letter winged its way to Lexington, Madeleine's distress grew.[8]

Spurred by Madeleine's threat of exposure, Breckinridge reached out to the Washington chief of police, Major Moore. Full of self-pity for how the newspapers chewed over his personal life with "malicious notes" and "innuendo," he railed against what he termed Madeleine's letter-writing campaign, in which she shared her engagement news with friends. Breckinridge grumbled that he had enemies who would be only too happy to publish "if she gives the papers and scandalmongers the opportunity." Breckinridge asked Moore to watch for her return to Washington and to keep her from the press. He sent Madeleine a telegram: "Written Major Moore. See him before you make publication." She ignored his message.[9]

Preston Scott could not have been happy either as his sister's suitor's name was dragged through the paper, and the whispers around Louisville grew louder. The news about this Pollard woman was most upsetting, let alone unseemly. He had reputations to protect: his widowed sister's, his good family name. Scott pressed Breckinridge for a wedding date. He would dispel the rumors and force clarity in the fog of gossip. On July 14, Scott joined the newspaper fray with a page out of Madeleine's playbook: he marched down to the Louisville newspaper office with an announcement that his sister, Louise Scott Wing, was marrying Congressman William C. P. Breckinridge. The editor hesitated—hadn't Breckinridge and Scott denied such an engagement in the editor's office? Scott replied testily, "The marriage would occur."[10] And the following day, on Preston Scott's authority, the newspaper reported that Breckinridge and Louise Wing would wed in Washington on August 2, just before the opening of a special session of Congress. In the fall, Scott had revealed, Breckinridge and Louise would visit the World's Fair.

The *Louisville Courier-Journal* remarked that the news caused a "pleasant flutter" among society people. The *Cincinnati*

Enquirer reported that Kentucky residents had been "much agitated" over whom Breckinridge would marry. Louise Wing, the papers enthused, was perfectly fitted in every way to be a congressman's wife. Still, the *Enquirer* offered, Wing was a surprise. Some still believed Madeleine Pollard would be the lucky bride. The Stanford, Kentucky, *Semi-Weekly Intelligencer* concluded Breckinridge was "sly, devilishly sly."[11]

Sly indeed. As tongues wagged, Louise Wing swung between joy and fluster. She had barely two weeks to plan a Washington wedding. Instead of offering support or reassurance to his fiancée, Louise's future husband insisted on a new plan, overwriting the August 2 date her brother likely selected. Breckinridge had decided they would marry this week. Wing hesitated; Breckinridge insisted. He was doing what was best for him.

And so, three days after their engagement had been announced, Louise Wing married Breckinridge in Louisville on the evening of July 18. Close family and a few local friends gathered at Dr. Scott's home for the evening ceremony. A light dinner followed. Wing wore a simple white dress with a bridal robe of white chiffon over which was draped a Parisian bridal veil. The newlyweds left on a late evening train for Harrogate, Tennessee, where they would rest at a resort hotel before traveling to Washington. The newspapers buzzed excitedly, reeling from the back-to-back engagements, the denials, and the surprise wedding. The Louisville papers reported that Wing was a lovely bride and that now, as a married woman, she no longer appeared as ill as she had of late.[12]

While Wing felt relief with her claim on Breckinridge solidified, her husband remained wary. Newspapers pondered the reason for the sudden wedding just days after the engagement announcement. One suggested that Wing's recent poor health necessitated the hurried-up date, speculating that Wing's physician brother had urged her to leave Kentucky summer heat for cooler climes. Left undiscussed by the papers were the advantages the congressman gained; Madeleine no longer had a claim on him. Surely, Breckinridge believed, she would now see the futility of her quest. She had lost. And if she moved on, they could both escape stigma and shame, an affair lost to history. A clean slate, starting over—he with a new wife, she with whatever she would find to do next.[13]

Did Madeleine learn of the wedding from the newspaper, or did a sympathetic friend send a telegram or note? We don't know how she discovered her dream had been crushed, that instead of a congressman's wife, she was now a congressman's former mistress, a onetime fiancée, a jilted woman humiliated further with each newspaper story on the lovely Louise Wing. The *Frankfort Roundabout* concluded that the previous announcement of Pollard's engagement must have been a mistake.[14]

The Virginia social set claimed to be "considerably surprised" by the Breckinridge-Wing marriage as they had long known, the local paper asserted, that Madeleine would wed Breckinridge. The *Cincinnati Enquirer* reported that nothing had been heard of Miss Pollard since the wedding.[15] How stunned Madeleine must have been to open that newspaper; how astonished were the Blackburns, having trusted their summer guest was engaged. Julia Blackburn had warned Madeleine that Breckinridge—that men—could be cads if they chose. The congressman indeed proved a cad. He had misled Madeleine, and he had deceived Blackburn. Intentionally. Deviously. Slyly, devilishly so.

On her honeymoon in Tennessee, Louise Wing Breckinridge claimed she was happy despite "wedding haste and wild confusion." There had been no time to invite anyone from a distance; her husband had insisted on speed, she apologized to her sister Ella. "I was so out of health," she wrote, "that I made no remonstrance though I was much upset." At the Four Seasons hotel, the Breckinridges would rest and recover away from gossips and prying reporters. Surely, Louise projected, time and distance would steer their marriage onto a good course. Toward the end of her letter, the new Mrs. Breckinridge reasserted that she was in good health, assuring herself as much as her sister that she felt better. She was very happy and devoted to her husband, and he was attentive to her. Still, she reported to Ella that she was nervous. Soon, though, they would be in Washington, and Louise would take her rightful place as a congressman's wife. There was so much to look forward to—society events among the powerful, a home of her own, a cosmopolitan life in the nation's capital, and the devotion of a good husband.[16]

As August began, Louise Wing Breckinridge's marriage launched her into a promising new life as a congressman's wife. On the twelfth, she joined her husband and other distinguished guests in Philadelphia to witness the launch of the steel-hulled cruiser *Minneapolis*. At two thirty, Minnesota senator William D. Washburn's daughter, Lizzie, smacked a champagne bottle against the carmine and dark-gray hull. The foaming bubbly glistened in the sun, a cannon boomed, thirty thousand spectators shouted, and fair-skinned women in summer dresses waved white handkerchiefs. The ship catapulted forward into the Delaware River.[17]

The crowds dispersed as waiting tugboats moved the *Minneapolis* to its new home. The shipbuilder, Charles Cramp, welcomed the Breckinridges and other special guests to a luncheon laid out in his offices. Even in these gatherings with several hundred officials and influential people, the congressman enjoyed prominence, and Louise basked in her new status. Newspaper coverage of the launch listed Breckinridge among the most noted men in attendance. Most articles, but not all, recorded Louise's presence as well. Their marriage was but three weeks old, and the couple had just returned to the capital for the special session of Congress. They were still news.

Louise looked forward to reestablishing herself in Washington. As a diplomat's wife, she had mingled in society circles before but had been out of the social scene since her first husband, Edward Rumsey Wing, died in Ecuador in 1874. Now, she expected an active social life. A congressman's wife had duties; hers centered in the home. The teas, dinners, and calling hours Louise would host were opportunities to press her husband's political agenda among the wives of the influential, who were equally eager to secure political alliances for their husbands over tea and cakes. First, she would call on those women who outranked her in the capital's social circles, and then she would receive the women of lesser status obligated to call on *her* in the hierarchy of Washington social custom. The complexities of society etiquette reinforced the rigid social hierarchy; serving the right tea, visiting the right women, and making the right comments served as a litmus test authenticating a woman's social place.[18]

The Breckinridges had taken rooms at the Cochran, a residence hotel favored by members of Congress. Still, Louise was eager to take up housekeeping, renting a home befitting their rank. In the coming social season, she knew she would be the center of attention, touted, feted, and celebrated for her fine match. A burst of light pushed aside the dark days of early summer.

On August 12, 1893, the luncheon at Cramp's shipyard completed, the Breckinridges boarded the special train back to Washington, flush with the excitement of the celebration and the boisterous crowd. Breckinridge spent most of the journey conversing with the secretary of the navy in cheerful spirits. But while the Pullman cars made their way south from Philadelphia, in Washington, the Breckinridges' new happiness was perilously near the end of its short life. Louise Breckinridge's first official event as a proud congressman's wife was also her last.[19]

While Breckinridge made ceremonial appearances, Madeleine Pollard attended to her future. The one-two punch of humiliation had not abated. In June, Breckinridge's repudiation of their engagement had made Madeleine an object of pity, and in July, the congressman's hastily arranged marriage made Madeleine the fool. On top of that, he dared try to buy her off using Major Moore as an intermediary: one hundred dollars to erase the last decade of her life? Pollard's fury grew into a hardened determination. She would not face this humiliation alone.

Madeleine hired two of Washington's most prominent lawyers, Calderon Carlisle and Jeremiah W. Wilson. Carlisle was the attorney for the British and Spanish legations, among other diplomatic clients. Wilson had spent years as a circuit court judge before representing Indiana in the US House of Representatives. By the 1890s, he was managing a highly successful Washington, DC, law practice. He was a brilliant man and a shrewd criminal lawyer and cross-examiner.[20]

Carlisle and Wilson worked fast. Barely three weeks after Madeleine's hopes for marriage died, her able attorneys walked to the Superior Court of the District of Columbia and filed a sheaf of paperwork. Madeleine V. Pollard charged W. C. P. Breckinridge with breach of promise for his failure to marry her. In doing so, the suit alleged Breckinridge had stolen her youth and ruined her future.[21]

The loss of Madeleine's past and future was not mere romantic rhetoric. Breach of promise established that jilted women suffered injuries, depriving them of the financial security and the social and economic advantages a marriage brought. Developed primarily as a remedy for white, middle-class women, breach of promise law recognized women's social humiliation and the economic, psychological, and social costs of having been abandoned.

A woman's security was her reputation, which was built on the notion of respectability. For much of Victorian society, female respectability entailed chastity—this was, particularly for single women, their most significant asset as they sought the economic safety of marriage. A jilted woman was suspect due to her tarnished reputation; a seduced woman was considered ruined. Future opportunities for marriage diminished, ultimately presenting financial loss and harm. Madeleine could receive monetary compensation if successful in court, but more importantly, the court could make whole her damaged respectability. They could deem her respectable once more.[22]

Suing for breach of promise was a bold move. Women did not typically bring forward lawsuits; the courtroom was a male bastion. But in doing so, Madeleine took active control of her life, yet, ironically, in a way that required she be depicted as Breckinridge's passive victim. She would need to face her accuser and name his crimes without being so bold and aggressive as to suggest a woman strong enough to have resisted his advances. But a meek presentation in court might also leave her voiceless, unable to explain and advocate for her life's path. She would have to walk a fine line between boldness and reticence to win over the jury.

Madeleine's perceived social class presented a challenge as well. When a man and a woman of the upper classes engaged in a sexual transgression, social arbiters deemed that the woman had a reputation that could be restored. But in a liaison between an upper-class man and a woman of a lower class, she, it was understood, had no reputation to be restored. In court, therefore, Madeleine's lawyers would attempt to depict her as a legitimate member of the leisured class; the defense would argue that she was a pretender, a lower-class woman trying to jump social categories. Madeleine was taking an enormous risk: her closest-held secrets were about to be laid bare for all to see, but then again, so were Breckinridge's.

On August 12, just hours after Madeleine's attorneys filed their documents, the late-afternoon Washington papers revealed the nature of the lawsuit and what had transpired between Breckinridge and Madeleine. Perhaps Carlisle and Wilson tipped off the press, offering a savory lead on what they knew would be breaking news. Or maybe a newspaper reporter lingering at the courthouse recognized the prominent attorneys and stumbled on to the colossal scoop. What is certain is that while Breckinridge's train chugged back to DC, in the House of Representatives, House members already huddled in small groups around their desks, their talk of Breckinridge's perfidy pushing aside the debate on whether silver or gold should anchor the US economy.[23]

The first short newspaper accounts laid out the stunning allegations: Breckinridge had promised to marry Madeleine Pollard but had reneged, marrying Louise Wing instead; Pollard and

Breckinridge had engaged in a nearly ten-year affair, begun when he seduced her when she was but a seventeen-year-old maiden, a college student bent on a literary career. From that time, the suit alleged, she fell under his complete domination: when she became pregnant, he forced her to give up the resulting infants; when she sought an education abroad, he forbade her to leave; when she attempted to end their illicit affair, he persuaded her to abandon her plans. And consistently and repeatedly, he swore he would marry her. But then he had married someone else.[24]

The Breckinridges returned to Washington in the early evening of the twelfth and walked from the train platform to the carriage entrance, chatting cheerfully with fellow passengers. They rode to the Cochran Hotel in the contentment of ignorance. No one on the train knew of the breaking scandal; the Breckinridges were blissfully unaware that they were already the hottest gossip in the city. On the short ride to the Cochran, they thought only of washing up and having supper in the hotel dining room.

Their carriage arrived at the hotel. As they stepped from the vehicle, a friend intercepted the congressman, pulling him aside to speak privately: Madeleine Pollard had entered a lawsuit, he said. She had sued him for breach of promise. Evading reporters, the Breckinridges ate a subdued meal in the public dining room. As they crossed the lobby afterward, however, time ran out on the congressman's secret life. A nervous attaché from the marshal's office approached and handed the congressman papers: he had been served.

Journalists stationed in Washington had the immediate scoop, but telegraph, telephone, and train quickly spread the news. By the following day, newspapers from New York to San Francisco reported the tale: "Sensational Charges," "Trifled with Her Affections," "Romance with Bitter Realities," "A Congressman in Trouble." The *Times* of Philadelphia reported knowingly that this great sensation had been brewing for weeks and quietly making the rounds of society. Headlines established the battle lines of this suit. Some championed Madeleine—a schoolgirl, cruelly tricked; others defended Breckinridge from the adventuress bent on blackmail.[25]

As the newspapers churned out excited headlines, Louise, one imagines, engaged in a difficult, private conversation with her new husband as they sat sequestered in their room. She faced an uncomfortable truth. He had lied to her; he had assured her in June when Madeleine's engagement announcement appeared that she represented only a lovelorn woman—someone to be pitied, not feared. Now Louise knew Madeleine had been his lover. He had been an unfaithful husband to the second Mrs. Breckinridge—had he been to the third?

The revelations crushed Louise. The bestselling author E. D. E. N. Southworth, who lived in Washington and moved among the city's best people, described Louise's social fall: "*Now*! While political circles were in eager expectation of the meeting of the extra session of congress, social circles were looking forward to the arrival of the celebrated statesman . . . and his beautiful bride—*he* a leader in Congress, she a queen of society. But they had not been here a week before the most disgraceful scandal was exposed that has ruined them socially, if not financially and politically. The poor lady who expected to queen it here is prostrated with grief and mortification although she is not to be blamed but very much to be pitied."[26]

The pity was evident whenever Louise left her room. In the public dining room, hotel guests took surreptitious glances at the humiliated newlywed. Kentucky senator William Lindsay wrote to his wife, relaying his surprise at finding the Breckinridges still at the Cochran: "I don't know whether they are permanently located and hope they are not."[27] Lindsay's mother-in-law joined the senator in Washington and endured an awkward scene when the Breckinridges' attempt at small talk with the Lindsays fell flat. The Breckinridges moved across the room. The senator's mother-in-law described the difficult social situation: "They both looked embarrassed. I am only going to be polite. I don't think we will enjoy anything *closer.*"[28] She wrote her daughter that Louise Breckinridge looked thin but youthful and wore a perky sailor's hat. In early September, she explained that the Breckinridges were keeping to their room: "They came in the parlor last week several times but were left so alone that they do not come now at all."[29] Three days later, she and the senator reported that Louise was sick from worry and mortification.[30] Breckinridge's letters to his confidants indicated that Louise's mental and physical health was failing.

Breckinridge had said little to the press, opining only that this charge was the result of "vindictiveness, vexation, and perhaps, blackmail."[31] Madeleine hid, equally reticent to speak on record. Reporters staked out her boardinghouse, a fashionable residence in a well-known block called Grant Row, just beyond the Capitol. Washington detectives attempted to follow her around the city, although she proved elusive. Detective James Greaves reported, "Things have been very quiet here, and I have seen that party but once. I have been on the lookout at her old place on K Street [St. Ann's] and my father has also taken up the watch, and not seeing her I think she has changed residences again."[32] He once spotted her on the corner of Fifteenth and Pennsylvania Avenue talking to a stylishly dressed man with a fast appearance. The two were deep in conversation, but Graves couldn't say anything about what and who the man was.

C. E. Sears, a reporter from the *New York World,* did locate Madeleine, and his reward was a rare interview. He crowed to his readers how the Washington correspondents had failed to pin her down but the *World,* he bragged, had succeeded. Seeing a weary interval before her story could be heard in court, Madeleine declined a formal interview but offered to write a detailed narrative. Her attorneys supported this savvy move; in writing her essay, Madeleine would control her story, setting out the argument her lawyers would make.

Madeleine invited Sears to her sparsely furnished room. She charmed the reporter. She is, he wrote, of average height, and while her figure looks spare at first glance, one soon sees a sense of perfection in her outline and grace. He praised her sparkling face and dark and abundant hair, braided and coiled firmly at the back of her head. Her nails were neatly cut and highly polished. She wore a dark dress with a dark-blue silk waist adorned with many ruffles. She wore a stiff straw sailor's hat, black, with a delicate veil that fell over her face. Madeleine's voice was clear and resonant as a bell. When she was moved, he observed, her voice grew low and quiet, her body stiffened, and she clenched her hands.[33]

Madeleine sat at her desk and wrote her statement as the reporter looked on, his presence verifying Pollard's authorship to *World* readers. Her white hand glided over the pages, frequently returning to an earlier passage to insert a word or revise an unclear sentence. She wrote quickly and confidently, without pause or conversation. When she finished, Madeleine stood quickly and shared her work with the reporter, resisting his suggestions for amplification of some passages and arguing successfully for brevity. The printed page was to be hers; she knew what she wanted to say.

On Sunday, September 17, 1893, Madeleine's essay appeared on page 19 of the *World*, the entire sheet a full-page spread of tiny type, eight columns of her sad story in a newspaper eighteen inches wide and nearly two feet high.[34] She neither asked for nor expected to be paid for her piece; she wanted only the chance to make a statement, countering the barrage of information carried in the daily papers that had speculated wildly on her life. This essay, she wrote, was one of the few ways left for her to redeem herself for the years of falsehood and deception she practiced in her misguided devotion to Breckinridge. Her impulse to tell this story and reveal the truth, she wrote, was irresistible.

The *World* piece could be summed up easily: promises, promises. Madeleine crafted a narrative arc of a sheltered schoolgirl longing for education when she crossed paths with Breckinridge, a man who took advantage of her youth, naivete, and lack of a father and used his powers of persuasion to ensure her devotion, manipulating and controlling her until he tired of her, cast her off, and married another. She had intended to devote her life to him, become educated and a credit to society, and marry him. Breckinridge broke that dream.

The *World* essay fired public curiosity, and reporters besieged her. Pen-wielding men followed her to her boardinghouse, making a scene her landlady could ill afford. She ran a respectable place, she said, and she would not risk her reputation with a boarder of Madeleine's character. The landlady asked her to leave.

Madeleine turned to St. Ann's on K Street, but the matron refused her; the house welcomed only the pregnant and unwed. Instead, the matron suggested she go to the House of Mercy next door. In September 1893, the House of Mercy, called the "Home" by residents, was under the management of Mary Gray Talcott, a fifty-six-year-old single woman. When Madeleine requested entrance, she didn't have enough money for streetcar fare to travel to her attorneys' office. Talcott sympathized with her impoverished state, but Madeleine's history had preceded her. Talcott reluctantly admitted her and took it on herself to collect money from some of Madeleine's "lady friends" to provide for incidentals. But those friends read the newspapers, too, and quickly and quietly drifted away.

Later in the fall, the House of Mercy changed managerial hands, and Madeleine, already in residence, became an inherited boarder. The problem of Pollard passed from Talcott to Sister Dorothea, the new matron. In short order, Sister Dorothea realized how dearly she would have loved to evict Madeleine. Madeleine was broke and notorious. She had managed to elude the press, avoiding unwanted attention to herself and the Home, but her perpetual lack of funds led to upset. She owed a week's board at her previous rooming house, and the landlady, so quick to evict her now-notable tenant, pursued the insolvent Madeleine to the House of Mercy, demanding payment. Frustrated by the repeated intrusions, Sister Dorothea gave the landlady five dollars just to be relieved of her annoying visits. Dorothea also provided streetcar fare and meals for Madeleine, expenses that added up to thirty dollars, funds the charitable organization was hard-pressed to spare.

To Dorothea, although all the residents were fallen women, Madeleine was a contaminant, and the House of Mercy matron was none too pleased to have her residing among her young, impressionable charges. She allowed her to stay but only under an alias—if she wished to leave the residence, she must ask permission, and she would work as a teacher to earn her board, and never, Dorothea demanded, could she tell her story to any of the residents. The lawyers assured Dorothea that Madeleine's tenure there would be short.[35]

But it wasn't, and as the weeks ticked by, antipathy grew.

Just days after the scandal broke, Madeleine's attorneys, Calderon Carlisle and Jeremiah Wilson, sent investigators to Lexington, seeking evidence of her good character and of Breckinridge's failings, and throughout the fall, they worked to gather the evidence to support her claims.[36] Washingtonians spent much time speculating on who was footing the bill for her high-priced attorneys. Several reports suggested Julia Blackburn was behind at least one campaign to provide funds to Madeleine. One story cites an unnamed society woman who reported that Blackburn had written to the women of her social circle, appealing for funds to assist with the plaintiff's legal expenses. The goal of this support was explicitly not to condone Madeleine's behavior but rather to condemn that of Breckinridge. To Blackburn and her circle, this was not simply a he-said/she-said debate. Breckinridge's crime was about the sanctity of the home and parlor and the risk to women's pride and reputations that men endangered when they played these foolish games.

It was likely the extended Blackburn family had urged Madeleine to sue—they had the legal connections and knowledge to counsel her next steps. In July 1893, when the congressman married Wing and the Blackburns entertained Madeleine at their summer residence, they were under the assumption she was a jilted legitimate fiancée. Madeleine had no father to defend her, no wealth for lawyers, no social status of her own—in short, no resources on which to make an effective response. Women without resources just had to take what fate had given. But she did have, at least at that difficult moment, her connections to Julia and Terese Blackburn. This proved to be her most valuable asset in the summer of 1893.

Blackburn claimed she learned the depth of Madeleine's duplicity from the newspaper when the scandal broke. She was shocked and hurt when the papers announced the mid-July wedding to Louise Wing, livid that Breckinridge made her a fool in convincing her to chaperone a woman whom he later discarded without the promised marriage. But in August, once the extent of Breckinridge and Madeleine's relationship was revealed, Blackburn was apoplectic that the congressman imposed on her a common mistress—and one who had been pregnant, multiple times, out of wedlock. Indeed, as Julia would later learn, a pregnant Madeleine sat in her parlor on Good Friday, playacting an engagement. Urging Madeleine to sue for breach of promise, for the Blackburns, was not to help Madeleine salvage her reputation but for Julia Blackburn to recover hers.

When the scandal broke, General Basil Duke was one of the first of Breckinridge's friends to defend him in the press. Duke was quick to disparage Madeleine and deny that Breckinridge had ever seduced any woman. Blackburn wrote to Duke and in no uncertain terms acquainted him with the facts, which, she insisted, if he had known, he would not have made his supportive statements. Breckinridge, she said, had "polluted the parlor." If her husband were alive, she wrote, he would hold Breckinridge responsible for this offensive insult. "Outraged" and "Indignant," the newspaper headlines read, and as a result, Julia Blackburn would not hesitate to appear in court to vindicate her name and make Breckinridge pay.[37]

In the months following the eruption of scandal, Breckinridge's challenges mounted. The Blackburns' anger seeped into elite circles, and friends who defended him in August drifted away by December. Louise Wing's mental health continued to decline, and Breckinridge struggled to attend to demands of family, the lawsuit, and his duties in Congress. In addition, his finances were severely strained, and he fell deeper and deeper into debt. He had assembled a large legal team, a mix of attorneys from Kentucky and Washington, but Breckinridge planned his three-pronged defense: he would demonstrate that Pollard was older than she claimed, prove that she had been no virgin, and find evidence that he was not her only lover. This would remove from Breckinridge the fatal stain of seduction while proving that she was, he would later say, not the kind of woman a man would marry—no matter what he had or had not promised.

Charles Stoll grew frustrated with the congressman's seemingly single-minded focus on disproving seduction. In months of interviews, Breckinridge's investigators had yet to find a smoking gun, an eyewitness, or a document exonerating the congressman. Late in 1893, Stoll met with the famous Pinkerton detective agency to seek assistance in ferreting out Madeleine's past. Breckinridge's independent investigators had gathered hearsay tales of fast times and loose talk from men across Kentucky who claimed to have known Madeleine. The Pinkerton agent was unimpressed and warned Stoll not to bother with testimony from intemperate men who frequented brothels; the judge will throw it out, he cautioned. Stoll knew Breckinridge was wasting time, money he didn't have, and energy pursuing unprovable rumors about Madeleine's youth. The trial was slated to begin in March, and their team had yet to create a credible defense. With little time remaining, in January 1894, Stoll met with the congressman and his son and pushed forward a bold idea to get the truth directly from Madeleine Pollard. And Stoll knew just the young woman who could help.[38]

4

No Mistakes

Charles Stoll's trip to Boston was a mission of desperation. By January 1894, Breckinridge's constituents and colleagues who had pledged their fervent support when the scandal broke the previous August had drifted away in the wake of Madeleine's accusations—three pregnancies, abandoned infants, and cheating on Issa Breckinridge, his much-revered late second wife. Breckinridge's attorneys floundered in their preparation, hamstrung by inadequate funds and their client lacking a credible defense. So far, attempts at a settlement with the plaintiff had failed.[1] Breckinridge had stubbornly resisted advice, failing to fully grasp the consequences of his team's legal blunders and missteps. In a letter to Breckinridge's son, Desha, Stoll noted that his father, "like all great men, is not a great adviser for himself."[2] But Stoll had a plan, and on January 12, he shared it with the Breckinridge men in person. Desha later wrote to his father, "What you will decide, I don't know. I have never seen a man more in earnest, I think . . . as to his suggestions, I have no opinion, but he is wise, shrewd, and with superb nerve."[3] He was not the only one for whom nerve would be needed.

Four days later, Stoll sent the congressman an update. After a stop in New York, Stoll would board the midnight train to Boston for a face-to-face meeting with Jane. This was the only safe way to pass along critical, and secret, details of the job. "I doubt," wrote Stoll, "the wisdom of telegraphing the young lady."[4] While

Breckinridge pushed his team to hire Pinkerton detectives in multiple elaborate schemes, the cost was prohibitive, and Stoll had confidence in his plan.[5] He also had great confidence in Jane Tucker, their Hail Mary pass—a last-ditch attempt to give the defense an edge.

In Maine, Jane hurriedly prepared for a job she knew little about. She made a pretty dress and had a new black serge coat sewn and trimmed with Persian lamb.[6] She looked distinguished and stylish. Her mother had come around to this opportunity. Stoll's letters and telegrams had just kept coming. Jane had no recourse, Mollie wrote to Mame, but to accept or "lose the friendship of a very powerful friend & the only kind & considerate employer she has ever known."[7] Mame agreed that it was quite the compliment for Stoll to want Jane, although she worried about Jane's illness and whether her departure would leave her parents in the lurch. "As long as you and Father feel that you can spare her," Mame wrote to her mother, "why it's all right for her to go," as if the decision about a household she had assiduously avoided joining was hers to make.[8] Jane's fatigue gave way to excitement: her appetite returned, she slept well, and her mother reported to Mame, as Jane left for Boston, her bowels were regular.[9]

Under gray winter skies, Stoll revealed the details of the clandestine task.

Given Stoll's preference for New York's luxurious Astor House and Park Place Hotel, it's likely he met Jane at one of the finer Boston establishments, perhaps the Copley Square House or the Parker House, where hotel bakers invented the Parker House roll and made Boston cream pie iconic.[10] Decorum required a public meeting place for a married man and a single woman, but the need for secrecy may have pushed them to a far corner of a hotel restaurant. Stoll quietly and carefully broached the delicate subject.

Stoll explained that his lifelong friend, a congressman, had become "complicated" with a young woman, Madeleine Pollard. She had sued him for breach of promise, a failure, she claimed, of a vow to wed. There were other claims: seduction, for one—and Stoll, a Southern gentleman, likely blushed to speak of this unseemly topic with a young woman. Jane nodded, intrigued. Stoll pulled out a cabinet photograph, and Jane studied the image: a young woman with dark hair. She was rather plain, one might say, not conventionally pretty. How, Jane likely asked, can I be of assistance?

We are confused, Stoll admitted: Madeleine was a complete riddle. Why would a woman publish to the world her sordid shame to seek damages from a man she knew had no money? And why would a woman seeking damages reject his offers of a liberal allowance that would permit her to start a new, honorable life? Frankly, Stoll told Jane, "We are puzzled to know what is at the bottom of this affair."[11]

This is where Jane could help. What we have in mind, he told her, is in the line of detective work. We need someone trustworthy who can create and carry out plans. We need someone who understands human nature and one whose judgment, honesty, and fidelity are without question. We need an expert stenographer. We need you.[12]

Jane listened. Madeleine, Stoll explained, was in Washington, living at the House of Mercy, a charitable home run by the Episcopal Church. He wasn't sure of her role: she might have entered as an inmate, prepared for a life of seclusion and repentance. She might be an employee exchanging light work for room and board. Or she might be in hiding, staying out of sight while plotting her trial strategy. Jane's mission: find Madeleine Pollard, become her friend, and extract her secrets. Stoll wanted her to discover what sort of woman Madeleine was and see if Jane could convince her to settle for a monthly allotment. In the event of a trial, Stoll added, Jane would keep the defense team informed of the plaintiff's plans. What they needed, he said, was a spy.[13]

Here was the great adventure Jane had yearned for in her youth; here was the escape from family duty she craved as a young woman. Her task started now. She would leave Boston for New York first thing in the morning, then take the midnight train to

Washington, DC. Once in the capital, Stoll directed, take a green streetcar up Pennsylvania Avenue. Get off near Washington Circle, on I Street. Then walk up Twenty-Fourth Street to K Street and seek out number 2408, the House of Mercy.

And then? Jane asked.

Stoll hesitated. It would be best if she had a pitiful story to get inside that cloistered realm, he told Jane. That was the only advice he could offer. Beyond the location, he had no information on the institution's inner workings and no guess on how long she might have to stay there. What might happen was unpredictable; next steps would depend entirely on Jane. Secrecy was vital. Jane must work incognito. She would need an alias. Stoll worried that the Kentucky lawyers—defense and plaintiff—involved in the trial might recognize Jane from her stint in his New York City office. Jane had to keep out of view. No one, including her family, could know her mission. No one could know her location. No one could know her real name.[14]

Stoll offered some final directives. Get settled at the House of Mercy, he said, and rent a post office box under a fictitious name. He said to send him the key and box number, and that's how they'd communicate—only in writing and using aliases. Not even Breckinridge would know her name—only him. Meeting in person was too dangerous. Write every day, if possible. The most important things, Stoll urged, were to proceed slowly, be exceedingly cautious, and make no mistakes. Jane took the job.[15]

Stoll hurried back to Washington and then on to Kentucky; Jane headed to Boston's Beacon Hill, head likely reeling as she left her former, and now once again, employer. Detective work, spying—these were hardly proper occupations for a respectable young woman, but Jane was hardly the model of Victorian womanhood. And what an adventure! She stayed with Etta Bailey's family, and, making an exception to the need for secrecy, she and Etta talked long into the night, mulling over this peculiarly stunning task. Jane was unaware of the scandal, but Etta had followed developments in the newspapers and told Jane what she knew.

Stoll had warned Jane not to read up on the case to avoid developing any preconceived notions about Madeleine, but the story was too rich for Etta not to share.[16]

Out of earshot of her mother and her mother's boarders, Etta told Jane how Madeleine Pollard had been a schoolgirl, naive to the ways of men. She had sought Breckinridge's help, and instead, he seduced her. Their affair continued through three pregnancies and almost ten years. Etta continued. He promised her he would marry her. Despite her secret life as a mistress, Miss Pollard had made a life in Washington, moving in good circles with respectable people as she prepared to take her place as a congressman's wife. But Breckinridge broke his promise and married someone else.

Etta sympathized with Madeleine, and after hearing Etta's perspective, so did Jane. Who knows what temptations were in her path, Jane surmised, and if she was now in a Christian home, perhaps she has repented. Yet true repentance and entering a lawsuit seemed at odds. Perhaps, mused Jane, Miss Pollard has abandoned her plan to appear in court and pushed the suit forward to force a reasonable rapprochement. In that case, Jane thought, she could be a hero by negotiating a settlement and preventing the damage such a sordid public trial would bring—and she would have helped a fallen, forlorn woman lead a better life.[17]

Neither Etta nor Jane had any idea what the House of Mercy would be like. Although they both lived urban lives, they could hardly be expected to have familiarity with the fallen. Etta thought the facility might be like the YWCA, with moral uplift, educational programs, and resources for young women who needed a hand. Jane recalled how a New York City YWCA had recommended a boardinghouse for her housing, which worked out fine. The House of Mercy, she rationalized, wouldn't be so bad.

Pragmatically, on this mission, there was money to be made. The new business venture with Etta, which Jane had intended to resume after regaining her health, was lucrative, but it was hard to predict how much business would come their way. Six weeks of espionage would net Jane generous and much-needed funds in short order. There would always be court documents to type. Jane could join Etta later in the spring once her detective work was done and her coffers were replenished. Jane pushed aside her lingering misgivings.[18]

Jane and Etta brainstormed ways that Jane could record and share her observations with Stoll while also keeping her intel hidden from prying eyes. Jane would need to take daily notes—and detailed ones at that. Writing in shorthand would prevent at least most people from reading her notes. It would be faster and save space on paper as well. To prevent fellow residents from finding her notes, Jane would crib them on tiny slips of paper and hide them in a small bag, looped around her neck and tucked into her dress. This would lessen the chance of theft, if a wayward resident pawed through Jane's things. Stenography had suddenly become much more than a mere avenue to paid clerical work in the big city.

Stoll had suggested he and Jane exchange information via a postal box, but Jane thought it might seem suspicious to those at the House of Mercy if she, a supposed newcomer to Washington, mailed frequent letters to someone within the city. But what if Jane's messages went to Boston? She could set her "pitiful story" there, and anyone surveilling her correspondence would see simply letters sent back home. Envelopes addressed to Etta could be easily explained—a school friend or a cousin, typical recipients of a young woman's letters. Caught up in the excitement of having a role, albeit hidden and unpaid, in the biggest sensation of 1894, Etta eagerly agreed to be the middle envoy of this scheme. She would transcribe the loops and curls in Jane's shorthand notes and send the decoded message to the fictitious John C. Johnson's postal box, where Stoll would retrieve it. If the plaintiff's team got wind of a spy, it was unlikely they'd suspect letters from Etta Bailey of Boston.

On Monday, January 29, 1894, Jane thanked Mrs. Bailey for her kindness and hugged her partner in espionage. She packed her tiny pencil and some paper and bought *Harper's* magazine. Jane boarded the train for New York. Excitement was colored by moments of self-doubt. Had she brought the right clothes? What did one wear to tell a pitiful story?

Jane sent her mother a reassuring letter, the first of many misdirections in her new role. Mr. Stoll's business, she wrote, was to help an employer of his. "There is trouble somewhere," she said. That was the reason for all the mystery. Jane downplayed her role, but in the next breath she took on a darker tone, telling her mother that no one could know she worked for Charles Stoll or where she was. When people asked about her, her mother should just tell them she didn't know which city she would settle in. The gold, wrote Jane, "is too scarce to let a good chance slip to make it and I shall enjoy the spring better if I have something in my pocket over my debts." Jane concluded her letter, "I hope I've told you enough so you and Daddy won't worry, but don't tell a soul outside that it is more than just an ordinary position as stenographer." And then ordinary Jane Tucker got on a midnight train to Washington.[19]

The steam-driven train thundered through the night; Jane was too excited to sleep. Stoll had told her that Madeleine Pollard had literary pretensions. Jane pulled the *Harper's* from her bag and studied the essays, articles, and short stories by the leading (largely white male) literary voices. When she arrived in Washington six hours later, she stepped onto the platform as Agnes Parker, undercover detective.

She walked through the crowded station into the bright Southern sunshine. Harried travelers rushed, men wrestled trunks onto carriages, and horses clop-clopped along cobbled streets. Jane gathered most of her things and exited the station, leaving a bag behind at the luggage storage desk. She glanced around, getting her bearings. Springlike warmth had replaced the slushy snow of Boston. The dome of the Capitol gleamed white, a beacon calling visitors to the Hill. She spied a respite, the St. James Hotel on the southeast corner of Sixth Street and Pennsylvania Avenue. She was tired but excited, adrenaline-fueled but hungry. In the St. James' dining room, Jane ordered breakfast. The last three days had been a whirlwind of telegrams and travel, and Jane no doubt enjoyed sitting in a leather chair that did not sway with the motion of transportation. But no dining partners would join her; there would be no clandestine rendezvous with Stoll. She was entirely alone; from then on, Jane Tucker—Agnes Parker—would stay in the shadows.[20]

While Jane Tucker filled her stomach and settled her mind, Madeleine Pollard awoke in her single room on the third floor of the House of Mercy, the window to her quarters directly above the heavy front door. Her sleep was typically restless, the hard mattress and the approaching trial preventing pleasant dreams. She washed in a basin of cold water and turned to her closet. Her custom dresses and one-of-a-kind hats had been winnowed down to a sedate few. Today, like most days, she would meet with her attorneys. Madeleine chose a simple black dress. On the days she remained at the Home, she donned a plain blue serge dress and a dotted white muslin cap, a teacher's garb.[21] In 1888, six months after first arriving in Washington, she had bartered teaching at a Catholic convent for room and board, a relationship that worked for three years. But at the House of Mercy, she struggled. As the inmates worked toward redemption from their sins and prepared for lives of domestic service, they kept their distance from Madeleine, known at the home as Miss Dudley, whom the girls felt carried a subtle air of superiority. Madeleine found the girls flighty, and some were downright rude, offering only a modicum of the respect she thought she deserved. The teachers were no better. They knew Madeleine's story and refused to eat meals with her. The nuns barely spoke to her. The headmistress abhorred her. She received no visitors. She could not wait for the trial to begin; she could not wait for it to end; she could not wait to leave this cold place of little mercy.

Jane stepped out of the St. James and caught a green westbound streetcar. A first-time visitor to Washington, she gazed at the White House as the car moved along Pennsylvania Avenue. Jane pulled the bell cord near Washington Circle and stepped onto the street. Experienced with urban transportation, Jane had no trouble navigating Washington's alphanumeric grid system of streets, but she had little idea what to expect in a home for fallen women.

She climbed the stone steps at the House of Mercy and paused at the threshold. Three stories of light-gray brick rose before her. Curtains covered all the windows, closing the interior to prying eyes and preventing inmates from viewing external temptations. A large gilt cross loomed above the door. An eight-foot wall topped with shards of glass surrounded the property. The polished brass doorplate gleamed. Jane's courage wavered; she could still turn and run. The heavy door was locked. To enter this sanctuary, she knew she needed a story, a lie—a falsehood that she would later call a *big one*. Jane Tucker had no experience in espionage, no training as a detective; she was a stenographer. But Breckinridge needed her. Stoll was counting on her. She took a deep breath and rang the bell.[22]

5

PITIFUL STORIES

The stenographer-turned-spy stood alone in a parlor, heart pounding, palms sweating. The faint musty odor suggested a front door that rarely opened. As Jane Tucker—alias Agnes Parker—waited for the House of Mercy matron, she corralled her racing thoughts. She must gain admission to this home, she told herself. She must identify Madeleine Pollard and then entice her to reveal compromising information. Anything less was a failure. Anything less would disappoint Charles Stoll. Jane steeled herself—the clack of Sister Dorothea's keys announced the matron's arrival.[1]

Sister Dorothea possessed a sweet face and no-nonsense attitude. She ran the House of Mercy with order and discipline, a calling to which her superiors found her "eminently adapted."[2] For ten years, the Episcopalian Sisterhood of St. Mary's had provided a Christian home to the fallen and outcast, a place of refuge and reformation where young women could improve their lot. In the K Street home, once a Gilded Age residence, the inmates, as they were called (although Dorothea was quick to emphasize that the place was not a prison), received an education and training for a respectable livelihood that would save them from a life of continued shame and a miserable death. Few tales of woe surprised her. She looked at the young woman standing before her and waited for her story.

"I've come from Boston on account of my health," Jane began. "I am not strong enough yet to work and cannot afford a boardinghouse until I can earn some money." The matron said nothing. "I would be willing to pay a small amount for my board," Jane offered, growing nervous. Sister Dorothea, a fortress in black fabric, gave her a hard look. "You had best come to my private office," she said sternly, the warmth of her earlier greeting fading as she led Jane to the office. Jane sat down stiffly, nervously. Dorothea closed the door.

"My child," she said, turning to Jane, "you do not understand the character of the house you have come to; you should have gone to the Young Women's Christian Association. This, my dear, is a home exclusively for fallen women." Consternation flooded over Jane as the matron took her seat. Her mission was ending before it even began. "We do not," the sister continued, "take anyone into the Home who has not committed this sin. The Home is carried on wholly to reclaim these poor creatures."

Jane cringed; Stoll's scheme was off to a bad start. Her story of ill health would not do. She needed a lie, and she needed a big one. She took a deep breath. "Sister," Jane began again, "I know the character of this house and because of its character came here. I want to have the example of my fallen sisters to help me lead a better life." She wept into her hands. "I, too, have sinned." Jane fumbled in her pocket, tears dripping, the matron watching. Sister Dorothea urged her to continue, and she obliged, pulling a fake tale from the depths of her handkerchief. She was all but an orphan, she explained between sobs, with only a few cousins to call family. Jane paused—Sister Dorothea understood all too well how the vulnerable became victims. Her physician, Jane continued, urged her to leave Boston and start a new life elsewhere. She paused again, the silence hinting at a tale best left untold: seduction, an unwed pregnancy, or, worse, the specter of abortion. Jane let the matron reach her own conclusion.

Dorothea took Jane's hand. It was clean and unblemished but not without evidence of work—a callus where she would hold a pencil or needle, the faint trace of ink. She studied Tucker, taking in her carefully kept clothes, a slender form that hinted at a feminine frailty, and her pale skin unsullied by the sun. The matron saw a weepy young woman of refined circumstances and standing that was respectable but, she assumed, for one unfortunate moral error. The girls at this Home were coarse, rough, and ignorant. These girls, she explained gently, protectively, were not worthy models for emulation; they would offend her genteel sensibilities. No, the matron told Jane, this lazar house of souls was not the place for her.[3]

Jane ducked her head and wept, stymied and stalling, her white linen handkerchief growing damp with crocodile tears. Stoll, Breckinridge, the fifteen dollars weekly salary—this mission could not end here. Sister, Jane pleaded with a hitching voice, "I can stand it; I can be with these poor souls." The matron softened. This one seemed determined and brave. Few young women had tried to argue their way into such a place; most begged to be released. Here, thought Dorothea, was a soul worth saving, a young woman who could be guided back to the straight and narrow. Perhaps, the matron considered, the presence of such a woman would lift the humble residents. And she had offered to pay for her keep—her presence would not strain the too-tight budget. Sister Dorothea gazed at her guest, now quietly weeping. She admired her resolve. The matron conceded: "I generally require these girls to be placed with me for at least a year, but if you care to come here for a week's trial, I will allow you to do so." Jane nearly laughed with relief, although her joy was short-lived. The stakes were high: at the end of the week, Jane either must leave—and risk failing in her task—or remain confined in the Home for one year. She dried her eyes and stashed her sodden handkerchief. "Thank you, Sister," she said.

The road to redemption would not be easy. For the next week, the matron explained, Jane would wear a dull uniform. She would sleep in a dormitory on a narrow iron bed covered by a thin, hard mattress. She would spend her days performing domestic chores. The sisters would read all mail sent and received. Her meals would be spare and eaten in silence. Jane could not leave the grounds without permission, and she could never go alone.

Roll call would be taken each evening at eight. Discipline, the matron preached, was the foundation of redemption: work and study inculcate habits of industry, cleanliness, and punctuality in her miscreant charges.[4]

Jane would enter the House of Mercy that very day. But first, she explained to the matron, crafting yet another lie in this morning of falsehoods, she must return to the railroad station to retrieve a misplaced bag. She thanked Dorothea for her trust and hurried along, retracing her steps, eager to contact Charles Stoll.

In the cavernous station, passengers raced by, hurrying to catch departing trains. Friends and family greeted one another, and conductors shouted, "All aboard!" Jane grabbed her bag and searched for a private corner, pulling out the fountain pen and paper she had stashed in the bag for this moment. She wrote two short letters, eyes on the clock, mindful of the need for a quick return. Jane crafted an upbeat note to her mother, confirming her safe arrival in Washington; she had traveled first class and was in good health and spirits.

She pulled out a second piece of paper. Stoll would be anxiously awaiting news.[5] Jane wrote quickly, adrenaline flowing. This letter held none of the forced cheeriness of her note home. She shook her head. She had been naïve, and Stoll had been ill-informed. The House of Mercy was no YWCA, and Jane could not simply swoop in and play the hero as if the star of a melodrama. Challenges abounded. First, she explained to Stoll their plan to exchange daily letters in a post office box would not work. Forced to remain within the Home, Jane could not retrieve notes unseen or send them unread. Don't write me, she warned Stoll, until I write you. If you must reach me, sign your letter "Doctor" and know the nuns will read it. Once she entered the Home, Jane would be secluded, segregated, and entombed. She would have to find another way to get information out.

Jane raised a more troubling concern. Sister Dorothea had told her a story, she reported to Stoll, a cautionary tale. "I want to warn you about your treatment of these girls," the matron had said. "We had one girl here who was above the others in education and breeding, and she was so unkind to them we were obliged to send her away." The matron told Jane to "be very careful and not show your contempt of them in any way." Red flags waved. Was the unkind girl Madeleine Pollard? Had she slipped beyond her grasp? And one more thing: it had been difficult enough to get into the House of Mercy; it would be even more challenging to leave. She would be under constant scrutiny. Sister Dorothea held the key to the front door, dangling from a silk cord tied around her waist. Imposing stone walls enclosed the grounds. Madeleine Pollard had vanished behind those walls; she might too. If Stoll didn't hear from her in three weeks, Jane pleaded, he should send a telegram that someone is dying. Certainly an impending demise would loosen the matron's hold on the front door. Jane paused—it was an apt ruse, as she felt like she was going to her own funeral.

Her fellow penitents were no happier to be there. They were shop girls seduced by leering customers, hometown girls fooled by false promises, and domestic servants abused in the household. Some girls had been in love, and some girls had not; some young women had been virgins before their fall, while others had been experienced. But all of these women had crossed a line; tricked, cajoled, deluded, or raped, they were unmarried, and either as agents or victims, they had been caught and crucified in an age of moral absolutes. The residents of the House of Mercy were fallen women—girls who had transgressed the pervasive imperative of a woman's purity. Jane Tucker, though, had not fallen into this home; she had leaped.

Luggage in hand, she returned to K Street. The heavy door shut behind her, enclosing her, she later wrote, like remains in a family crypt. One of the sisters ushered Jane into the parlor. Dishes rattled as the sisters and teachers enjoyed their meals in the next room; Jane's dinner arrived on a tray. She ate alone, the clink of silverware keeping company with her thoughts. A nice lamb chop, mashed potatoes, jelly, and a good cup of tea—the sinking feeling wrapped around her heart loosened. At least she would not go hungry. Perhaps this stint would not be so rough after all. She looked at the meal and hesitated. She was no longer Jane Tucker, stenographer; she was Agnes Parker, fallen woman. A true sufferer would not have a hearty appetite. She left most of the meal uneaten.[6]

Sister Dorothea joined Jane, keys clinking as she crossed the room. She had another story to share, she said, this one about a woman currently in residence. The matron leaned forward with a confidential air. "You would find this out for yourself," she told Jane with lowered voice, "and I think it is better for me to tell you about her." This woman served as a teacher but was here under pretenses. Dorothea spat out the distasteful truth: Miss Dudley was a notorious woman. Dudley was not even her real name. "It was a great mistake," she said bitterly, "to permit her to come here at all." She warned Jane not to tell the woman her story, and not to listen to hers. The worst feature of this woman was that she told her miserable history to anyone who would listen.

Jane nodded thoughtfully, taking in the matron's story. Who could be more notorious than a congressman's mistress? So what the matron intended as a warning, Jane took as an invitation.

In the midday quiet of the dormitory, Jane rested on a cold metal bed, excused this first day from afternoon lessons and chores. The cheerless room was bare: whitewashed walls and rows of closely set beds crowded the space. There would be no privacy here.

Jane turned her thoughts to her mission. If Madeleine was here as a true penitent—as some newspapers had hinted—then Jane could surely find her among her dormmates and amenable, in her penance, to a compromise with the congressman. But if Madeleine was Miss Dudley, then it sounded as though she wasn't penitent at all. Jane had to consider every possibility. Stoll's admonition to make no mistakes echoed in her head.

Miss Grey, the dormitory matron, arrived to supervise Jane's transformation—at least in dress—from wayward woman to repentant inmate. No fashionable clothes were worn here—all sinners were equal in the eyes of the Lord. Under Grey's pointed gaze, Jane removed her street clothes. She shivered in the cool air. Grey handed her a well-worn uniform: a blue gingham dress, a gingham apron, and a white cap. A molasses stain dribbled down the front of the dress, and the fabric emitted a peculiar odor, sour and astringent and reminiscent of the dye pot. If she needed to leave in a hurry, Jane realized, she would be quite the sight in the dreadful clothes. Grey locked Jane's traveling clothes and luggage in the attic. Even her new serge coat and jaunty hat were gone. But under her ugly dress, Jane had tucked a little leather bag, evading Grey's inspection. Inside the tiny pouch, she hid the tools of her new trade: a tiny pencil, a little money, stamps, and scraps of paper awaiting her coded notes.

By evening, Jane dearly regretted her uneaten lamb chop. Supper was parsimonious: bread, butter, and a cup of tea that she judged wet but had little else going for it. She sat with two dozen resident girls, the newcomer and the old hands scrutinizing one another in the silence of the meal. Jane sipped her tasteless tea and glanced around the long table: too young, too blonde, too short, too coarse. At seventeen and eighteen, these girls were much younger than she had expected—and too young to be Madeleine Pollard. Stoll had offered scant details on the case, but Jane knew Pollard was in her late twenties, well-educated, and had long brown hair that reporters seemed to agree was her very best feature. None of these girls resembled the woman in the photograph Stoll had shared in Boston. If Pollard was masquerading as an inmate, she was not among those present.

After the meager meal, the residents retired to the sitting room. Jane followed and mapped her surroundings. The good-sized room held a table for hand sewing and two wardrobes that stored games donated by do-gooders and McGuffey readers, textbooks that infused middle-class values in lessons in reading, vocabulary, and spelling. A few plain chairs provided seating. The girls were noisy; a day's worth of pent-up laughter and shouts bounced off bare wooden floors and plaster walls. As the matron had warned, these girls were rough and ordinary, but few were vulgar. They were, Jane thought, untamed. She saw little evidence of earlier education or training; the dated schoolbooks and keep-busy hand sewing would be hard-pressed to turn so many sows' ears into silk purses. Jane winced at the increasing din. Still, she played board games with the girls, glancing surreptitiously and surveying the room.

Then Sister Dorothea determined to make Jane's trial week count and called her for yet another chat. Jane tried not to roll her eyes as Dorothea thrust religious tracts into her hands. She dutifully consented to read the material, hoping to be excused quickly from their private tête-à-tête and rejoin the Home's residents.

Released at last, Jane returned to the sitting room. Several teachers had joined the girls, their dark-blue dresses and white caps dotting the room. Jane scanned the parlor; her eyes landed on a young woman. She sat at the table, leading the girls in a game of checkers. Sister Dorothea followed Jane's gaze. "Agnes," said the matron evenly, "I would like to introduce Miss Dudley." Jane's breath caught; she glanced from Dorothea to Dudley, a smile growing. "So pleased to meet you, Miss Dudley," said Jane, halting her smile at a congenial angle, trying not to grin. Dudley rose and offered her seat. "Please finish this game for me. I never could play checkers," she said with a laugh.[7]

Dudley pulled up a chair. Jane moved a checker. She sized up her adversary. Miss Dudley was homely and common-looking, and her teacher's uniform did little to improve the picture. Jane thought her coarse face verged on repulsive: her gray eyes were far apart, and her brows were heavy and black. Her nose was turned up and presented two round nostrils. Her thick upper lip extended over the lower, and her face was doughy and expressionless. Her hands were too large. Yet when Dudley smiled, her face lost its hardness. Her voice was musical with a soft, Southern drawl. She spoke with careful diction, like a schoolmarm, and her conversation was charming. Her nails were nicely manicured, and her hair was indeed her crowning glory: thick bronze-brown braids were gathered and coiled at the back of her head. *A notorious woman masquerading as a teacher*, the matron had said. *Dudley is not even her real name.*

Jane had to be sure. She finished the game and took a seat in the parlor. Jane pulled out her *Harper's*—Grey had not objected to her keeping the magazine. She slowly flipped through the pages, studying the articles as if reading with rapt attention, studiously not glancing back toward the girls and games. Dudley ambled over. She joined Jane on the settee. Side by side, they looked at the illustrations. Dudley scanned the table of contents. William Dean Howells had published a farce. "I knew Mr. Howells and his family very well," she said. She had met them when she studied in Cambridge, Massachusetts, hinting at a connection to Harvard's women's college, Harvard Annex. They were very kind. And she knew Charles Dudley Warner, the *Harper's* editor, "very well indeed." He was so entertaining; she had visited his Hartford, Connecticut, home. She had enjoyed many dinners in the North with literary people. She pointed to the latest installment of a Western tale. Frederick Remington, its author, was a friend, too. She called him Fred. Miss Dudley seemed determined to impress Jane with her place in a cultured world.

"What a great thing it must be to have such talent," Jane offered. Dudley smiled—she had written some herself. Really? Jane replied in astonished artifice, urging her to say more. Dudley declined, but perhaps, sometime, she would show her something.

While the younger girls galumphed around the room, Dudley sat bolt upright, stiffly erect with an achingly perfect posture. She spoke carefully and precisely, as if determined always to do the perfectly correct thing. Jane found it painful to watch.

Across the room, Sister Dorothea watched this conversation carefully and not happily. Her face grew hard. "Miss Parker must be tired from traveling," she announced. "She should retire." It was not a suggestion.

Jane left the *Harper's* and the sitting room, thwarted by Dorothea's interruption but not entirely disappointed for the chance to be alone. Clues crowded her head. In the cold, dimly lit dormitory, she pulled her tiny bag from her dress, removing a slip of paper. She scratched her shorthand notes. It was a relief to set her thoughts on paper; she had guarded every spoken word so carefully. Go slowly, Stoll had said. She had found Pollard, she was sure. Dudley's age, appearance, and education matched Stoll's description of Madeleine. Her fondness for literature and the famous names she had casually dropped—Jane recorded each one, capturing potential clues for Breckinridge's team. And her final piece of evidence: the matron's rueful story of the notorious Miss Dudley's unwelcome presence. Neither the matron nor Miss Dudley had revealed her real name, but it must be Madeleine Pollard. She had to be Pollard. Jane tucked her notes into her leather bag.

Sleep eluded Jane: the husk-filled mattress was uncomfortable and the day's events so very strange. Surrounded by the snores and wheezes of the night, she plotted her next move. She had succeeded where male detectives had failed. She had located Madeleine Pollard, but now the more crucial task began: getting her to talk. Really talk. Jane needed confirmation from Dudley's lips that she was who Jane thought, that she was—had been—Breckinridge's lover. And she needed answers to the questions that bedeviled the congressman. Why *was* this woman publicly humiliating herself? What was her history? Who was supporting her? And what, Breckinridge was desperate to know, was she after?

Jane had to gain Madeleine's confidence and trust. They must become fast friends and quickly. This was no easy task for the stenographer, who had been known to pepper her youthful diary with insults to the "fiends" and "brats" who crossed her path. Charm was not her strong suit. Jane had six days.

———————

Morning came too soon for the sleepless. A large, loud bell announced the start of the daily routine. The sun had not yet risen; many girls crowded around but few washbasins. Tiny mirrors reflected pieces of penitents as they donned their dull dresses by gaslight. Jane was cold and cross at morning prayers. Her body ached; her stomach growled. Breakfast discouraged her: the oatmeal was coarse and the coffee weak. She ate a prisoner's meal: bread and hot water. Her daily chores called. Jane made beds. Stoll, she thought, had no idea what he had asked.[8]

Classes followed chores. Miss Dudley, although a novice with the needle, sat and sewed with the girls. She was in a talkative mood. As the girls hemmed linens, she shared her history with the newcomer, or a version of it. Jane, a highly skilled needleworker, listened carefully as Miss Dudley spoke of her father's death and the family's sudden poverty, how she had lived with a succession of aunts, and how she studied Latin, German, and botany with a tutor. She shared indignities too. Once, her grandfather had failed to rise when she walked into a room, and Dudley had refused to sit, angered by his lack of respect. That is why she always rose when a superior entered the room, she explained, and she taught the girls here to do the same. Jane nodded encouragement, offering sympathetic *oh*s and approving *ah*s to keep the words flowing. Aunts, tutors, pride: Jane memorized each clue.

Miss Dudley shared a story from her youth. When she was a little girl, she had blurted out, much to the amusement of adults purchasing a horse, that "a Kentucky thoroughbred is the best horse there is, and the best is none too good for me." How her family loved to tell that story; she laughed, saying they called her a "wee little thing." Jane smiled at this account of Dudley's endearing precocity. Just that morning, she had insisted that her mattress not be turned so that the cotton-covered side remained facing up. She explained to Jane, "The beds are hard enough anyway, and I intend to have the best I can get out of them." Jane made another mental note: horses or mattresses, Miss Dudley expected the best. On the other hand, Jane thought, good tip about the bed. Her first night at the Home had introduced her only to the "soft side of a pine board."[9]

The noontime meal separated predator and prey. Jane joined the inmates, seated at their long table, a dozen girls to a side. The teachers and staff ate in the adjoining dining room. As a teacher, Dudley enjoyed tastier and more generous meals than those served to the resident girls. But for Dudley, the benefit of better food came with the sting of social snubbing. As Jane ate, she watched the Ladies' Table, but Miss Dudley did not appear. None of the teachers or sisters would eat with her. They knew who she was and what she had done. Dudley ate alone: breakfast in her room and dinner at the Ladies' Table after everyone else had eaten. It appeared to Jane that she had no friends and no visitors. Her students neither respected nor admired her. No wonder she talked so openly with Jane: she was lonely. Jane knew she could fill that void if she could get Madeleine alone.

But finding time and space for private conversation was easier said than done. Most days, their paths intersected only in the presence of others. So Jane connected with her however she could. In the evening, Dudley taught the girls how to write, spell, and compose letters, and occasionally she played the piano and sang. Jane joined in, drawing on her moments on the Boston stage. Together, they taught the girls the Virginia reel. As they sang and danced, Jane picked up pieces of Dudley's story—her earlier singing lessons and how diphtheria had ruined her voice, as well as a claim that she had lived in Paris. The information sputtered out in dribs and drabs as they wheeled and marched around the room. Jane needed to get closer to her, away from the noisy, nosy girls and the ever-watchful Sister Dorothea. Alone, she could turn Dudley's dribble into a stream. Five days remained.

On February 1, Jane's third day, she finished her sparse, cold breakfast and turned to her assigned chore—making the teachers' beds.[10] Helped by a young woman named Alice, Jane flew through the dull domestic task and suggested a quick walk in the yard. The day was warm and sunny, but a fresh-air jaunt was not her goal. Jane wanted to look at the possibilities the walled-in yard presented, just in case she needed to make a sudden departure. She was quickly discouraged. The brick wall was at least six feet tall and topped with jagged glass from broken bottles. Alice explained that the glass was to prevent escapes, but, she scoffed, some girls still tried it.[11] Jane eyeballed the wall; her youth had provided another valuable skill: tree climbing. Older and wiser now, though, Jane saw how the glinting glass eliminated that route. The front door was always locked, and the yard was blocked in—Jane was a prisoner. Escape, if needed, would have to be facilitated from the outside.

Dudley longed to talk; Jane longed to listen. She was certain she had located Madeleine Pollard. And so, when Jane returned from the yard and Madeleine, hovering downstairs, offered her a quick communicative glance, the two young women sprinted out of the matron's view like schoolmates skipping class.

Jane studied Madeleine's small but well-appointed room. The narrow bed stood in the corner. As a teacher, Madeleine enjoyed the relative luxury of a bureau, washstand, table, and rocking chair. Books crowded a bookshelf. A tiny photograph of Madeleine's sweet-faced mother was her only connection to home. There was a small corner closet—Jane saw that Madeleine had few clothes and no pretty toiletries. If wealthy benefactors were paying her bills, those patrons neglected her sartorial needs. The room lacked heat, but it was homey.

Madeleine and Jane talked out of sight of Dorothea and away from the girls. They each proceeded cautiously, Madeleine gently pushing for openings to shared confidences, Jane gingerly eliciting her history. Madeleine discussed literature; Jane matched her book for book, her fondness for reading serving her well in a task she could not have imagined when she had perused the pages of *Little Women*, *The House of the Seven Gables*, and *The Count of Monte Cristo*. They reminisced about favorite works—Jane favored Dickens and Madeleine George Eliot. Madeleine pulled *The Scarlet*

Letter from her shelf. Jane flipped through the novel. The copy was heavily marked. Madeleine explained that she had critiqued a recent stage version of Hawthorne's classic for the famous actor Richard Mansfield. She claimed to have been at the play's opening amid a sold-out performance and an audience full of literary luminaries. That a globally known actor would ask Madeleine for a critique seemed hard to believe. Still, Jane wondered about the underlined passages—did Madeleine imagine herself a modern-day Hester Prynne? An outcast sentenced to suffer her shame alone on the margins of society? Jane made yet another entry on her mental notepad. Madeleine offered Jane the book; Jane had read it in 1885. She took it and said nothing.[12]

Duties and midday dinner interrupted the chat, but tentative ties encouraged both women. Jane had not been in contact with Stoll for two days. She could not mail a letter, nor could any letter leave the Home unread. But if she could craft a code, she could pass information to Stoll right under Sister Dorothea's nose.

Jane had scratched a shorthand message on a tiny scrap of paper in the darkened dormitory: "She is here but will remain only a few weeks. Will try to go when she does, but if you hear nothing in three weeks, telegraph." She inserted random errors into the text, hoping to stymie interlopers should her message be intercepted. She hid the note in her little bag tucked under her dress and walked downstairs.

Jane approached Sister Dorothea: "I should alert the doctor of my safe arrival." The matron agreed, handing her newest resident a sheet of paper and an envelope. Jane sat at a table and composed a carefully worded letter as Sister Dorothea hovered. Any slip-up—a misplaced word, a deviation from Jane's big lie— would be a costly mistake. Compiling a coded message with a nun watching over your shoulder was no easy feat. Jane concentrated on writing naturally without extended pauses of the pen and composing her letter, as the 1893 *Stenographer's Guide* suggested, "in concise and well-chosen language."[13]

Washington, Thursday p.m. [February 1, 1894]
Dear Doctor:-
   I suppose you will be relieved to know that the girl you have been anxious about is here and safe for the present at least. I do not know for how long. Frankly, there are times when I question the benefit of it all, but I will try to do my best and shall stay as long as I can hold out and as long as I feel there is any real good in my stay.

You have no idea, she continued, "how much you asked me to do." Redemption from sin was hard, she implied as she pledged to stay as long as her health allowed, at least a week or two. Dorothea would have nodded in approval. This young woman was no quitter.

Jane then reassured her "doctor," writing that she had not mentioned his name or address. Instead, Jane wrote, she would send the letter to him by way of his niece, Henrietta.

Stoll knew of Jane's Boston partner, Etta Bailey; this comment told Dorothea why Jane did not address her envelope directly to the doctor who had sent Miss Parker to this Home. "I would be glad if Henrietta would write me," Jane wrote, teasing her Boston friend, "for I used to think her a very tiresomely good girl but shall not think her so anymore."

Jane then tossed a sliver of hope to Sister Dorothea, now unabashedly reading as Jane wrote, remarking on her newly awakened conscience. But Jane didn't seek religion; she was building an exit plan, lest Dorothea trap her in the home for the mandatory one-year stay. Jane created a fictitious relative, an invalid on death's door. If "cousin Mary" should suddenly perish, she hinted, she hoped the doctor would notify her of the funeral. "Of course," Jane explained, "the Sisters read all my letters, so do not refer to the past any more than is necessary." Yes, Dorothea would have agreed, let past sins be. Don't blow my cover, hinted Jane.

Under Dorothea's shadow, Jane promised Stoll she would not let him down.

I came here to please you, and I mean to stay and try—
oh, so hard—but there are so many doubts in my mind.
Thanking you for all past kindnesses, believe me,
Very sincerely,
Agnes Parker

Sister Dorothea reviewed Jane's letter. She nodded approvingly, a worthy young woman struggling upward on her way to redemption.

Jane enclosed her letter in an envelope, asked for a stamp, and, when the matron turned her back, pulled her tiny note from her secret bag and slipped it into the envelope. She sealed the envelope and handed it to Dorothea, who would mail it.[14]

Jane's first spy report was on its way to Boston. Bailey transcribed the shorthand note and forwarded Jane's message to Stoll via the decoy post office box. The time lag worried Jane, but the news Bailey sent delighted Stoll. "Miss Parker is quite clever," he gushed to Breckinridge as he told him about her coded communication. "She is able to keep up her end of the line."[15]

Stoll sent Bailey a letter outlining his response to the "doctor's" letter. She got right to work—no longer a "tiresome" girl as Jane had slyly joked. Bailey sent Stoll's letter to Agnes Parker, penitent, House of Mercy, along with several issues of *Harper's*, picking up on a hint Jane had encoded in her letter. Stoll was pleased. This plan might work.

Dorothea had taken note of Jane's neat handwriting and set her to work on the Home's account books. The matron liked having all the records written in one consistent hand, putting an inked order to the reality of chaotic lives.[16] The accounting was minimal: the Home received charitable donations, and the inmates' needlework generated additional funds. Congress provided some funding; annual reports noted the efficient and effective work of the Home under Sister Dorothea's charge. The matron hoped

Congress would soon approve an additional appropriation as she had plans to expand. In a city like Washington, one such annual report pronounced, "with probably more than its proportion of fallen women, the field for its operation is almost illimitable."[17]

As Jane rewrote the ledgers, Sister Dorothea took the opportunity for another chat. "Miss Dudley has been asking about you," she said to Jane. "She was quite curious about your story." Jane kept her hand steady, suspecting where this conversation was headed. Dorothea reminded her not to share her tale or seek Madeleine's. Jane copied the figures from one volume to another, ignoring the jingling keys as the matron walked away. Contrary to Dorothea's mandate, Jane determined to gratify Madeleine's curiosity as soon as possible, offering the same pitiful story she had told Sister Dorothea. At least, she hoped she remembered the tale accurately—but given the tension between Madeleine and the matron, they were unlikely to compare notes.

Later that afternoon, Jane and Madeleine evaded Sister Dorothea, taking refuge in Madeleine's room, the third floor empty as the teachers and girls attended to the daily routine. Jane opened up and told a sad, vague tale, captivating her new friend with a hazy story of seduction and flight from Boston. Jane may even have squeezed out a tear or two. It worked. Madeleine nodded sympathetically. "My own life," she whispered, "has not been as it should have been." Jane held her breath. Madeleine offered an edited version: a man, unnamed, whom she had dearly loved, had betrayed her. And now she was trapped in this cold, heartless home. She had business to conclude soon. The details, she held back. "I promised Sister Dorothea not to tell my story to any of the girls here," she continued, "but when you get ready to leave, I will tell it to you," a tantalizing promise that got Jane thinking. Perhaps she need not be entombed past one week. She might get more information out of Madeleine if she left the House of Mercy.

Shared intimacies had lightened Madeleine's burden. "Aggie," Madeleine said, "we are made for each other," and Jane readily agreed: two congenial women with a similar past who could find a better future together. Jane was a ray of hope on Madeleine's dark horizon. After her business in Washington was concluded, she told Jane, they must live together. Jane nodded with enthusiastic guile. "Where," Madeleine asked, "would you like to live?" Jane thought of her late sister, Patty. "West," she suggested. They should head West and start their lives anew, maybe even marry— Jane dangling a hook to see what fish she might catch. Madeleine leaped onto this fantasy: "We will go out and catch some big-hearted Westerner, and whichever gets married first shall help the other; if you get married first, you will have to let me live with you until I catch someone."

Or, Madeleine suggested on further reflection, maybe they would move to Europe. Once, she began, she had almost gone abroad. Jane took careful note of dates and names as Madeleine reminisced about how she had been invited to attend a prestigious private girls' school in Germany to study and become a writer. Her words trailed off, the story unfinished. Madeleine did not tell Jane how Breckinridge had offered to pay for the trip but refused her his name. She did not share that she then refused to go or tell Jane how that disagreement in the fall of 1892 had pulled at the threads of their relationship until it had frayed beyond repair, until Breckinridge had sought another's company, until Madeleine was humiliated and abandoned and forced to sue.

She shook off the sad memories. Yes, Madeleine said, they would go abroad, and she would study. She would rewrite her life with her new friend, returning to the road not taken. Someday, she told Jane, she would make a name for herself and return to the United States famous. No one would dare sit in her presence; she would be so well regarded that everyone would rise when she entered a room. Madeleine paused, regaining her composure. She returned to her happy vision: They could take a walking trip through Europe. She had a brother who could accompany them. Jane mentally noted: a brother still on friendly terms.

Madeleine admitted, though, she had no funds. She had lost considerable money the year before when an investment went sour; a European journey might be a stretch. There was New York, a city both women knew well. Perhaps, she mused, they could rent a flat in the city: Jane would work as a stenographer, Madeleine's brother would find a job, and Madeleine would keep house and write. But, she added, her present business in Washington might also replenish her coffers and help them find stable footing. This was a grand plan. Jane agreed, lying through her teeth. She shook Madeleine's hand; their futures were now linked. Both women beamed.

That evening, the House of Mercy residents enjoyed a rare treat of ice cream. Madeleine and Jane sat together and talked of favorite foods. She told Jane that she made a very good Welsh rarebit, obliquely referencing a favorite snack of late nineteenth-century college girls and implying her possession of the era's must-have appliance for women who entertain—the chafing dish.[18] She could also cook lobster "á la Newburgh," hinting at her familiarity with the crustacean that had at century's end risen from food for the poor to a meal for the privileged.[19] In New York, Madeleine planned, they would attend plays, and she would prepare after-theater suppers, what a very proper friend of hers called "champagne shrieks."[20] We will live a Bohemian life, she said, eyes sparkling with anticipation. The arts, interesting people, the luxuries of life—without them, she sighed, life was not worth living. Jane forced a smile, her face a portrait of anticipation for a future that would not be.

Sister Dorothea watched as Jane and Madeleine finished their dessert, laughing and smiling. Her expression grew cold. She had told Miss Dudley not to spread her story and warned Miss Parker not to listen. Now Jane appeared caught in Madeleine's charismatic web. Keys jingled. The matron stepped forward, forbidding the pair to meet in Madeleine's room or to converse privately. She would not have Miss Dudley contaminate Miss Parker. This would not do; this would not do at all.

6

The Stenographer's Guide to Spying

The stenographer should be systematic in everything. Other things being equal, the one who pays the strictest attention to details, and the minutest details, at that, will become the best stenographer.

—THE STENOGRAPHER'S GUIDE (1893)

Three days after Jane had arrived, Sister Dorothea watched her and Madeleine like a hawk, determined to keep them apart. Madeleine was unwilling to let go of her new friend. They simply had to be more careful—the resident girls repeated everything they overheard. Jane readily agreed to a quest for privacy, relieved to have Madeleine as an unwitting ally. Madeleine had teaching duties this Friday, but her students had grown restless and tired of lessons. At noon, she released the class into the walled-in yard for some fresh air and a game of prisoner's base. Jane followed.[1]

Madeleine returned to the fantasy flat in New York. "It may be some weeks before I shall be able to leave here," she said, asking Jane how long she would be willing to wait, testing the boundaries of this new friendship. Jane saw an opening. She stepped closer to Madeleine; at the end of the week, she confided, she planned to leave. Come with me, Jane invited, dangling Madeleine's wish in front of her. We will get a nice room in a pleasant part of Washington. Don't worry about money, Jane said; she had enough to live on until they could go to New York.[2]

Madeleine knew she couldn't; her legal case would be stronger if she remained at the House of Mercy, away from gossip about an unrepentant lifestyle. She couldn't share her reason with Jane, still eliding the names and details of her story, so she gave her a vague answer. No, she told Jane, she could not leave until her business was completed. Still, she suggested, seeing a respite from the Home's restrictions, Jane could rent a room, and Madeleine could visit; they could even hire a caterer to provide a solid meal now and then. Madeleine had seen a room for rent on a recent trip to her lawyer's office—she promised to look it over. And in return, perhaps Jane could help her: "You might watch for me and . . ." trailing off to silence with a favor unasked. Jane waited. Madeleine had said too much—but about what? Suddenly distressed, Madeleine turned the conversation to a forlorn hope that her brother would arrive soon, and she prayed silently to herself that he would take her away from the House of Mercy, from the trial, and from notoriety. Then, they could all live together, and she could leave her current troubles behind.

Jane knew Breckinridge's team struggled to prepare for the coming trial. The plaintiff and defense lawyers battled over depositions, hiding from each other key deponents and failing to give adequate notice of interviews. Attorney Enoch Totten, hired for his expertise in the District of Columbia court system, had become ill and relocated to Florida for his health. Every day the mail brought letters offering leads on men who claimed to know Madeleine's allegedly seamy history, and Breckinridge attempted to follow them all, at a considerable cost of money and time. Jane saw the defense's scattershot approach and Stoll's frustration; she determined to extract from Madeleine the piece of the puzzle that would prove the congressman's innocence, that he had not seduced Madeleine Pollard, that there had never been a promise of marriage. So far, she had gained nothing that would condemn Madeleine or exonerate Breckinridge.

For Madeleine, her lawyers' preparations were no less problem-filled. Several potential witnesses for the plaintiff, particularly women, refused to testify—some withdrawing at the command of their husbands, others removing themselves to avoid notoriety. Madeleine had been counting on schoolmates who could speak to her intellectual ambitions, women physicians who cared for her postpartum, and Lizzie Fillette, with whom Madeleine had lived. When she learned that Fillette had left Washington for parts unknown, she returned from her attorney's office in a foul mood.

Jane found her in the parlor after supper, staring out the window as the girls played, lost in thought. "Things have gone wrong all day," Madeleine complained to Jane. "I am not myself." She snapped at the girls and pushed them away. When one resident presented Madeleine with a newly cleaned ink pot, Madeleine brushed off her generous labor with nary a kind word; when another got on Madeleine's nerves, she held her against the wall and scolded her until the girl shook with shame. Jane paid close attention; Madeleine's bad mood was a bellwether of the progress of her case, signaling points of anger and hurt that portended a personal revelation.

Madeleine turned to Jane. She had been ruined by a man thirty years her senior, she said. Jane listened, stock still. Madeleine said she'd truly loved this man and had given him the best years of her life. He made her believe he loved her in return, but he did not, and now he acted like a coward. She spoke bitterly and wanted revenge. The restless girls grew noisy, drawing Madeleine away from the moment and her confession to step back into her role as evening chaperone.

Madeleine and Jane took some games from the closet to redirect the room's energy and quiet the girls. Madeleine chose a board game based on Nellie Bly's recent trip around the world, attempting to beat the fictional Phineas Fogg's record of eighty days. Bly did it in seventy-two. Madeleine asked Jane what she thought of Bly. "She showed a good deal of pluck," Jane answered as she helped set up the game board, counters, and dice.

Bly was an investigative journalist, a stunt reporter who gained fame when she faked mental illness to be committed to the insane asylum on New York's Blackwell Island. And what, Madeleine asked Jane, had she thought of Bly's undercover work. Jane admired Bly's courage and endurance, adding that her work in the asylum had done great good in changing laws to protect the mentally ill. Madeleine did not share Jane's high opinion of Bly's subterfuge. Before Madeleine could elaborate, she was called to the visitors' parlor. As she left, she asked Jane to tell the girls more about Bly's exploits. Madeleine's mood was black. Jane turned cold.[3]

Madeleine's brother, J. D. "Dudley" Pollard, had called to see his sister. Dorothea allowed the visit. They spoke privately. He shared some of the stories circulating in the press, including hurtful fabrications about the Pollard family. A reporter himself, Dudley knew that wild tales sold papers. Accuracy was a luxury. A kindhearted man, he was as distressed to share the stories as Madeleine was to hear the baseless tales. When Dudley left, Madeleine returned to the playroom and set the now-quiet girls on to their evening lesson. Jane sat near Madeleine, sensing her anger. In a low voice, Madeleine castigated the press: "I hate reporters. They have no heart or consideration for a person. All they care for is to get up something sensational and to fill up a certain space in their papers, without regard to the personal feelings of their victim." Madeleine clenched her fingers. She had a friend, she told Jane, who was a society reporter for a New York paper. She had shared secrets with her in the strictest confidence, but the so-called friend published their entire conversation. Another promise breached.

Madeleine still seethed. She turned her ire toward Sister Dorothea. She hated the woman, she told Jane, and was "not one bit afraid of her." Dorothea had no authority over her, Madeleine insisted. This was a contest of wills. If they dared to put her out, she said, she would jump in the river, and her death would be on their conscience.

Jane sensed a breakthrough. She steeled herself to stay still. But before Madeleine's rage could boil over, her anger deflated to a simmer. She eyed Jane coolly, the pain of recent betrayals still fresh. Jane felt the temperature shift. Danger was in the air. What had Madeleine detected? Aggie, said Madeleine in an even tone, if you are going to leave at the end of the week, you best go to Sister Dorothea and tell her. She will need time to prepare. Jane agreed with Madeleine's wise counsel and left the room before she could make a misstep.

The next morning, all was apparently forgiven when Madeleine asked Jane to come to her room after breakfast.[4] She wanted to lend her a play by Richelieu, but when Jane joined her in her room, she saw that was an excuse. Madeleine was distracted, moving from bed to dresser to bookshelf. She picked up the photograph of her mother and showed it to Jane. "She would not speak to me if I were dying, yet she is my mother."

Jane heard sadness and anger; she made a quiet remark: "A mother ought to go to her child, no matter how great her sin."

"You don't know mine," answered Madeleine. Mine hates me. She put the tiny photograph back on her dresser.

Madeleine left for her day's business—Jane knew Madeleine went to Attorney Calderon Carlisle's office even though she continued to hide her destination. Jane worked on the account books in the matron's office. Trying to sound appreciative, Jane told Sister Dorothea that her trial week was almost complete and that she planned to leave at the end of it. She had enough money to support herself for a month, and she was sure that she would find work soon. She said that she felt so much better in body and soul.

Dorothea mixed the sad with the stern. We'll miss you, Miss Parker, she said, but then cautioned that the routine would not be eased in her remaining days. Jane rationalized that a few more days cleaning the dorm, sewing, and eating spare meals would do her no permanent harm, and she still held out hope for a secret revealed.

By midafternoon, Jane had taken to her bed. Although feeling ill, she forced herself not to doze off and concentrated on listening for Madeleine's return. Late in the afternoon, Madeleine stormed up the stairs; Jane called out from the dormitory bed. Madeleine's footsteps revealed she was peeved, and Jane wanted to know why.

Madeleine sat next to Jane's bed on a hard wooden chair. She refused to discuss her long appointment. She fastened her eyes on Jane, searching her fevered face. Nellie Bly was on Madeleine's mind. "Agnes," she began, "I had such a strange dream about you last night; I thought you were Nellie Bly." Jane froze; Madeleine's look was mean. Jane forced a casually cheerful voice. "Oh yes! And that I went around the world with nothing but a handbag!" She rattled on nervously, "But I tell you, I should want to stop in places longer than she did. I always wanted to travel but should not care to skip through the cities of the world and see nothing of them." Light, upbeat, tamping down nervous laughter.

Madeleine shook her head and looked directly at Jane with cold gray eyes. Jane shivered. "Oh no," Madeleine began evenly, "I don't mean that at all. I thought you were one of those dreadful reporters and that you had come here to take down everything I said to you and write it up. I was so scared and thought how much I have been talking to this dreadful woman! She will write it up for the papers. How could I have talked to her as I have?"

Jane knew this was no dream. The tiny leather bag felt like a mail pouch; surely Madeleine could see it through her clothes. With studied nonchalance, Jane called the dream unpleasant and hoped Madeleine would not be troubled with any more disagreeable thoughts. Besides, Jane continued, "There was nothing worth writing up in this place, even," she added, "if I had brains enough to do such a thing, which I certainly do not have." And Jane rattled on, "I cannot recall anything you have said that would interest anyone beyond the Home." "Oh," Madeleine replied, "that is because you do not know me. The newspapers would be very glad to get hold of any facts about my life." Jane deflected, asking, What was this mystery? She moved close to Madeleine and grinned— Was she a Russian agitator engaged in a nefarious plot? Madeleine laughed, and the tension broke. She reiterated her promise: I will tell you my tale when you leave the House of Mercy.

On Sunday morning, Jane still felt ill, shaken by Madeleine's suspicion and felled by the spring fevers endemic to the warm, wet city. She spent the day in bed. Madeleine visited that evening, once again cross after meeting with her attorneys, glancing around the cheerless dormitory. Her hair cascaded down her back in thick auburn waves. The dormitory light was dim in the evening hour, and Madeleine recounted the many sad incidents in her life, a tragic tale. Jane listened and nodded. Then Madeleine suddenly shifted, taking Jane's hand: "See how strong I am, Agnes? I could easily crush this little hand of yours." Jane understood the painful warning: the Richelieu play about secret plots, the Nellie Bly dream, the society reporter. This was a loyalty test. Madeleine squeezed harder. Jane steered the conversation to cheerful topics, an attempt to redirect this silent contest toward neutral ground.[5]

Madeleine ignored Jane's babble and returned to the story of the still-unnamed man who had ruined her life. She was a sheltered and innocent girl, she insisted, a virgin when they met. She had no other beaus. He treated her well and with respect, just like he treated his own daughter. Madeleine went on, lost in the past: I was careful and guarded my reputation; I was not a whore. I went into society with an esteemed chaperone. No one ever suspected anything improper or found out about my secret life. Until he ruined it all.

Madeleine continued, and Jane felt encouraged: instead of nostalgic stories of her childhood, Madeleine was finally revealing details of her affair. Her lover was proud of her, she said, and he was at her command. Once, she told Jane, when he was in the West, she sent a telegram demanding he return to Washington, just to see if he would come. She commanded him, but he also commanded her. Madeleine grew sad, her anger drained. She gave up two children, she said quietly, hands slowly clenching. They died as infants. She gave up everything for him; she enjoyed a respectable reputation, lived a pleasant life in Washington, and she was a society woman. She had lost it all: bitterness had replaced love. Jane nodded in faux sympathy.

In the dim dormitory, in a nearby bed, a curious girl feigned sleep.

Noisy inmates tromped up the stairs. Madeleine grew quiet.

———————

On Monday morning, Madeleine's secret turned fodder for the House of Mercy residents. Jane tried to warn her, but she already knew. The girls had told Dorothea, and the matron called Madeleine into her office. Dorothea lectured; Madeleine refused to shrink in shame and told the matron she didn't mind that the girls knew. In fact, she told Jane after escaping Dorothea, I would have told my story to them long ago, beginning to end, if not for Dorothea's prohibition. And now she would not be cowed by the truth.[6]

The girls were having a field day. The sewing class was all atwitter during the afternoon session, girls sneaking peeks at a disgraced Madeleine and giggling into their piles of linens. Miss Ellis struggled to maintain decorum and keep the focus on stitching. Despite her superior airs, Miss Dudley, the penitents smirked, was no better than any of them.

While Madeleine endured the sewing room, Dorothea called Jane into the parlor to meet one of the Home's trustees. The "lady trustee" tried to convince Jane of the benefit of spending a year at the Home. But their conversation was interrupted by the noisy fervor in the house as the girls continued to chew on the tastiest piece of gossip they had heard in a long time. Dorothea explained to the trustee the unfortunate conversation overheard by the girls and the identity of the teacher, Miss Dudley.

The trustee took Dorothea to task. Miss Dudley, the trustee opined, should never have been allowed to speak to anyone in the house, and further, if the trustee had been in Washington when Dudley had first arrived, she would never have allowed her in the Home. It was a grave mistake to have let her stay. Sister Dorothea waited as the trustee continued her lecture: Dudley was a bad, notorious woman. She turned to Jane and admonished her to not have anything to do with Miss Dudley after she left. But to the trustee's horror, Jane stuck up for Madeleine. Jane wasn't sure what to make of Madeleine at this point, but she answered to Charles Stoll, not some holier-than-thou rich lady. Avoiding Madeleine would put her undercover work in jeopardy. Without apology, Jane told the trustee that she hoped her friendship with Madeleine would continue. Dorothea was no fan of Jane and Madeleine's friendship, but she must have enjoyed, just a little bit, the snapback to this officious woman.

The trustee was aghast. Female trustees assisted those leaving the Home with finding respectable lodging or a domestic job. But Jane had pushed her over the edge; the trustee told Dorothea she could not help Miss Parker. Jane nodded in faux agreement as if she had just lost a great honor, but really, she was relieved. The last thing she needed was some do-gooder watching her every move or showing up at her boardinghouse while she was writing a report for Stoll or entertaining Madeleine.

———————

On Tuesday, February 6, Jane's last morning at the House of Mercy, she washed her face in the basin of cold water and shouldered her way to a sliver of the mirror. She put on her molasses-stained dress and made her bed, pulling up rough sheets on the thin, hard mattress. Leaving was risky. From within the House of Mercy, she had had daily access to Madeleine Pollard. Once outside, could she reenter the one place Madeleine was guaranteed to be?[7]

In her week's stay, Jane had confirmed that Madeleine remained in Washington and would not settle—she was determined to go to trial, and her attorneys, with their daily meetings with Madeleine, were hard at work in preparation. In their conversations, Jane heard the same outline of events discussed in the newspapers—the older lover, her literary friends, the lost babies. Madeleine had professed her affair was a relationship of love, until her paramour deceived her. She was hurt and mad. Jane suspected there was more to her story.

Jane had learned to listen and to watch Madeleine's hands—
she clenched her fingers when she was upset, and when Madeleine
was angry, her guard fell, and she was more likely to spill a secret.
As for Madeleine's past lovers, Jane knew nothing. There was much
yet to uncover. But in the wake of the revelation of Madeleine's
story, Dorothea had forbidden Madeleine and Jane from speaking
to each other at all, and the idea of remaining at this Home for a
year was intolerable. For the sake of the mission, Jane had to leave.
She went downstairs for her last House of Mercy meal.

Breakfast was a trial. Madeleine held her head high in the
face of the sneering, laughing girls. She refused to let these girls
shame her; she would be respected. Jane forced down the cup of
bitter coffee and dry, day-old bread. Madeleine sat down next to
her as the girls ran off to their morning chores. Was she leaving
today? she asked. Yes, Jane told her. Madeleine opened a newspaper and looked over the rooms to let. She marked those in good
neighborhoods, those that would be safe. She turned to Jane in the
empty room. I promised to tell you my tale, she said, all of it. Jane
held her breath.

Miss Dudley whispered: My name is Madeleine Pollard.

Jane stayed stock still: I don't recognize it.

Madeleine spelled her name slowly: P-o-l-l-a-r-d.

Jane put on the face of one trying to recall a memory just out
of grasp. Perhaps, she said, I've seen it in the periodicals—a byline
on something you had authored?

Madeleine turned blunt: I am suing Colonel William Breckinridge, the congressman from Kentucky, for breach of promise.
My whole story, she told Jane, has been printed in the *New York
World*. I wrote it, she said. It came out in September, but you can
still get a copy at the newsstand near the Ebbitt House. Read it,
she urged. This trial, she said, rising from the breakfast table, is
going to be a very bitter fight. Very soon, the newspapers will be
full. Madeleine seemed pleased.[8]

Madeleine needed to head to her daily business; Jane needed
to take the next step in enacting hers—both women masking to the

other the work that filled their days. Jane told Madeleine that, even though Sister Dorothea had tried to warn her away, she would try to get her new address to her. They must stay in touch. Madeleine promised to visit Jane. Jane hoped that was true.

In the late morning, Miss Grey, the dormitory supervisor, appeared as Jane packed up her few things. Jane followed her to the attic and removed her ugly uniform. Grey returned Jane's luggage and clothes—the red dress she had made in Maine; her jaunty, stylish hat; and her new serge coat with the lamb's wool collar. Grey liked Jane and regretted her departure; the staff thought her a good role model for their wayward charges. As Jane dressed, transforming from penitent to young woman, Grey grew friendly, no longer attempting to wield authority over an inmate. Grey said that she didn't understand why Miss Dudley wanted to talk of her sinful life. What good did that do? And what good could come of the suit? Miss Dudley had said she wouldn't touch a penny of his money. She was only out for revenge and to ruin the congressman. Everyone knew the congressman had no money. Grey didn't understand—Miss Dudley's actions were incomprehensible, exactly the puzzle Jane was hired to solve.

Sister Dorothea made a final effort to convince Jane to stay. Despite her infatuation with the Home's most infamous resident, her soul was worth saving. Jane could be helpful in Dorothea's mission; where Madeleine's presence contaminated the girls, Jane's good breeding could cleanse them. Like a realtor eager for a commission, the matron showed Jane a private, third-floor room, directly across from Madeleine's, in the teachers' section of the house. Before Jane could contemplate the value of this proximity, the matron warned her: if she stayed, she could not visit Madeleine's room. No, thank you, answered Jane.

As Jane said her goodbyes to the teachers and staff, a disappointed Sister Dorothea pulled her aside and begged her not to see Madeleine in the city. She knew that Jane helped her from a kind heart, but Madeleine would bring only trouble. Jane politely demurred. She offered a compromise—she would leave but would continue working on the House of Mercy account books. When she came to write the ledgers, the good sisters could provide moral guidance. Dorothea agreed.

In a callback to her arrival and the lost-bag-at-the-train-station scheme, Jane left her bags in the House of Mercy dormitory—an excuse to come back and see Madeleine—while she looked for a room. She rented a comfortable place on Connecticut Avenue, near K Street and the House of Mercy, and convenient to the trolley line that traveled near the post office and the courthouse and along Madeleine's daily path as she trekked back and forth to her attorney's office. Once again, Jane drew on her recent illness, informing her landlady that she had come to Washington for her health, but how long she would remain depended on whether the climate agreed with her. Jane's thin frame from her earlier health troubles and her light diet at the House of Mercy sold her tale and encouraged sympathy, and a month-by-month lease, from the landlady.[9] Jane had one more errand to complete before returning to K Street to get her bags. She hurried.

Jane returned to the Home and ran upstairs for her bags. She passed by the dormitory and went to Madeleine's room. She left the two gifts she'd picked up on her errand: a stack of magazines and a box of candy. Jane opened the box and hid her new address inside. Madeleine had promised to visit and to write often. Jane's success depended on it.

Sister Dorothea, Miss Grey, and the housekeeper walked Jane to the door. Dorothea pulled the key from the clanking bunch at her waist. She placed the key in the lock, turned it, and opened the door. Sunshine illuminated the street. Jane was free to go. She took a deep breath of freedom. She had survived the House of Mercy. Jane Tucker *was* Nellie Bly: courageous, quick thinking, and confident. She had convinced Sister Dorothea that she was repentant, convinced Madeleine that she was a friend; she had shown Charles Stoll she was clever and capable. Jane was more than a dutiful daughter subject to the family claim—she was a sleuth, a detective, a spy.

7

So Darned Clever
in My Work

Jane Tucker sat in the restaurant of the National Hotel and breathed a sigh of relief. After seven days of weak tea, bland food, and meager servings, she ate like an Arctic explorer just returned to civilization. Between slurps of soup or bites of meat, roasted potatoes, or lettuce with French dressing, Jane pulled out a pen. Having managed to send only a single letter from inside the Home, she owed Charles Stoll an update.[1]

Jane emptied her memories of the past week into her report. Her close observations and private conversations with Madeleine had given Jane unique insight into their adversary's motivation for the trial, the question that bedeviled Breckinridge. Madeleine was an actress, Jane wrote, and bent on revenge. She had honed her tale of woe and could weep on command. Madeleine was eloquent and quick-witted. The congressman's lawyers would have their hands full with Madeleine on the stand.

Madeleine was of two minds, Jane observed. She both complained about and sought newspaper notoriety. And, Jane reported, a savvy Madeleine knew the importance of her public appearance and was "much too smart to do anything now that could be used against her on the trial." At present, noted Jane, she was living a correct life—escorted by her brother when out in public and only going to her attorneys' office or on the occasional shopping trip. Despite a lonely existence and ill will from Sister Dorothea, Madeleine would not leave the House of Mercy until the trial ended.

She had few supporters in Washington: her brother, Sarah Ellis, and Sister Ella, the first from family duty, the latter two out to save her soul.

As for what Madeleine wanted—she wanted her day in the spotlight. She wanted to tell her story. She wanted to be seen, to be heard. There was no chance of a settlement. Madeleine anticipated, even looked forward to, the "great fight" to come. Breckinridge, Jane warned, needed to prepare for trial. And for her to provide him with critical intel on the plaintiff's team's strategy, Jane needed to find access to Madeleine beyond the House of Mercy where they could speak uninterrupted and in private. Jane finished her meal and mailed her report to Stoll.

Out of the House of Mercy, Jane traversed unfamiliar territory. How did one spy? While a handful of female Civil War spies had published their memoirs of daring acts and secrets betrayed, there was no espionage equivalent to *The Stenographer's Guide*. Yet, as the Northern and Southern wartime agents had learned, attention to every detail, patience, and quick thinking served as effective techniques. Like the women before her, Jane would learn on the job.

With a week in Washington under her belt, Agnes Parker, Jane mused, had made headway with this faux friendship, but Madeleine could run hot and cold—one day inviting Jane to share confidences, the next eschewing her visits. In addition, Sister Dorothea presented a barrier to visiting, an impediment to the mission with the matron's misguided quest to keep Madeleine and Agnes apart.

Jane got to work. William Worthington, Breckinridge's clerk, delivered a copy of the September 17 *New York World*, and Jane studied Madeleine's self-described history and how she framed her legal complaint. She also read the almost-daily newspaper stories about the case to develop topics for seemingly casual conversations: articles on Madeleine's male friends, for example, suggested Jane create some past lovers of her own and then ask Madeleine about hers. Madeleine's schooling and travels provided an opportunity to investigate her ambitions, and mentions of elite literary friends offered Jane conversation starters on literature and Madeleine's potential financial supporters.

Preparation was key. Jane wrote out her diary from her tiny shorthand notes scrawled in the dark House of Mercy dormitory and sent a copy to Stoll. In return, she asked him to send her more information on the case. He had kept her in the dark, sharing details on a need-to-know basis. Jane pointed out that the more she knew of Madeleine's life, the more shared backstory she could create and the more information she could gather when fate next placed Jane in Madeleine's vicinity. She instructed Stoll to send material to her at the postal box Worthington had arranged, lock-box 586, and to use the name John C. Johnson.[2]

Jane settled into her room. Restful nights and better food helped keep her clear-eyed—the proprietress provided good meals twice daily. Jane ate an orange every morning, and her digestive illness abated. On Sundays, she watched the "swell teams" trot past on the broad, treelined expanse of Connecticut Avenue, a private parade of the city's best horses. Jane reassured her parents that her fellow boarders—mostly foreign government workers and two spinsters from Connecticut—were decent people.[3]

In her furnished room, Jane awaited Madeleine's promised visit.

But Madeleine never came.

———————

There is a power in the invisibility of women's domestic lives. Female spies in the Civil War hid notes in corsets, shoe heels, and elaborate hairdos, private spaces no decent soldier would search. Women glided by adversaries unsuspected, delivering food, washing laundry, or eavesdropping on officers quartered in their homes while they went about their daily chores. Jane found feminine spaces, the mundane objects of a woman's daily life, and domestic labor as fortunate instruments in her detective mission. And she had a knack for turning happenstance into an opportunity to gather intelligence.

Buying underwear provided an opportunity no male detective could exploit. While Jane shopped at Woodward and Lothrop, two days after leaving the Home, she found Madeleine examining the display of ladies' underthings. It was no surprise to Jane that Madeleine favored this establishment. The store stocked a wide variety of goods, including the latest fashion from Paris. Feigning delight at the apparent coincidence—one suspects that Jane followed Madeleine to the department store—the two women chatted as they examined bloomers, corsets, petticoats, and other items of intimate apparel. Madeleine conversed pleasantly enough, but Jane detected a decided chill. Harried, Madeleine explained she was leaving for Cincinnati that very afternoon. Distracted, she tried to push Jane off. Perhaps, Madeleine suggested, they could wait until after the trial to renew their friendship. Once that all-consuming event was behind her, Jane would see what a good friend Madeleine could be. Jane realized Madeleine had no intention of visiting her room; she was dropping her. Jane thought fast.[4]

The attraction of a department store was the wide variety of goods offered, all under one roof. Indeed, these new multistory buildings were designed to keep women there for extended visits. Department stores offered tea rooms, parlors for rest, live music, and attendants to wrap, carry, and deliver one's purchases. Seeing that Madeleine had no pocketbook, Jane insisted on buying her one, delaying Madeleine's departure as the two inspected drawstring reticules, tapestry purses, and frame handbags. Jane no doubt slowly weighed the merits of fashion and function of each before selecting an appropriate bag. She spent two dollars on what must have been a very nice purse. The impromptu gift thawed Madeleine's frost. "Jane," she invited, "come with me to pick up my new hat at Morez et Cie."[5]

As they entered the H Street millinery shop, Miss Susan, the milliner, greeted Madeleine warmly. Miss Susan had made Madeleine's Parisian-style hats for years, and Jane listened carefully as Madeleine paid eleven dollars for a hat with a sticker price of fifteen. She wondered about the curious financial arrangement and totaled the morning's shopping: Madeleine had twenty-nine dollars and change in hand to start; she spent nine and a half dollars at the department store and had placed that expense on account; she spent eleven on her hat. Her purchases totaled more than Jane made in a week and were of nicer quality than the bargain buys Jane favored by necessity. Madeleine had pleaded poverty—who was providing the cash for custom-made hats, new underwear, and expensive attorneys? After they left the shop, Madeleine turned to Jane. "Please," she said, "don't mention this purchase to Sister Dorothea."[6]

While the morning's purchases added to the mystery of Madeleine's finances, her trip to Cincinnati took precedence. Who did she plan to see in Cincinnati? And for what purpose? Had the plaintiff's lawyers discovered something new? Jane was itching to alert Stoll.

The excursion to Morez et Cie completed Pollard's errands, but now she was running late and still needed to retrieve her traveling bag from the House of Mercy before boarding her train. A sympathetic person might politely excuse herself and take her leave, recognizing the press of last-minute tasks Madeleine faced. Jane made no move to bring their day together to an end, willfully naïve to Madeleine's schedule. She offered to buy lunch, and Madeleine agreed to meet her at the train station, where they could dine before her 2:00 p.m. departure. Lady Luck offered Jane another gift shortly thereafter: although Madeleine arrived at the station late, she came with her brother, Dudley Pollard. Jane knew of Dudley, but she had yet to speak with him. If Madeleine's Cincinnati mission raised questions, perhaps Dudley could provide the answers.

At the busy train station, Madeleine kept to the shadows. Her face and name were readily recognized, a public visibility she not only disliked but had grown to fear. On this Thursday, February 8, Dudley escorted his sister onto the Cincinnati-bound train. Jane followed as he guided Madeleine to her stateroom, a private space where she could avoid passengers' gawking stares on the overnight

journey. Dudley offered to walk through the train cars to identify reporters or other interested parties, but Madeleine declined.
Her brother's offer embarrassed her, and she seemed impatient for
him and Jane to leave, their protective ministrations only highlighting her situation. Jane eyed Madeleine; Madeleine watched
Jane watching her. She broke the moment's spell, redirecting the
conversation. Now the sister embarrassed the brother, Madeleine
exclaiming he looked seedy and needed a decent overcoat, tasking
Agnes to help him pick one out. Jane graciously accepted Madeleine's inadvertent gift: they would shop for a coat, and in their
polite conversation, Jane would see just what Dudley knew.[7]

The brakes released a giant sigh, and the Washington and Cincinnati Special chugged out of the Baltimore and Potomac station.[8]
Jane took stock of Dudley. He appeared unsophisticated and guile-
less, traits Jane could exploit. Although brother and sister had not
lived in the same household for almost twenty years, he dutifully
protected her. He tried to negotiate the impasse between mother
and daughter. Madeleine, unwilling to forgo the lawsuit and stand
alone in disgrace, refused. Whenever their mother sent Dudley a
bit of spending money, he gave half to his sister, a generous gift but
certainly nowhere near what she needed for her shopping, travels,
and legal fees.

The sudden death of his father in 1876 had shaken young
Dudley's life as much as his sister's. While Madeleine lived with
her Aunt and Uncle Cowan in Pittsburgh, Dudley spent nearly ten
years at the Masonic Orphans and Widows Home in Louisville,
along with his brother Horatio and sister Rosalie. There, he was
educated and learned the printing trade. Dudley left at age eighteen. A personal note appended to his record commented on his
kind nature and how he and Horatio were very fine young men of
outstanding character.[9]

As the Cincinnati-bound train disappeared from view, Jane
seized the moment, asking Dudley if he had seen the Washington

sites. He had no plans for the day, so the pair purchased a guide-book, readily available from vendors at the busy train station.

Jane had played the roles of a repentant young woman and adoring new friend. She added first-time tourist to her repertoire. The pair strolled up to the Capitol. From the visitors' gallery, Dudley and Jane watched the Senate in session, and Dudley pointed out the men he recognized. They crossed under the Capitol dome and through the National Statuary Hall to the Chamber of the House of Representatives. They discussed the most well-known men. Jane asked Dudley to point out Breckinridge, hoping this might stimulate a private comment. Dudley identified the colonel, a democrat, seated at desk 90, in the middle of the fifth row from the front and in the middle section of five on the east side of the Representatives' Hall. Seeing Breckinridge made Dudley uneasy, and he worried about his sister. He asked Jane, Would Madeleine want to know that Breckinridge was in the city?[10]

Oh yes, said Jane eagerly and they returned to the station to send Madeleine a telegram. Dudley wanted to ease his sister's mind, but Jane had an alternate reason: Stoll would want to know of Madeleine's departure, and Jane had yet to find a private moment to send her message. She helped Dudley compose a brief message with no superfluous words, just as *The Stenographer's Guide* would advise.[11] Dudley asked Jane to send the telegram in her name, Agnes Parker, to foil reporters and gossip spreaders who might see the communication and recognize his surname. Dudley's apprehensions took the bloom off their adventure. Jane made an excuse to end the day. As soon as he left the station, she sent Stoll a special delivery letter detailing Madeleine's itinerary—a travel plan that suggested new witnesses were about to be deposed.[12]

Stoll would be grateful for the information Jane sent, alerting the defense to a possible new angle in the plaintiff's team's attack. Depositions—the sworn out-of-court testimony of witnesses—provided the evidence to support, or refute, Madeleine's legal claims. Lawyers from both sides drew up lists of potential witnesses and were required to share this information with the opposition. A date and place were set, and the plaintiff, defendant, and their attorneys (or representatives) attended. Questions were asked, and the deponent's responses were recorded by a court reporter, who then shared the transcript with both parties. The information gathered helped determine what a witness would say in court and how valuable (or damaging) their recollections might be. It also gave the opposing party insight into the argument that would be made. If a witness could not appear in court, the deposition would be read into the record in their stead. But those witnesses who gave a particularly compelling deposition would find themselves begged to appear in person. The deposition of Julia Churchill Blackburn was compelling.

Blackburn's outrage had not faded in the months since the revelation of the scandal, and although adopting a pose of feminine modesty, she quite willingly agreed to be deposed. The deposition was taken at her Washington home in early February, the day Jane left the House of Mercy and two days before Madeleine headed to Cincinnati. Blackburn had endured public scrutiny before. Her insistence on propriety and doing the correct thing may very well have been the legacy of the midcentury downfall of her late husband, Luke Pryor Blackburn.

The Blackburns met in Paris in 1857. Twenty-four-year-old Julia Churchill was on the Grand Tour—the excursion to Europe's historic sites, great art, and cathedrals providing refinement and Western cultural knowledge for an elite young woman. Physician Luke Blackburn was visiting hospitals, undertaking a study of the treatment of contagious diseases. They married by year's end. When the Civil War erupted, Luke Blackburn acted as an independent agent supporting the Confederate cause. At the end of the war, a spy accused the physician of having plotted to bring disease-infected clothing and linens to Northern cities, with one bundle directed to President Lincoln. He was acquitted but unpardoned, and the Blackburns remained in Canada until a yellow fever epidemic raged in the US South.[13]

Despite the danger, the Blackburns returned to the United States in 1867. Luke Blackburn originated the practice of quarantines during epidemics and was credited with saving countless lives—taking the first steps that would restore his tarnished reputation. Exonerated of his alleged crimes and returning to Louisville, Blackburn and his wife rebuilt their respected positions through philanthropy, public service, and politics. In 1879, Luke Blackburn was elected governor of Kentucky. He died in 1887, leaving Julia without a husband for protection, highlighting the vulnerability even of wealthy women and the social disruption Breckinridge's selfish activities created.

Newspapers published Blackburn's deposition. "Her testimony appears to be strongly against Colonel Breckinridge," the headline judged. Desha Breckinridge agreed that her deposition was detrimental to his father's case but nonetheless hoped the plaintiff would put her on the stand. Desha, likely imagining a soft-voiced widow, an elderly woman nervous and hesitant in a male domain like a courthouse, told his father, "She is much more damaging in deposition than on the witness stand, I should think."[14] He thought wrong.

With each success, Jane's confidence grew. Stoll praised her work, clearly pleased with her natural abilities. "You are certainly a trump card," he enthused.[15] Attorney Benjamin Butterworth thought her "shrewd," predicting a future in the working world. Her early success was "indeed beyond [their] wildest hope."[16] Jane told her mother that the lawyers were under a delusion that she was smart and, without revealing the nature of her work, noted, "I shall think I am too."[17]

"My brain has to hustle," she wrote, "and it works pretty well considering." The work had been difficult and discouraging at times, but if Jane could get out of debt, she said she'd have no regret about this position. Moreover, detective work improved her health and well-being, and she was proud that she was good at this task. Indeed, she told her mother, "I think I'll write a book when I get through—it would be amusing, I can assure you."[18] When Mollie updated Mame on Jane's "bright cheery letters," Mollie admitted that despite her worries, she was glad Jane had the chance to leave Maine "to get away from this hard weather & dull life I lead."[19]

Jane had impressed seasoned lawyers, but she was less impressed with them. She castigated Breckinridge's clerk, William Worthington, for numerous missteps, including putting her name on the John C. Johnson post office box application and, after she moved to Connecticut Avenue, delivering documents to her in person. Certainly, snarked Jane, Madeleine would be suspicious if her former lover's clerk was seen with Agnes Parker. Even Stoll did not escape Jane's criticism. When she received his letter outlining the facts of the case, she noted dryly, "I should have been glad of the points contained in it before I entered the Home. However, I believe I did the best that could be done with the material I had to work with, while I was there" and, in a self-deprecating pose of faux feminine frailty, "these additional facts might have simply confused me."[20]

Madeleine returned from Cincinnati on the eleventh, after four days of travel and depositions, and returned to her routine. Day after day, since she had hired her attorneys in July 1893, Madeleine sat in Calderon Carlisle's office, honing her testimony, answering questions, and reliving intimate moments. She returned to the House of Mercy each evening exhausted from the rehearsal of her life. She liked her attorneys, two well-regarded men who, they claimed, had taken on the case in a gallant effort to vindicate a wrong. Madeleine described Carlisle as a true and noble man. He dressed well, and his hair shone; his eyes were gendarme blue. He was heavy-chested with thin legs and a florid face. Wilson was a leader of the Washington, DC, Bar, tall and angular with a straggling beard, large bony hands, and a plain face.[21]

The plaintiff and her attorneys met in Carlisle's office in the Fendall Building on D Street, a castlelike fortress complete with turrets and a crenelated facade. As to the fees for her knights in legal armor, Madeleine had no means to pay. And their work piled up, with hundreds of hours spent preparing for trial as they took dozens of depositions, traveled between Washington and Kentucky, and hired private investigators to dig into Breckinridge's activities. Some speculated that Breckinridge's political enemies provided the funds; others imagined Carlisle, a wealthy man, donated money from his assets. Some said it was Carlisle's wife behind the donation in retribution for a slight from Breckinridge. Still others assumed that Julia Blackburn and her brother-in-law Senator Joseph Blackburn were paying the bills, the former humiliated by Breckinridge's attempt to thrust his mistress on her as an equal and the latter to eliminate Breckinridge as a rival for his Senate seat.[22]

Newspapers reported that Kentucky Masons were furious at Breckinridge's treatment of the daughter of a fellow Mason and collected money on her behalf. The same was said of Kentucky Odd Fellows, raising funds in tribute to their former leader J. D. Pollard, Sr. Breckinridge imagined Charles Dudley Warner supported Madeleine. Multiple sources identified a society of (unnamed) women as her monetary donors. Perhaps a group of nominally sympathetic women sent a few dollars her way, supporting her cause for calling out the double standard and helping her maintain a respectable sartorial appearance in the courtroom. It's unclear who supported Madeleine's financial needs. Wealthy or modest, male or female, her benefactors remained behind the scenes. Breckinridge was desperate to know.

Appearing in public was excruciating. Women snubbed Madeleine, and men stared. When she traveled to Cincinnati, the train conductor recognized her name from her ticket. When the train reached its destination, reporters, passengers, and the curious, alerted by telegraph in advance of her arrival, had formed a corridor on the platform, a gauntlet of gawkers for Madeleine to pass through. On the return trip, seated in the passenger car, Madeleine endured a parade of male travelers strolling past her, taking time for a long sideways glance—and once they arrived at their destinations, hurrying off to tell their friends how they had laid eyes on the country's most notorious woman.[23]

Dudley provided a barrier between Madeleine and the gazing, gaping public, but Madeleine wasn't sure what to make of him. Her brother was an experienced journalist. He'd found work as a stringer for the *Washington Evening News*, earning five dollars a column. But despite his reporter's instincts, he had no interest in using his reunion with his sister as the basis for an article. In fact, he diligently avoided reading about the case and disliked listening to his sister discuss it. He was supportive but disinterested in his sister's legal woes. His distancing made her wonder if he even loved her.[24]

The House of Mercy was both protection and prison. One afternoon, Madeleine asked Sister Dorothea to unlock the front door. She needed to get out, to clear her head away from mocking girls. Ever since her whispered story had been broadcast through the residence, peace eluded her. She no longer instructed the girls; any authority she had once been accorded had evaporated. She slept poorly, and her anxiety in advance of the trial grew. All she wanted was a breath of fresh air, a walk in February's weak but warming sunshine. Sister Dorothea grilled her: What was her destination? Her purpose? Madeleine said she had an appointment with a minister. Dorothea begrudgingly permitted her to leave. As Madeleine pushed past the witnesses to yet another humiliating scene, she tried to hide the tears welling up in her eyes.[25]

————————

The game of spy and quarry, predator and prey, detective and detected continued. Jane reviewed her strategies. She was good at lying to Madeleine, Sister Dorothea, and her mother. She knew Madeleine responded to flattery, admiration, and gifts. With no little sarcasm, Jane told Stoll, "I have succeeded pretty well so far in giving her the idea that I think she is a most remarkable woman, but it was not a difficult thing to do."[26] Jane was quite the actor, accepting religious tracts from the nuns and promising to read them while condemning Madeleine for what Jane assumed was a "pretended goodness" in Sister Ella's religious discourses. Jane continued to exploit her delicate physical appearance. Her pale skin, thin frame, and tales of recent illness were understood among the upper class as an indicator of genteel refinement, which thus encouraged sympathy from Sister Dorothea and her staff and gave Jane a continued welcome at the Home.[27]

With Madeleine busy with her attorneys each day, Jane turned to Dudley as a source of information. Initially, he was reticent, polite, and a perfect gentleman as they visited the Army Medical Museum, the zoo, and the botanical gardens. As Dudley grew more comfortable, he had taken to visiting Jane at her boardinghouse. They'd sit in a parlor among other residents and talk or play card games.[28] One evening, just two days after he met Jane, Dudley was unusually excited and told her in confidence that a junior editor of a Kentucky newspaper had written to his sister's counsel with a new bombshell against Breckinridge. "It will be a great card for them," Dudley gushed.[29] The plaintiff's lawyers were delighted. Further, he told Jane, the informant hated Breckinridge and offered to do whatever he could to help Madeleine's case. This was all behind the scenes—the informant's boss was strongly pro-Breckinridge. But in secret, Dudley said, he could try to get testimony. Jane asked about money—was this one of his sister's financial sources? Dudley hedged. No, he said, this man didn't have money to spare, but the information he could offer was much more valuable. Dudley grew quiet. Jane thought he looked scared to death.[30]

Dudley assisted Madeleine's attorneys with several tasks, and in return, they had arranged a room for him just four blocks from their office.[31] In a letter to Stoll, Jane expressed surprise that he worked endlessly for the attorneys, willing to tackle any task, as if she weren't doing the same for the defense. Jane reassessed

Dudley. He was a tough nut to crack: when she asked him his age, he replied twenty-five next October. He went silent when she followed with a question on Madeleine's birthday. "I could see," she reported, "that he had been carefully trained on the subject of age."[32]

Dudley occasionally sent regrets when he could not join Jane on an excursion. One day, they planned to watch the elephant walk around at the zoo, but either Dudley's editor or his sister's attorneys claimed his time. Jane remained hopeful. Dudley seemed to like her, and she kept up the illusion of a budding friendship. She wrote Stoll: "While he knows very little about the suit, he forms a connecting link and enables me to ascertain his sister's movements and whereabouts; and that is quite important."[33]

Meanwhile, Madeleine had grown more cautious, guarding her answers on those days, increasingly infrequent, that she had time for Jane. On one February walk, Jane and Madeleine pondered how to fund renting a New York flat. Six months of expenses could run near $500, Jane suggested. Madeleine knew how to pay for it: "I have a friend," she said, "who has promised me that much or more." Jane perked up, attentive to what assistance a wealthy friend might provide Madeleine. Madeleine had an idea: they would borrow more than they needed, and a banker friend of hers could invest it. It would be risky—Madeleine had previously invested her savings from her civil service positions in the stock market, a progressive move for an independent woman but one that, if successful, would increase her savings faster than a woman's wages. Anticipating a marriage and setting up a household, or perhaps thinking about European travel or wisely protecting herself, Madeleine had placed her funds with S. V. White, a Wall Street broker. When the market crashed in the Panic of 1893, Madeleine lost her entire investment, her insolvency adding an additional imperative for securing marriage to Breckinridge. When Jane pressed for the identity of this generous friend, Madeleine clammed up, taking great care not even to reveal the gender of her future benefactor.[34]

Spring weather gave more opportunities for walks. On more voluble days, Madeleine was chatty, and Jane pressed her to give up the lawsuit, hoping that in her expected refusal, Madeleine would reveal her motivation. "I cannot give this up now," she said. "It is a part of my life. I have gone too far to drop it. I cannot draw back now. I *must* go on." Her frustration and anger roiled to the surface: "This man has ruined my life. I gave him all the love in my heart; he was a coward and a villain. I hate him, and he shall suffer what he has made me suffer."[35]

Jane wondered what a victory would mean for Madeleine's future; she asked what she would do if she was awarded money. "Sometimes," Madeleine admitted, "I think I will take it and study abroad," as a woman of good social standing had advised her. Breckinridge's shadow loomed large over Madeleine. "But," she continued, fists clenched, "I never can touch a penny of it. *He* shall have nothing to do with my future; I will make it my own."[36]

Jane tried to discover if there was a future mate waiting in the wings for Madeleine. She cautiously inquired about the men in Madeleine's history, revealed in her essay in the *World*. Of James Rodes, she spoke fondly. He was a rough diamond, she offered kindly, and she was the only woman he ever loved. Madeleine, though, had had no interest in polishing that diamond and kept their relationship chaste. No, none of the men in her past held a candle to Breckinridge, she said. He was the one she wanted to marry. *Had* wanted to marry.[37]

Jane offered the banal fish-in-the-sea scenario, but Madeleine was adamant. Marriage was not in her future. Jane suggested that she drop the trial and go somewhere where she was unknown and begin again with a good man. Madeleine scoffed. She must have stared at her oblivious friend. Did Agnes not understand how infamous she was and how unlikely a "good man" would seek out this onetime mistress for marriage?

Jane's ploy had failed.

These walks had given Jane Madeleine's romantic dreams of life in New York and tough pronouncements about refusing

Breckinridge's money. But Jane was feeling the press of time, and what Madeleine might do in the future was less important now than discovering what she had done in the past. The trial date had been set, March 8, barely three weeks away. Jane desperately wanted to find what Breckinridge desired most: the name of Madeleine's seducer, the benefactor paying her legal bills, or proof that another man fathered her three pregnancies. Jane dutifully sent her nightly reports to Stoll, but of late, she was frustrated with the dearth of information to report.

Three weeks after leaving the House of Mercy, Jane had reached an impasse. Madeleine spent all day with her attorneys, and although detective Jane hovered in Washington Circle hoping to intercept Madeleine on her return to the House of Mercy, on those occasions when Jane did encounter her, the plaintiff was often too exhausted and not interested in walks, carriage rides, or heart-to-heart talks. By the end of February, Dorothea was tightfisted with the keys, refusing to allow Jane's visits, peeved by her continued friendship with Madeleine and her refusal to adhere to Dorothea's advice to drop her friend. As for Dudley, he was apparently too busy to see Jane. Frustrated with the lull in detecting and in herself, she wrote Stoll she feared she had failed.[38]

Jane took to her bed, ill with malaria and impatient with the dull, fruitless days. Stoll came to her aid, offering a Kentucky remedy—whiskey—and sent a case to Worthington, who was tasked with delivering a bottle to Jane. He discarded his first idea—sticking a bottle in the post office box—and instead sent it by messenger after removing all the labels in an overabundance of caution and taking Jane's earlier criticisms to heart.[39]

In a generous mood, and to bolster Jane's flagging spirit, Worthington took the occasion to praise Jane and let her know how much everyone appreciated her hard work: "I want you to know that we feel that if we don't accomplish as much as you hope for, sometimes it is not your fault and that you are working it to the very best advantage."[40] Breckinridge's team had not given up on her. Louise Wing Breckinridge and the colonel's daughter, Sophonisba, bolstered her spirits, too, sending flowers and candy during this difficult period. As for her next assignment, Worthington passed along a note from Stoll with a request for information on three potential witnesses for the plaintiff about whom the defense lawyers knew nothing. Mr. Breckinridge, Worthington promised, would send more points for her to raise with Madeleine. If, Jane thought, she could weasel her way back into Dorothea's good graces.[41]

On March 1, with the trial slated to begin in one week, Jane recovered in her room, the malaria mitigated by whiskey and rest. Jane anticipated that the court battle would produce piles of papers that the attorneys needed transcribed, typed, or indexed. The men trusted her to organize the depositions, daily transcripts, correspondence, and lists of questions. Moreover, they looked to Jane to recognize in the material patterns or overlooked details. In addition, she would add to the document pile her reports on her conversations with Madeleine. Stoll had advised Jane to keep duplicate records, so, discarding notions of genteel debility in favor of working again, she escaped her sick bed and rented a typewriter to facilitate her nightly memos, after testing the machines herself.[42]

Jane was cautious to leave no trace of her undercover work visible in her room. She read, memorized, and returned any letters Stoll, Breckinridge, or Worthington had sent. After noting relevant facts in shorthand, she would place her tiny notes in her money bag and hide it under her dress. In case she needed to reread a letter, she numbered each missive and the corresponding notes. She did keep a copy of the *World* with Madeleine's autobiography in it, ever hopeful that Madeleine would visit, even though a month had passed since she made that promise. Jane reasoned that it would not harm the case if Madeleine saw the paper in her room; indeed, seeing that Jane saved that issue might signal to Madeleine Jane's loyalty.[43]

Jane's room was not the only arena she needed to secure. One by one, Jane's family members had caught the scent of her employment, recognizing Charles Stoll's name in the newspapers and gleaning Jane worked in some secretarial capacity on the biggest trial of 1894. In letters to each other, Mame and Mollie worried that with her previous connection to Stoll, Jane might have to appear on the stand to testify, although on what topic they imagined is unclear. Will Patterson guessed her connection to the case, as did Jane's brother Bill and her grandmother; they all worried about Jane's reputation working on such a seamy, disgraceful subject.[44] If Jane appeared on the witness stand, Mollie wrote to Mame, "I believe I should collapse."[45]

In a letter to Jane, Mollie patted herself on the back for solving, she thought, the mystery of Jane's employment. Jane chided her mother: "You take *my* advice and don't get a swelled head about your powers of guessing—in fact, don't make wild guesses and then worry over these because if you'll have patience 'til I get home, you'll know all about it." Jane had to keep the details of her work confidential, she told Mollie, and begged her "not to say a word to anyone of what you may think or guess at."[46] Mr. Stoll did not want anyone to know Jane's job, and, she reiterated, her success depended on this silence.[47]

Six days before the trial that would determine his personal and political future, Breckinridge sent a letter urging Jane to keep after Madeleine about her relationship with Charles Dudley Warner. This could be essential to the case, he alone advised, with his attorneys' attention on other subjects. Breckinridge also sought information about a Margaret Norris in a Rhode Island insane asylum. Her brother, Breckinridge believed, had been an intimate friend of Madeleine's. He suggested that Jane create a pretend insane friend and bring her up in conversation to get Madeleine to talk about Margaret, which would give Jane an opening to ask about Margaret's brother.[48] Jane no doubt saw this plan for what it was—a desperate grasp at straws as the clock ticked down.

With his letter, Breckinridge had gone a bit rogue, ignoring the careful procedure Stoll, Worthington, and Jane used to communicate. Sending a letter under his own signature urging a duplicitous plan was dangerous; should it be intercepted, Stoll's secret plan—and Breckinridge's folly—would be revealed. Moreover, Stoll had cautioned the congressman to adhere to Pinkerton detective Doughty's advice from January not to bother with testimony from Madeleine's alleged past lovers. As Stoll astutely knew, such evidence would be circumspect at best and, more to a point Breckinridge could not seem to see, who Madeleine had slept with was not on trial: the issue was Breckinridge's promise to marry her.

Newspaper articles grew in tandem with eager anticipation of the start of the trial. Jane scrutinized the chatter, looking for nuggets of truth, hints, or leads she could follow with Madeleine or Dudley. She pored over a story about Madeleine's aunt, Mary S. Oliver, who, the papers accused, had been involved with Senator Simon Cameron of Pennsylvania, Lincoln's secretary of war, and had attempted blackmail. Liaisons with powerful politicians seemed to run in the family, newspapers opined. Jane contemplated how to verify this family history.[49]

As the start of the Great Fight, approached, Jane redoubled her efforts to get answers to nagging questions, but she struggled to see Madeleine in the days immediately before the trial. Her frustrations grew. "There is so much to learn, and I get on so slowly," she complained to Worthington.[50] In five weeks, Jane had infiltrated the House of Mercy and befriended Madeleine. From her faux friend, Jane learned that Madeleine could not be bought off, and she had confirmed much of what Breckinridge's team already knew of her past liaisons, pregnancies, and history in Washington. But nothing new had been revealed, frustrating Jane, who suspected a smoking gun lurked just beneath Madeleine's closely held surface.

Madeleine was frustrated too. She had been spending long days with her attorneys, reviewing the evidence, honing her testimony, and fine-tuning their trial strategy. These lengthy sessions exhausted and angered her, especially when the lawyers suggested she should not testify. On these days, she stormed upstairs, and

Sister Dorothea denied Jane a visit, fearing that she might further aggravate their difficult resident. Jane's irritation grew in tandem with Madeleine's—a lost opportunity as Madeleine's anger provided an inroad to her truths. Jane advised Stoll to make the plaintiff angry on the stand: "Her real self always comes to the front when she gets angry, and this always happens when things don't go to suit her."[51]

Jane turned creative. If she couldn't get into the House of Mercy, she'd find Madeleine beyond it. On Sundays, a church provided the most likely venue for an encounter. Jane was not a regular churchgoer, but on Sunday, March 4, four days before the trial would start, she sat through two services. At the end of the second service, Jane spied her prize, Madeleine, away from the watchful eyes of Sister Dorothea and freed from Carlisle's office. Jane approached Madeleine casually as if meeting by happy accident. They chatted, Jane attuned to any task or favor she could provide—any excuse to stay in her orbit. Madeleine mentioned the most recent issue of the *World*, and Jane offered to get her one at a newsstand; when Madeleine asked her to fetch Dudley so they could all go for a ride in the country, Jane hurried away, strategizing the topics she could raise with the Pollard siblings.[52]

She returned with the newspaper and Dudley, who greeted his sister but announced that he had too much work and could not join them on their ride. To Jane's relief, Madeleine was still game. They boarded the streetcar and headed toward Tenleytown in northwest Washington, near the Maryland border.

The streetcar rumbled and swayed, windows open in the warm weather. Jane turned to Madeleine and posed a question, but she brushed it aside. Jane changed topics, tried again, and was again rebuffed. Madeleine made very little conversation on the streetcar, whispering that she was afraid of being overheard by reporters. Jane might have dismissed what she thought of as paranoia, but Madeleine knew her story was a commodity. Reporters were eager to turn any scrap of information—whether accurate or not—into a quick payday.[53]

Once they reached Tenleytown and walked for some time, leaving fellow riders in the distance, Madeleine opened up. But Jane's hope for the smoking gun was quickly frustrated. She skipped polite chitchat and raised the issue she knew bedeviled Breckinridge: how Madeleine met Charles Dudley Warner. Madeleine claimed she had sent one of her stories to Warner, which greatly impressed him. When he came to Washington to write about the city for his series "A Little Journey in the World," they met. Madeleine described their mutual friends and how Warner and his hosts frequently invited her to dine with him, painting a portrait of her life in elite literary circles filled with elegant meals and being a favored society guest.

"Madeleine," Jane begged, mimicking the confidence between close girlfriends, "you must tell me what Warner was like. He must be young and very attractive." Madeleine laughed: "Not at all. He's old and focused on his health." Jane persisted. "Did you ever care for him?" Madeleine mused: Warner had flattered her and introduced her to "charming literary people," but no, she had no love interest in him. It was Breckinridge that she had loved.[54]

Jane prodded Madeleine, saying she doubted the possibility that Madeleine had never flirted with any men other than Colonel Breckinridge. "No," said Madeleine. "I had opportunities and plenty of nice male friends, but they were simply friends." Again, it was only Breckinridge.[55]

Jane launched more conversational arrows, but they failed to elicit anything of use. They boarded the trolley car back to Georgetown. Jane asked whether Madeleine had kept Breckinridge's letters and how many she had. Madeleine cut to the chase, her voice increasingly hard, annoyed at a conversation that perhaps felt more like a cross-examination: Madeleine said she had many, but she didn't need letters to win, "for he cannot get out of the fact that he took me to Mrs. Blackburn and asked her, as an old and valued friend, to chaperone me as his future wife," and she could prove it. "That," she concluded, "is enough to win the case."[56] Madeleine's stony silence told Jane to back off. They continued the ride without speaking.

Jane let the silence linger and then returned to her questions, unable to ignore her desperate need for answers and worried that Madeleine's assessment might be right. But minutiae on Fillette's house, Carlisle's wife, and convent life meant little. As they neared their stop, Madeleine spied a small house for rent not far from the House of Mercy and asked Jane to see how much it was. It would make a lovely home for them and Dudley, she said. Jane agreed. But, Madeleine cautioned, she shouldn't tell the sisters their plans; she made Jane promise, and Jane did.

Although Jane hadn't secured any shocking information, another afternoon with Madeleine might prove fruitful—perhaps more personal revelations on her time as Blackburn's protégé. Jane began thanking Madeleine for her delightful company, and said they should spend more time together. Madeleine suggested another Sunday after church; she would evade Miss Ellis or Sister Ella, her usual bodyguards, she said with a laugh. They could walk and talk after the service. In the meantime, they agreed to meet tomorrow for a drive. The streetcar arrived at their stop.

On Monday afternoon, March 5, Jane went to retrieve Madeleine for their carriage drive, hoping the more private conveyance would be conducive to shared secrets. Sarah Ellis met Jane at the door and told her that Madeleine had gone to her lawyers' office. Stalling and crafting an excuse so she could return to the Home later, Jane offered to take a sick girl out for a ride to revive her spirits in the fresh air. Jane had already rented the carriage, she explained, pointing to the waiting vehicle. When Ellis went to get the girl ready, Jane slipped into the Home. Sister Dorothea called her into the parlor.

Agnes, she said, Madeleine is getting ready to go to her lawyers and cannot go with you. Jane puzzled: Had she gone to the lawyers, or was she getting ready to? Dorothea continued: Madeleine told me of your plans to live together. She asked me to tell you she does not see how she can carry out this plan. A warning bell sounded in Jane's head.

"Sister Dorothea, I don't see why Madeleine couldn't have told me this herself." The matron had no answer: "I surely do not know why Madeleine asked me to tell you this or why she told me of the plan to begin with," said the matron.[57] Jane turned to leave.

As she walked to the boardinghouse, Jane puzzled over this surprising turn of events. They had spent the previous afternoon together and, for the most part, had a pleasant conversation. Jane felt hurt, the unexpected emotion surprising her. "What an ungrateful and changeable disposition she has!" Jane wrote to Stoll.[58] Did Madeleine take some pleasure in wounding her friends? Or had Jane's barrage of questions reawakened Madeleine's suspicions? Did she suspect Aggie was not the friend Madeleine hoped she'd be? Madeleine's warmth had turned cold, and it appears that Jane did not see Madeleine again before the trial began.

Meanwhile, the night before the trial, Congressman Breckinridge penned a letter to his daughter, Sophonisba. He needed a trusted person to care for and be a sympathetic companion to her new stepmother. The trial would be brutal, he anticipated, and her health was already weak. He explained to Nisba that Louise's poor health and the humiliation of the newspaper stories have prevented her from socializing and making friends. He was worried and in need: "I do not know where to turn to find somebody to be with her."[59] His dutiful daughter answered the call.

Breckinridge had just moved from the hotel to a rented house at 1725 Q Street NW. Along with Louise, Sophonisba, and Desha, John Shelby and Charles Stoll would live there as well. During the trial, the private quarters would allow the defense team to brainstorm and strategize without being overheard in hotel parlors and thin-walled guest suites. Jane, veiled and taking steps to avoid being followed, would meet there on occasional evenings or weekends and report directly to the men.[60]

Once the trial began, Jane would play a crucial role. Despite Madeleine's now cool demeanor, Jane would attempt to visit each evening. She was the eyes and ears of the defense: she would study Madeleine's emotional state, warn of surprise witnesses, and alert the lawyers to changes in the plaintiff's strategy. Jane wanted to believe she could tip the balance and provide a Breckinridge victory. But with the nation focused on the trial, protecting Jane's secret identity was paramount. If Stoll's scheme unraveled, the social outcry would irreparably harm the congressman's standing, thwart his reelection bid, and perhaps even jeopardize the trial, not to mention the consequences that would befall Jane. As Madeleine moved into the limelight, Jane retreated into the shadows. To succeed, she must become invisible. "Success," she knew, "depends on silence."[61]

8

A Fellow Woman,
Ambitious and Smart

On Thursday, March 8, Madeleine awoke rested and ready. She prepared carefully for her court appearance, setting aside the plain blue dress of a House of Mercy teacher and donning her sedate but fashionable clothes. She selected a dark dress and tailored blue serge coat with wide, gathered sleeves and a double row of buttons. She wore black gloves. Her auburn hair was braided and interlaced into smooth knots gathered neatly behind her head, a low black hat secured with a ribbon tied in a small bow under her chin. A decorative gewgaw topped the cap, sitting on the front like a tiny tower, and a dotted veil hung down, barely covering her smooth, clear skin. She wore no jewelry save for a gold hat pin. She ate a light breakfast and went downstairs. Two friends accompanied Madeleine: Sarah Ellis, the House of Mercy sewing teacher, and Dr. Belle Buchanan, Madeleine's physician from Cincinnati. Buchanan wore a fashionable olive outfit; Ellis dressed so severely in black that the press mistook her for a nun.

Excited and nervous, Madeleine waited across the street from the courthouse, ensconced in Calderon Carlisle's office. She paced the room, peered out the window, and gazed at the crowd below, milling on D Street and pressing at the columned portico of City Hall. Madeleine could look down onto the East Wing and into the courtroom windows from her perch, perhaps catching a glimpse of the silver-tongued, white-haired defendant. Buchanan and Ellis sat with her making small talk and keeping her calm. She would not enter the courtroom until Carlisle was about to make his opening statement. Madeleine would wait until called. All eyes would be on her. Her entrance would be dramatic.[1]

———————

Spectators did not wait. Determined men and courageous women marched up D Street, braving the raw March weather in eager hopes of winning a rare seat on a hard bench or a scratchy cane chair. The marshal had secured the larger of two courtrooms in the District Courthouse, anticipating enormous crowds. One thousand people had requested admission tickets, and two hundred members of the bar had already claimed seats.[2] The empty courtroom stood ready in the East Wing of the old City Hall building, quiet in the early morning hours. Sixty by 40 feet and largely unadorned, the courtroom had witnessed history: assassins of presidents, murderers of rivals, and desperately aggrieved lovers had been tried there. Three arched, 8-foot-wide, 15-foot-high windows on each long wall brought light. Looking south down Four and a Half Street, a distracted spectator would see the 555-foot-tall Washington Monument, the second tallest structure in the world since the Eiffel Tower (1,024 feet) opened in 1889. The room did not lack color: two-toned walls of blue and olive—in some light, the latter turned the color of mud. Only a clock and a row of clothes pegs marked the walls. "It is all bare, old fashioned, commodious, and plastery," described George Townsend, reporting for the *Cincinnati Enquirer*.[3] This was a serious room, the architecture said; this was not a stage for a public craze or airing of social opinion. And yet the trial was all that, counter to the gravity a courtroom embodied. The lucky few who would win an uncomfortable seat in the rear of a crowded, stuffy room would witness Madeleine Pollard's day in court.

Judge Andrew Bradley entered the courtroom. The buzz of excited conversation faded, and the line of lawyers rose. Breckinridge, Butterworth, and their defense-team compatriots sat facing the judge on his left; Wilson, Carlisle, and a seat for the plaintiff on his right. The marshal and court clerks were stationed on a raised platform facing the spectators. Judge Bradley perched above them on a big red leather chair under an arched indentation in the wall. The jury would be seated to his right on a raised platform, perpendicular to the cadre of counsel. Bradley wore an expression of benign boredom, although he anticipated this case would prove anything but.

The judge glanced at a slip of paper in his hand recording the name of the case: *Pollard v. Breckinridge.* He asked those assembled, "Are you ready for trial?" The spectators leaned forward. A dozen reporters, huddled around a diminutive table and crowded at one end of the middle rows of benches, opened their notebooks. Two tables of attorneys nodded. There would be no last-minute compromise. The plaintiff and defendant were ready to begin.

————————

Jane desperately wanted to go. She had begged Charles Stoll for a seat in the courtroom. Too dangerous for Agnes Parker, he replied. So many of the attorneys and spectators had Kentucky connections; even if she were veiled, someone might recognize Jane Tucker from her work with Stoll in New York. Sequestered in her boardinghouse, Jane had sighed reading the early morning response.

"Anyway," Jane wrote her mother from her position in the shadows, killing time with correspondence, "there are such crowds to go that it is next to impossible to get in."[4]

————————

Those hoping to witness this spectacle first had to pass by the marshal, Alfred Wilson. Like a doorman at a nightclub granting entrance to the young and the hip, Wilson controlled access to the courtroom, offering a rare seat to only a handful of male spectators; women were not welcome in Bradley's court with testimony he anticipated would be too graphic for the fairer sex. Members of the legal profession certified by the clerk of the court were admitted, as were the credentialed press. The marshal permitted a minister to attend as well. A scattering of congressmen attended each day. The only female spectator—an attorney—argued her way in. A court officer challenged a Black attorney standing in the courtroom to observe the trial. Refusing to acknowledge the attorney's proffered business card, the officer roughly escorted him out until the marshal at the door confirmed the gentleman was a certified member of the bar. The officer of the court stalked off without an apology.[5]

Curious onlookers pressed close to interior windows in the main corridor of the court building, which looked across a light well and into the courtroom. As one man left, another shouldered in to take his place.

Jeremiah Wilson launched a preemptive salvo, setting a contentious tone and embarking on a day's worth of arguing over depositions gathered in Kentucky. As the lawyers argued, the crowd shifted, bored and disappointed. Bradley made rulings and moved on. Hopes were raised as the marshal called the jury to the courtroom. Twelve white men took their seats, a plain brick wall to their backs. They had been drawn from a pool of twenty, plaintiff and defense each allowed to strike four jurors. Five Black men had been in that pool; all had been struck. Two carpenters, a steamfitter, and a painter joined a banker, two bookkeepers, a farmer, and an agent. Ferdinand Heitmuller dealt in produce; Josef Wyland was a merchant; Hugh Reilly sold paints and glass. These dozen men would judge a young woman's ambition and a privileged man's promise.

Calderon Carlisle now stood, ready to make his opening statement only to be interrupted by the defense asking for an adjournment, pleading that one of their attorneys had just joined the team after a lengthy illness, and with the new, and hotly contested, depositions arriving from Kentucky at any moment, both legal teams would need time for a thorough review of these documents. Madeleine's lawyers reluctantly agreed, and Madeleine, making her way to the courthouse, was intercepted by Carlisle's clerk, running across the street to tell her the news. Her anticipation wilted.

Miss Ellis and Doctor Buchanan guided her back to the House of Mercy. Disappointed spectators vacated hard-won seats. Reporters put away their pencils. Jane waited for the late afternoon *Evening Star*. Day one of the trial was not much of a day at all.

———————

On Friday morning, Madeleine awoke and steeled herself for her day in court. Once again, she donned her dark dress and serge coat and carefully fixed her hair. Today, she would enter the courtroom. Ellis and Buchanan met her near the door to protect her from the overeager curious on the streetcar and to escort her from the trolley stop, through the crowds, and into the courthouse. Reporters watched as she made her way into the courtroom and took her seat. They weren't sure who Buchanan was, but they thought they recognized a nun when they saw Ellis.

Madeleine sat at the plaintiff's table, awaiting the start of the trial and aware of the many eyes focused on her. She looked well rested and held her head high; her eyebrows were dark and arched, her cheekbones prominent, and her long neck sloped to her shoulders, "careworn yet genuine," thought the *Enquirer* reporter.[6] When she smiled, her face lit up. Her smile faded by the end of the day.

———————

Meanwhile, in her room, Jane typed a letter to Worthington. She reported that she was unable to see Madeleine last evening but she had seen Dudley Pollard. Last night, Jane wrote, Dudley had arrived later than expected at her boardinghouse, kept busy with tasks from morning to evening. She had questioned him on his daily routine. While court was in session, he had said of the first day of the trial, he greeted witnesses for the plaintiff as they arrived in Washington and escorted them from the railroad station to hotels or Carlisle's office. The plaintiff's team, he told Jane, had said publicly that they were annoyed that the first day's legal squabbling had delayed opening statements, but they had lied.

Dudley laughed—they were delighted with the extra day and the additional time for witnesses to travel to Washington. As to the identity of these visitors, that's all tight-lipped Dudley would say.[7]

Midafternoon, Jane haunted the downtown newsstands, awaiting the late afternoon and early evening papers with their report of the trial. The *thunk* of a string-tied bundle hitting the sidewalk signaled news, and Jane fished for coins in her purse. It was two cents for the *Evening Star* and one cent for the *Washington Times*, a morning paper reporting on the previous day. Newspapers in hand, she walked with a determined pace, not wanting to call attention to herself in her excitement. On the trolley, Jane resisted the urge to scan the headlines lest anyone see the front-page news stories and strike up a conversation about the trial. She walked from the trolley stop to her boardinghouse and climbed the stairs to her room—or maybe as the front door shut behind her, she raced up as curiosity got the best of her. Jane tore off her hat and gloves, unfolded the papers, and read.

Calderon Carlisle had made Madeleine's charge clear: Breckinridge had broken his promise to marry, a pledge three credible witnesses had heard. How Madeleine spent her youth, Carlisle argued in his opening statement, and the choices she had made were not at issue. The issue here, he said, standing before the jury, was whether Breckinridge had promised to marry and if that promise had been broken. Carlisle intended to prove it had.[8]

On that note, the courtroom paused, anticipation high. But jurors and spectators rode the roller coaster down to disappointment once more. Before any of Carlisle's witnesses could take the stand, the lawyers argued about a four-volume set of Washington Irving books that one-time benefactor James Rodes had given Madeleine in 1884 and that she had subsequently gifted to the Norwood Asylum. The defense lawyers had borrowed the books from the asylum nuns but had failed to share this evidence with the plaintiff's lawyers. Madeleine fidgeted. Defense Attorney Benjamin Butterworth played coy. Which books? he asked. The plaintiff rolled her eyes. The attorneys argued. Madeleine clenched her hands. Despite weeks of preparation for attending court, Madeleine broke courtroom decorum and asked in exasperation, "Why does he ask such questions? They are absurd!" Judge Bradley agreed and ordered the defense to give the volumes to the court clerk. Carlisle worked to quiet Madeleine. Miss Ellis held her hand. Everyone took a breath. Carlisle motioned to the court crier, who called the plaintiff's first witness. But as Jane read of Julia Churchill Blackburn's appearance, her heart dropped. The plaintiff's lawyer had elicited powerful testimony from Blackburn, but on cross-examination, the defense had bungled the case. On just the second day of the trial, Breckinridge was losing.

When Julia Blackburn took the stand, she exuded class, dressed in a black gown and furs that set off her white skin and rich black eyes. She "looked the lady," noted one reporter.[9] Her gray hair marked a woman of experience and wisdom, of respect and reputation. She was sixty-one years old, the former First Lady of Kentucky, and a widow. As she answered Calderon Carlisle's questions, she looked at Breckinridge and raised her voice above a parlor whisper. She did not want the jury to miss a single word. She wanted Breckinridge to hear too.[10]

The content of her testimony yielded few surprises. Her deposition had been published in the papers weeks before and had been the focus of much pretrial discussion from Washington to Kentucky. Yet in the courtroom, her refined presence added considerable weight to her words as her social status stamped her testimony unimpeachable. It was no accident Carlisle put Blackburn on the stand first. "The social superiority of Mrs. Blackburn to both [Breckinridge and Pollard] is felt by the spectators," Townsend wrote. In Carlisle's strategy, her testimony presented uncontestable proof of a promise breached.

Yes, she testified, Breckinridge brought Miss Pollard to her flat on Good Friday, 1893, and asked her to protect Miss Pollard, to provide a guiding hand to the young woman who would be his

wife. "I only remember the date," she said, "because of the per-
sistency with which they insisted on seeing me." Blackburn relayed
to the court that Breckinridge had said he expected to marry Miss
Pollard as soon as the appropriate mourning period for his late
wife had passed.

There were subsequent visits, she said, in March and April
1893, Breckinridge arriving without Madeleine on several occasions. She was shocked at his engagement with not yet a year
passed since his late wife's death. "I think," Blackburn had told
him, "it is a poor return for so much devotion from your wife
to become engaged so soon after [her] death." In the courtroom,
Breckinridge's already florid face flushed.[11]

Blackburn repeated to Carlisle the explanation the congressman had offered her for this uncomfortable social breach. "Colonel Breckinridge said, 'The reason I have become engaged so soon
is that I had discovered Miss Pollard's feelings toward me, and
as an honorable man, I thought I should ask her to marry me.'"
Blackburn continued her testimony, "I said, you have certainly
taken a very high view of your duty in the matter."

The words hung in the courtroom. Judge Bradley rocked in
his chair, his gaze resting on the brick wall above the jury. Madeleine whispered to her attorneys. Breckinridge fidgeted in his seat,
sometimes lounging back and at other times leaning forward on
his elbows. Blackburn went on to describe how Breckinridge had
asked her to take Madeleine to Europe and how he had strenuously dismissed the rumors of his engagement to socialite Louise
Wing. He begged her, she said, to publicly contradict the stories
of an engagement to Wing—a story, he said, that would pain his
children and injure him with his family. Blackburn described how
Madeleine had asked "Willie" to name the wedding date and how
he promised to do so in her presence. Blackburn faced the jury.
He said explicitly, "I will come back and tell Mrs. Blackburn of
the day I intend to marry the young lady to whom I am engaged."

Julia Blackburn reviewed the events of late spring 1893 when
Pollard and Breckinridge were discovered together in New York.

Although the day was dark and chilly, the room grew warm and stuffy. Madeleine flapped a paper fan. Blackburn described her anger with Breckinridge's repeated visits to Madeleine. "I told him," she said, "that if he continued to act without propriety, I would wash my hands of them both." When Madeleine told Blackburn of her growing suspicion of his continued attention to Louise Wing, Blackburn told Madeleine a hard truth: "If Colonel Breckinridge wishes to play the villain, you are powerless to prevent it." Carlisle yielded the floor to the defense.

Phil Thompson began his cross-examination, remaining seated in his chair. Thompson was young and powerfully built. Despite his youth, his hair was thin, almost balding. He addressed Blackburn: "You are the widow of the late Governor Blackburn of Kentucky, are you not?"

"You know that as well as I do, Colonel Thompson," she replied sharply, eliciting a sigh from the attorney. He put on his most gracious, Southern manners to continue the examination.

Thompson reviewed Blackburn's history with Madeleine, seeking an explanation for their unlikely friendship. Their acquaintance, Blackburn stated, began three or four years ago when Mrs. Lizzie Fillette, Madeleine's former landlady, introduced them. Madeleine was always very respectful and polite and began to call frequently. I liked her and found her agreeable, Blackburn offered. Her conduct was gentle and ladylike. Thompson pressed, Why would a much older woman befriend someone of Pollard's youth and lesser social standing?

"I found her to be an unprotected girl, a fellow woman, ambitious and smart," Blackburn said, and added pointedly, "and I extended to her the kindness that I would give to any unprotected young woman coming from my own State of Kentucky."

Blackburn was no easy witness. She did not suffer fools lightly. She was also very well aware of how her association with Madeleine appeared: like a silly woman who was easily flattered and fooled, an aging widow played by Madeleine, played by Breckinridge, or both. Thompson pressed for details; Blackburn resisted sharing personal moments. Reluctantly, she repeated Madeleine's private nickname for her: "the Duchess." Relentless, Thompson asked again about the closeness of their relationship. Blackburn grew indignant.

"There were no close relations," Blackburn exclaimed. "I felt sorry for her, just as I feel sorry for myself in being compelled to appear here and suffer this ordeal. She was unprotected, just as I am." Controlling her rising tears, Blackburn flashed a significant look at Breckinridge: "If I had the defense of a husband," the widow said deliberately, "it would never have been necessary for me to have come here."

Breckinridge flushed to the roots of his hair, and a courtroom full of men shifted in their seats at the indignity—and truth—of the scene.

Thompson continued. What had been Pollard's relationship with Lizzie Fillette, and what had Fillette told her about Miss Pollard and Charles Dudley Warner? Carlisle leaped to his feet: "Objection!"

Judge Bradley turned to face the court: "I have been surprised that this examination has been allowed to go as far as it has," he remarked. "Any conversation this witness may have had with any other person about the plaintiff is irrelevant to this case. The objection is sustained." Carlisle smiled; the defense fumed.

Thompson took a new tack and pressed Blackburn for the specific dates of each of Breckinridge's visits. Blackburn replied that she did not recall the dates beyond the Good Friday visit.

"Colonel Breckinridge was calling on his own business and not on mine," she said. "*He* can probably give you the dates." Thompson persisted, harping on the calendar.

"I have told you all about the affair," Blackburn said. "I can add nothing to it and take nothing from it. I have said everything there is to say."

Jeremiah Wilson jumped in to defend his witness, reminding Breckinridge's counsel that Blackburn had already said she could not recall the dates. "I do regret this line of questioning," offered Thompson, "and I am trying to be as courteous and gentle as possible, but the defendant deserved to have this information provided."

Blackburn looked at Judge Bradley: "Colonel Thompson knows what I have said is the truth. I know nothing more, and I want so much to leave." Her voice was earnest, her face tearful, but her heart was hard. Thompson continued his cross-examination. Did she know why Breckinridge had called on her alone?

"Do I know what actuated Colonel Breckinridge?" she repeated. "Of course not," she answered with annoyed inflection. "Ask him." The court took a recess.

When the afternoon session commenced, Julia Blackburn— cooler and collected—returned to the stand. During the break, Madeleine's attorneys had cautioned Blackburn not to take Thompson's bait. She shortened her answers, her voice dropped, and spectators craned forward to catch her words—but there wasn't much to hear. She identified two telegrams from Breckinridge to Madeleine and was released from her ordeal. If she glanced at Madeleine, her one-time friend and protégé, as she left the room, it was likely the last time. It's doubtful that they ever spent time together again.

Blackburn's bearing and testimony hit the mark. "Ladies who lecture," suggested the *Cincinnati Enquirer*, "should learn natural eloquence from Mrs. Blackburn."[12]

Jane kept reading the newspaper account, shaking her head at the mismanaged start. The defense should have been more aggressive, challenging Blackburn. But the attorneys' Kentucky roots dictated deference to the genteel, younger to older, men to a senior woman. Jane continued to read. Three additional witnesses had testified for the plaintiff. Mary Desha, the sister of Breckinridge's late wife, identified a sewing basket once owned by Issa Breckinridge. The basket had been a gift from Mary to Issa, purchased on a sisters' trip to Nantucket, and a keepsake said to be one of the late woman's favorites. Desha's testimony implied that her former brother-in-law had given this cherished possession to his mistress. When the congressman's lawyers attempted to cross-examine Desha, Breckinridge interrupted and waved them off, releasing her from the embarrassment of testifying further. It was a matter of honor; a Southern man protects his kin.[13]

Carlisle called District of Columbia Police Chief Major Moore to the stand to relay his encounters with Breckinridge and a distraught Madeleine Pollard in May 1893. The chief of police knew shorthand and had taken notes during his encounter with the aggrieved couple. His key contribution to the plaintiff's case came in his description of how, in Moore's office, Breckinridge named a wedding date, the last day of May, and, in a second visit, he confirmed that Pollard was pregnant, and he had fathered the child. Moore related how the congressman denied seducing her; "No!" Pollard interrupted, hearing Breckinridge's lie. Sarah Ellis tried to quiet her as she sobbed and shook.

The last witness for the plaintiff, Dr. N. S. Lincoln, a leading DC physician, had examined Madeleine in February 1893, when Breckinridge's attention to Louise Wing had come to Madeleine's notice. Lincoln described how Breckinridge had brought Madeleine to his office because he thought she was unreasonably jealous and excitable; he asked Lincoln to medicate her; the doctor refused. Lincoln had told Breckinridge there was another profession that could help her more. In his opinion, Lincoln implied, Madeleine did not need a physician—she needed a minister.[14]

Escaping the press and the crowds, Miss Ellis hurried Madeleine back to the House of Mercy, her charge exhausted from the day's emotions. Madeleine went directly to bed. No visitors. When Jane arrived at 7:00 p.m., the matron offered little sympathy. What did Madeleine expect? What was the point? Bah, she said, the trial was useless.[15]

In the absence of a face-to-face with Madeleine, Jane had little to report that evening, but she offered a pointed critique of the second day. The lawyers had been too gentle with Blackburn. I suppose, Jane mused, that "because she is a lady of high social standing . . . your side did not wish to appear, by your cross-examination, to doubt that she was telling the whole truth, or had any purpose to conceal any of the facts." Jane thought otherwise: "No woman who volunteers to become the chief witness in a case of this kind has a right to expect any other treatment, at the hands of the opposing counsel, than that which is necessary to elicit the whole truth." Other women would be called as witnesses: "Your mild manner of handling Mrs. Blackburn simply encourages them to tell what they want to tell and nothing more." Jane warned Stoll: women witnesses would run roughshod over attorneys worried about the modesty of ladies.

Jane had a point—the lawyers had worn kid gloves in questioning Blackburn, their upbringing and assumptions about elite women's tenderness and natural honesty getting in the way of their interrogation. When Blackburn's eyes had filled with tears on the stand and when she had pleaded with Judge Bradley to release her, those in the courtroom understood her emotional responses as evidence of her feminine frailty and delicate sensibilities. Blackburn must have been hurt to lose her young admirer, aghast that Madeleine had a hidden life she had hardly suspected, and angry that the mistress who had sullied her home was also the friend who admired her wisdom. She may have forced out her tears, or they may have been legitimate as she endured the gaze of so many men. Still, there's no mistaking her anger at Breckinridge. Women needed protection, she argued—elite widows from selfish men, and poor young women like Madeleine from liars and cads. Despite their different social classes, Julia portrayed Madeleine as much a victim of deception as she herself had been deceived. To protect her name and her hard-won respectability, Breckinridge had to pay.

Following Friday's session, the court adjourned for the weekend. Jane spent Saturday morning reading and writing letters home. Her mother had shared Wiscasset gossip about a fight between young women. Such hypocrites, thought Jane of the incident. Two sisters had made a fuss over befriending a young woman but later snubbed her. Well, Jane replied to her mother, "I would not pretend to be such a friend to a girl, and then the first chance I got to injure her, do it."[16] But yet . . .

Jane sent her mother Friday's *Evening Star* with its report of Blackburn's appearance. The opening day, she reported, did not go well for Breckinridge. But once he testified, Jane was confident he would easily beat the plaintiff. It was far from over, Jane thought. Of her new friend Madeleine, Jane described her as "about the best actress you ever saw."[17] Of her shaking and interruptions in court, Jane judged it acting and practiced beforehand. The plaintiff had scored an early win but, Jane thought, convincing herself as much as her mother, the defense had yet to say its piece.

On Saturday, Madeleine trudged once again to her attorneys' office. Jane desperately wanted to learn if and when Madeleine would be on the stand and what she planned to say, key information for the defense. But at the House of Mercy in the late afternoon, Jane faced a blockade of nuns who refused to let her visit the exhausted Madeleine for the third consecutive day. Jane's frustration grew.

She tried again on Sunday, sitting through two church services. Her persistence paid off. Jane spied Sister Ella leaving the church and hurried to intercept her. "Sister," she greeted happily, as if running into her was entirely unexpected. What could she pick up to spare Madeleine, or the good sisters, the need to venture out? Sister Ella admitted concerns about Madeleine's health. The strain of the trial was weakening her, but, she added, beef tea and perhaps a little milk punch each evening would strengthen Madeleine for the difficult days ahead. Jane readily agreed and volunteered to purchase the beef tea and the fortifying ingredient of the punch: whisky. Alcohol was justified in cases of nervous exhaustion.[18]

While Jane shopped for supplies, Madeleine spent Sunday with Dr. Belle Buchanan, her physician friend from Cincinnati. Buchanan had arrived as the trial began to provide emotional support and nightly restorative massages. The two old friends went for a carriage ride, escaping the city, the House of Mercy, and Jane.

Armed with whisky and bottled beef tea, Jane called to see Madeleine late in the day. Seeing the health-stimulating gifts, Dorothea permitted the evening visit but assigned Sister Ella and Miss Ellis as chaperones, leaving Jane scant time alone with Madeleine. Sister Ella made the milk punch, mixing a spoonful of sugar into milk and whisky. She gave it a good shake. Madeleine complained that it was tasteless. Jane took the hint and added another splash of alcohol. She later shared with Stoll, "She evidently likes her punch to be clearly defined in its flavoring."[19]

Whether the milk punch fortified Madeleine's strength is unclear. It did loosen her tongue, and a nervous Madeleine turned affectionate, offering Jane a kiss and, as the alcohol worked its magic, talking freely. She was in a good mood. Jane asked for her take on Friday's testimony. Madeleine had been delighted so far. Major Moore supported her claims of a marriage date, Mary Desha and Dr. Lincoln illustrated Breckinridge's caddish behavior, and Julia Blackburn proved to be a "great card," Madeleine's admiration clear for her one-time mentor and friend.

Jane reluctantly agreed. Time to probe. How, she asked, did she spend Saturday?

Madeleine sighed. Yesterday had been hard. In Carlisle's office, her attorneys prepared her for testifying, although, she complained to Jane, they had yet to decide whether to put her on the stand—worried for her mental and physical health. Nonetheless, Carlisle and Wilson had tried to anticipate questions the defense *might* ask her *if* she testified. Madeleine practiced precise answers to hypothetical questions over and over, offering names and dates she easily drew from memory. Madeleine's recall impressed the lawyers.

But those dates marked seduction, pregnancy, and heartache.

As the mood turned solemn and the milk punch took full effect, Sister Ella ushered Jane from the room, cutting the visit short. Madeleine, Ella ordered, needed to go to sleep.

———

Jane walked back to Connecticut Avenue, frustrated in failing to learn if Madeleine would testify or to discover the focus of the attorneys' questioning. In the boardinghouse parlor, Dudley waited for her, bitter and steaming. Everyone seemed to want a juicy morsel, he complained—acquaintances, journalists, crowds all wanted Madeleine's brother to talk, tell his story and his sister's. So hypocritical, he grumbled. After all of this, he said, he was heading North. If Madeleine wanted to stay here, she'd do it alone.

Jane made sympathetic sounds and then pressed, trying for her own juicy morsel. She asked when his sister would take the stand. Dudley offered nothing. He claimed he didn't know the lawyers' plans for Madeleine. Jane called up a note of worry into her voice as she told Dudley that Madeleine looked pale—was she ill? Dudley was pragmatic, even unsympathetic. "Well," he told Jane, "she will have to stand it now until the thing is over."[20]

Alone in her room on the top floor, Jane worried about the nuns' continued blockade and Madeleine's afternoon escape with Dr. Buchanan. Stalking Sister Ella in church had won Jane a small victory, but success in her mission demanded unfettered access. For victory, the defense needed to be a step ahead of the plaintiff, and, a frustrated Jane feared, it was looking like she would have to be the one to get them there.

She took a sheet of paper and rolled it into the typewriter.

At age fifteen, Jane Armstrong Tucker longed for a great adventure. (Courtesy of Historic New England.)

Castle Tucker, Wiscasset, Maine. The unique two-story piazza was a selling point for summer boarders. (Courtesy of Historic New England.)

Mollie Tucker and children.
(Courtesy of Historic New
England.)

Mary Mellus Tucker Clayton.
Jane's sister, Mame, performed
in a traveling theater troupe.
(Courtesy of Historic New
England.)

St. Joseph's Academy, Emmitsburg, Maryland. Jane Tucker's training in advanced needle skills served her well in sewing jobs in Boston and, later, as a tool for spying on Madeleine Pollard. (Print from a painting by L. Enke; Lith. A. Hoen and Co., Baltimore. Library of Congress, Prints and Photographs Division.)

Patience Tucker Stapleton. Patty's November 1893 death called Jane home to care for her grieving parents. (Courtesy of Historic New England.)

Jane Tucker scoured Boston for
bargains on clothing, food, and rent,
stretching her working-class salary.
(Courtesy of Historic New England.)

Madeleine Valeria Pollard as a
schoolgirl in Cincinnati, ca. 1884.

Martha McClellan Brown, vice president and faculty member at Cincinnati Wesleyan Female College, lectured her young students on decorum, etiquette, and virtue. (Courtesy of Wright State University Libraries' Special Collection and Archives.)

Cincinnati Wesleyan Female College. Madeleine Pollard delighted in the well-stocked library, literary society, and her classes.

Madeleine Pollard, 1892.
Jane Tucker enticed
Madeleine to confide
about her relationship
with Charles Dudley
Warner with gifts of
Harper's magazine.
(Library of Congress,
Prints and Photographs
Division, C. M. Bell
Studio Collection.)

Julia Churchill Blackburn.
Jane Tucker castigated
Breckinridge's lawyers
when they failed to
challenge Blackburn on the
witness stand. "Women,"
she wrote, "would run
right over them." (The
Filson Historical Society,
Louisville, KY.)

Dr. Mary Parsons supervised Pollard's second pregnancy. (Underwood and Underwood, Washington, DC, ca. 1910, Manuscript Division, Library of Congress.)

House of Mercy, Washington, DC. Jane Tucker became Agnes Parker when she entered this home for fallen women in her quest to befriend, and betray, Madeleine Pollard. (Courtesy of the Archives of the Episcopal Diocese of New York.)

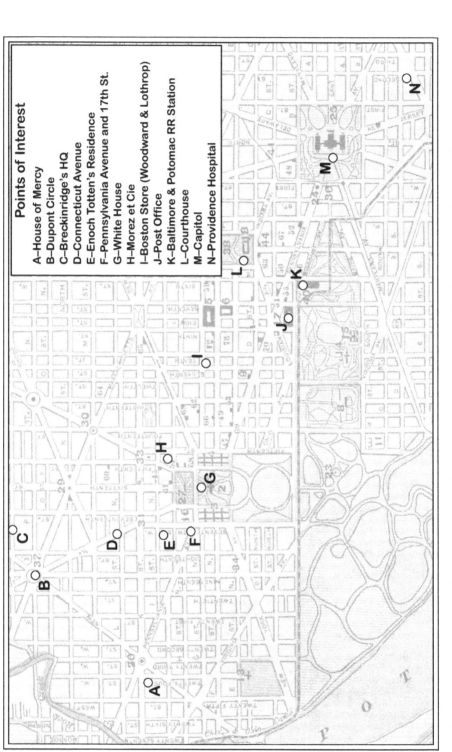

Points of Interest

A–House of Mercy
B–Dupont Circle
C–Breckinridge's HQ
D–Connecticut Avenue
E–Enoch Totten's Residence
F–Pennsylvania Avenue and 17th St.
G–White House
H–Morez et Cie
I–Boston Store (Woodward & Lothrop)
J–Post Office
K–Baltimore & Potomac RR Station
L–Courthouse
M–Capitol
N–Providence Hospital

Washington, DC, 1894. Points of interest in Jane Tucker's surveillance of Madeleine Pollard. (Map created by Dick Gilbreath, cartographer.)

"A Sensational Scandal in Court." Madeleine faints into the arms of Dr. Belle Buchanan and Sarah Ellis. Later, tensions between opposing attorneys erupt into a fistfight. (*National Police Gazette*, March 31, 1894.)

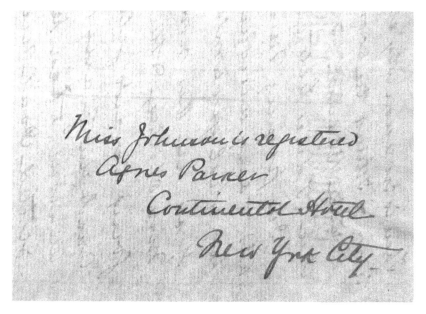

Jane Tucker used several aliases, including Agnes Parker and Miss Johnson. (Note to W. C. P. Breckinridge, June 1894, Breckinridge Family Papers, Library of Congress.)

Jane Tucker moved from the House of Mercy to nearby Connecticut Avenue, which gave her more opportunities to spy on Madeleine Pollard.

[ca. 1894]

Jane Tucker's invoice for five months of work for Congressman Breckinridge included charges for carriage rides, magazines, and tomatoes—tools of Tucker's detective work. (Invoice, page 1, ca. May 1894, Breckinridge Family papers, Library of Congress.)

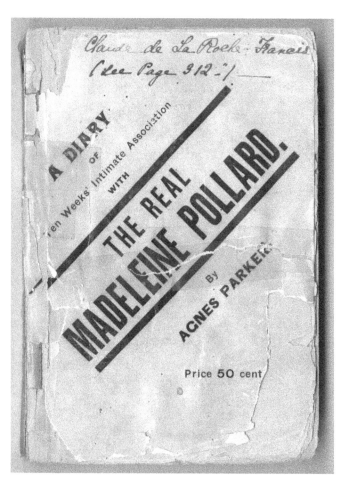

The fragile cover of Jane Tucker's book, *The Real Madeleine Pollard* (June 1894). (Courtesy of Lexington Public Library.)

Madeleine Pollard moved to England by 1897. From 1917 to 1940, she lived in a top-floor flat in this Chelsea building. (Author's photograph.)

Madeleine Pollard's unmarked grave, Lynton, Devon, UK. (Author's photograph.)

9

THE ONLY CHANCE
A GIRL WILL GET

With Julia Blackburn's and Phil Thompson's con-
tretemps widely reported in the previous day's papers, a throng
of hopefuls attempted to gain the marshal's favor. The seats filled
quickly; some sat in the windowsills at the rear of the courtroom.
Author and Washington wit Colonel Bob Christy eyed the crowd.
Considered to be of a philosophical bent, Christy opined to a
reporter that "where there is scandal, the wolves will be found
ready to fall upon the wounded."[1] Among the wolves were several
fashionable young women who managed to slip by the marshal.
They took seats in the front two rows, some on the bench ear-
marked for female witnesses. A few older women sat behind them,
all chatting and laughing at their good fortune and anticipating
the testimony they might hear. One of their number, a matron with
gray hair, carried field glasses. She intended to see every detail.

The waiting pack was soon rewarded. Madeleine Pollard
entered the courtroom and walked to her seat, Ellis and Buchanan
at her side. The women stared at Madeleine and made comments,
audible to reporters and certainly to Madeleine, who sat nearby.
She kept her back to them and spoke quietly with Attorney Jere
Wilson. Judge Bradley arrived. He glanced at the women and the
pressing, prurient crowd. No women except witnesses would be
permitted in his court, he announced and asked the marshal to
remove them. Faces flushed, embarrassed at the looming marshal
waving them away, the women retreated. They chattered in anger;

Bradley rapped his hand on the desk, calling for order. Breckinridge chewed on a quill toothpick.

The *Washington Post* declared that the Breckinridge-Pollard drama was both comedy and tragedy, and on day three, spectators were treated to levity during otherwise grim testimony. Following a morning of legal wrangling, the plaintiff called their first witness. Claude de la Roche Francis arrived in an excessively long overcoat with purple fur lapels and undressed black kid gloves. He carried a high silk hat with a deep black band around it. His gold-topped cane tapped on the marble floor as he walked to the witness stand. He claimed New York as his home but spent most of his time abroad, studying law and traveling. He pronounced his name *Frawn-cis*, lengthening his vowels and drawing out the first syllable to an elite length. Spectacles sat on his pale face, an effete contrast to the sun-hardened carpenters and farmers on the jury.

Francis took his seat. "Good awfter-noon," he said as he rested his cane against the table and described the first months of 1893 when he wintered in Washington. He had met Madeleine in February and then encountered her and Breckinridge frequently at the home of Mrs. Thomas, where Madeleine had lived in early 1893.

"Where did you see them?" inquired Mr. Wilson.

"In the drawing room," Francis replied. "They were usually sitting on a sofa," he said, "but sometimes they were standing up." The spectators tittered. He described a winter visit to the Thomas home. He had been standing in an entryway waiting to be announced when he overheard, quite accidentally, naturally, a conversation between the colonel and Madeleine in the parlor. Later, Madeleine confirmed the details of what he had overheard, a whispered fight about when to announce their engagement. Francis testified that Mrs. Thomas knew of the engagement too.

Francis was fond of small details, and in answering Carlisle's questions, he flew off on tangents; as one reporter phrased it, when he spoke, he put on trimmings and added a touch of parsley here and there. He delivered his testimony as if sharing a delightful story at tea. As Francis prattled on to the jury and spectators, captivating them with his affable manner, Calderon Carlisle sat back in his chair and smiled.

Francis continued, describing to the packed courtroom and the peering observers pressed against the hallway windows what he witnessed a year ago. Breckinridge and Madeleine, he believed, had a mutually respectful relationship until last spring. At that time, Francis testified, Pollard grew increasingly worried about Breckinridge's commitment. She thought she might kill herself if he abandoned her. Francis told her that Breckinridge was an honorable man, and besides, even if he proved not to be, there were plenty of fish in the sea, adding that he was one of those fish. The smiles on the courtroom spectators were audible. Even Breckinridge laughed.

The mood shifted from comedy to tragedy. Madeleine's lawyers called two well-known Washington physicians to the stand to document Pollard's second and third pregnancies. Dr. Joseph Tabor Johnson exuded gravitas as he testified to the events of May 1893. His head was broad, and he parted his black hair in the middle. He wore Russian whiskers and a goatee, very popular in 1894, and his gray hairs testified to his experience and medical lineage—his father was a prominent Washington physician as well. With Madeleine's consent, given at that moment in the courtroom, blushing as she conferred with Attorney Wilson, Dr. Johnson revealed that Miss Pollard had miscarried a two-month-old fetus on May 24, 1893.

In cross-examination, Charles Stoll pressed Johnson on the miscarriage, probing to elicit an unnatural cause, hinting at the specter of abortion. Johnson denied the charge. Her miscarriage was natural, spontaneous, and possibly the result of Madeleine's nervous worries. Stoll asked if the plaintiff's jealousy could have prompted the miscarriage—subtly shifting blame from Breckinridge's behavior to Madeleine's troubled mind. Madeleine sat still with her head bowed. It was possible, Johnson said, that distress of mind could have prompted the unfortunate event, but he could not know if that were so in this case.

Dr. Mary Parsons followed Dr. Johnson. She wore nice furs and appeared sensible, reporters noted. Parsons was more than sensible—she was highly accomplished and well-respected. Born in Colebrook, New Hampshire, in 1850, Parsons experienced two modes of studying medicine. Early on, she learned obstetrics at the elbow of her grandmother, a midwife. Like generations of women before her, she learned by observing and assisting. In the 1870s, there were few options open to women for formal study of medicine, which was variously thought to be too intellectually difficult, too emotionally challenging, or too unseemly for women. Nonetheless, Parsons found a path.

Parsons entered Howard University Medical Department in Washington, DC. Admission required good moral character, skills in English, elementary mathematics, and enough Latin to be able to write prescriptions and read medical terms. A college education was not a precursor to medical school; Parsons had graduated from a New Hampshire seminary, so, like Madeleine, she had enjoyed an education more rigorous than many young women undertook. Howard University was founded to provide education for and to uplift Blacks, but its charter specified that it welcomed male and female applicants both white and Black. Parsons, who was white, graduated in 1874 at the age of twenty-two, the second woman graduate, and began her practice.[2]

In 1888, Parsons charged five dollars for confinement, delivery of the child, and one year of infant care. Madeleine paid Mary and Wesley McKenzie eight dollars a month for room and board at their South Washington home. She stayed there until early March, about a month following the birth of her second child.

Wilson asked Parsons to speak louder, and she smiled as she raised her voice. She delivered Madeleine's son at the McKenzies' on February 3, 1888. Undernourished, Madeleine had difficulty nursing the child. Dr. Parsons advertised in the *Evening Star* and

Washington Post for a wet nurse needed immediately for a new-born; candidates, the ad noted, should be nice, genteel, and the "person and milk perfectly fresh."[3] When Jere Wilson pressed Parsons to establish paternity of the child, she deflected the question. Breckinridge paid the bills, she said, and she had been led to believe that he was Madeleine's guardian.

Wilson asked the fate of the child. Ellis reached for her smelling salts. Breckinridge had insisted Madeleine give it up. Madeleine had written on a tiny slip of paper, "Please name my baby Dietz Downing," a character in a Thomas Carlyle novel. Parsons had pinned the note to the child's clothing.

Dr. Parsons answered Wilson's question: "Mrs. McKenzie and I took it to an asylum." While Parsons waited in the cab, McKenzie brought the baby into the asylum and told the staff she had found the infant at her door. It was between 7:00 and 8:00 p.m. The baby was six hours old.

Parsons had visited the child once or twice. Wilson asked when the last time was.

Parsons hesitated, glancing at Madeleine. Baby Dietz had grown ill at the asylum, a not uncommon fate in a crowded orphanage. She answered Wilson: the last time she saw the child was at an undertaker's shop. As the implication settled on the courtroom, Madeleine began to shake and moan, and her low sobs filled the room. She threw herself onto the table, weeping, inconsolable. "Oh my God," she cried, "pity me." Miss Ellis and Dr. Buchanan gently lifted Madeleine, Ellis taking care that Madeleine's worn and ragged petticoat was covered, assuring her some dignity in her departure from the room of staring men.[4] As the trio passed through the doorway, Madeleine fell into a dead faint. A bailiff jumped forward to catch her.[5] Spectators craned their necks to catch a glimpse of Madeleine. Marshal Wilson hurried over and carried her to his office. Dr. Buchanan quickly closed the office door. Madeleine would not return to the courtroom this day.

Breckinridge ignored the scene and chatted with Stoll and Butterworth.

Judge Bradley called the court back to order, spectators settling down after witnessing the dramatic moment. Dr. Parsons finished her testimony, leaving the attorneys to wrangle, again, over depositions taken for the plaintiff in Kentucky. The defense believed the depositions were gathered improperly and thus invalid. The plaintiff's counsel complained that in Kentucky, agents working for the plaintiff had approached Shelby, Breckinridge's law partner, to assist in questioning the deponents, but he refused to participate. Further, the plaintiff's team alleged that notaries and stenographers needed for the process had suddenly, in Lexington, mysteriously become unavailable. All of this, Madeleine's counsel argued, was the defense team's bald-faced attempt to hamstring the plaintiff, one grievous action in a long line of underhanded moves the plaintiff's cosmopolitan attorneys sneeringly referred to as the "Kentucky way of practicing law." Tempers rose. Court was adjourned.

The attorneys gathered their things, muttering insults. Will Johnson called Shelby a liar. Shelby slapped Johnson's face; momentum moved all the attorneys toward the courtroom door, and the fight spilled into the lobby, where crowds and elbows competed for space. Desha Breckinridge struck Calderon Carlisle; the congressman got in between flying fists to separate the pugilists or perhaps to land his own blow. Carlisle swung blindly. Jere Wilson's silk hat lay crushed on the floor. The sounds of slaps and curses echoed in the marble hall. A pale man cried out, "Send for the bailiffs! Send for the judge!" Rotund, whiskered men in fancy suits pulled apart the combatants, the teams of lawyers now grouped as if in a schoolyard fight, tempers raised, eyes glaring.[6]

Judge Bradley stood before the red-faced, panting men, almost too outraged to speak. Will Johnson stuttered an explanation. The judge cut him off. He warned the attorneys: "I will have no such disgraceful acts in my court."

"Clear the lobby!" yelled the bailiff, and the spectators and the lawyers moved along, glaring at each other and muttering about who struck whom.

In the late afternoon, Jane hurried to K Street. Earlier, a hired cab had delivered Madeleine, Miss Ellis, and Dr. Buchanan to the House of Mercy following the plaintiff's courtroom faint. Madeleine went immediately to her room, attended to by her two stalwart friends. When Jane arrived, Madeleine refused her visit, exhausted from the trying day in court. Jane had expected this response. Dr. Mary Parson's testimony of the death of Pollard's second infant lacked only "slow music and dim lights," or so she told Stoll. She would like to have seen it in person.[7]

Refused entry, Jane returned to her room to bang out her nightly report.

Jane had read the evening headlines: "Gave Way to Emotion" and "Miss Pollard Weeps."[8] She didn't believe a word of Pollard's distress and told Stoll, "She knew perfectly well what impression she was making on that jury all the time this little scene was being enacted." Jane found it absurd—it was nothing but acting. You fell for it, she implied, as did everyone in the courtroom. She warned Stoll, "You can't handle this woman in an ordinary manner. She is not an ordinary person." And know this, warned Jane, "this is but a forerunner of what is to come."[9]

Jane rose early the next morning, Madeleine's faint on her mind. She skipped breakfast and her daily orange and hurried along K Street to catch Madeleine before she could don her courtroom persona.[10]

Jane ran up the stone steps, rang the House of Mercy bell, and talked her way in. Upstairs, Madeleine sat in bed in her bedclothes. Jane waited in the sitting room, ears to the hallway; when she heard footsteps, she hurried to the doorway to watch as Madeleine descended the stairs. She looked well rested, bright, and happy. Unaware of Jane's scrutiny, Madeleine appeared without a trace of grief or woe—greeting Jane brightly, pleased at her morning visit.

With the ever-faithful Miss Ellis, Jane and Madeleine caught the streetcar. As the car rumbled downtown, Jane pressed for Madeleine's thoughts on yesterday's faint. Madeleine praised Miss Ellis for protecting her dignity. She would have been horrified if, in her dire condition, her frayed petticoat was revealed. She'd recovered in the marshal's office, Madeleine shared. The court officers had hailed a cab for her. Jane later complained to Stoll that Madeleine could not have been all that ill if she was thinking about her undergarments, but Jane missed the point. In a trial about one's place and social class, and with reporters recording Madeleine's daily sartorial choices, the newspapers would not hesitate to share this embarrassing moment and see a worn and tired petticoat beneath a neat, fashionable dress as a metaphor for Madeleine as a society woman only on the surface.

As for the fistfight between the lawyers, Madeleine was unimpressed. She understood the stakes and the challenge of a quick temper. Kentucky men, she shrugged.

Jane nodded, ears on Madeleine but eyes keeping track of the stops, cautious not to get too close to the court building and the crowds. She left Madeleine and Miss Ellis at the next stop, offering typing work as an excuse.

Huge crowds pressed for admission. Older men who had nothing else to do rubbed elbows with younger men who skipped out on work and those with the privilege to set their own hours. Reporters described "bruisers and vulgarians" who hoped to see lawyers fight again; a few women dawdled on the sidewalk, perhaps hopeful of hearing more "filthy medical details."[11] Three women argued for admission with the marshal, but he refused. Two boys made good use of a day out of school and climbed the steps of the courthouse but left disappointed when they could not get in.[12]

Jane bought the morning papers and returned to her room. She reviewed the previous day's events, looking for contradictions, gaps, and openings for later conversation. She wrote Stoll at 11:00 a.m. and then set out for the House of Mercy around noon. Today she'd try a new strategy: sit and wait. When the sisters rebuffed her atypical midday visit, Jane offered to help Sister Ella with the backlog of sewing. With Miss Ellis attending court and Sister Ella catering to Madeleine's daily needs in the evenings, the sewing had languished, depleting one of the Home's few sources of income. Ella knew Jane was an adept seamstress. Dorothea might not have been happy with Jane's presence, but Ella welcomed her skilled assistance. Jane sat and sewed, waiting, and listening. And waiting.

For three hours, Jane hemmed linens, stitched tablecloths, and finished fancy goods. Shortly after 3:00 p.m., the heavy door creaked open. Jane hurried to the entryway to greet Madeleine, but Madeleine rushed by her, heading right to her room. She had no desire to talk, angrily refusing Jane's attempts to follow as the sisters blocked Jane's path. The only thing heading upstairs was Madeleine's beef tea and toast. Something must have happened in court. Jane fabricated a forgotten engagement and bolted from the House of Mercy, promising to return in an hour to finish her sewing.

Jane ran for the afternoon papers, skimming them quickly, reading reports of the attorneys spending hours reading depositions into the record. They read the testimony of Dr. Mary Street (now Logan), a Cincinnati physician who had treated the pregnant Madeleine in 1885, but there didn't appear to be anything shocking in her recollections. Sister Cecilia, who had been in charge of the Norwood Asylum in 1885, testified in person. Legal squabbling interrupted her testimony, and the day's session ended at three o'clock. Although there were questions about Madeleine's aliases, there were no bombshells. What had soured her mood?[13]

Jane read the articles again. Ah, she realized, Madeleine never made it to the courtroom. She had spent the day isolated in Carlisle's office, prevented from appearing in public and growing increasingly frustrated as a clerk ran back and forth across the street with updates. As far as the jury, the defense, and the public knew, Madeleine was ill in bed, a consequence of yesterday's heartbreak. Madeleine was an unhappy participant in a bit of legal theater as Attorney Wilson explained to the press that his client was better but had not yet recovered from her fainting spell and could not attend court.

Jane ditched the newspapers and hurried back, hoping to capitalize on Madeleine's anger. Just as she reached for the House of Mercy door, it opened. Jane jumped back as Madeleine stepped out with Belle Buchanan. The awkward encounter created a moment of silence, Madeleine suddenly uncomfortable face to face with the previously rebuffed Jane. Madeleine turned to Miss Ellis, still holding the key, and announced stiffly that she and Dr. Buchanan were going for a drive far out into the country. She would likely be late and miss supper. For the second time this afternoon, Madeleine brushed by Jane. Jane grumbled as the carriage pulled away from the curb. Was her fake friendship with Madeleine fraying? Without access to Madeleine, Jane's days as a detective might come to an end—as might her friendship with Stoll and her quest to grab some gold.

Now what?

Sarah Ellis lingered by the door, nervously fingering the key, neither closing the door nor retreating inside. Jane sensed a secret. She ventured a guess. "I see Madeleine did not appear in court today. That's odd, don't you think, Miss Ellis?"

"Oh no," she offered, "Mr. Carlisle and Wilson have made up their minds to keep Madeleine out of the court room, as far as possible."

"But why?" Jane prodded.

"Well," confided Miss Ellis, drawing closer to Jane, "She is so nervous and excitable [and] as yesterday's outburst revealed, she is so difficult to control." They have decided not to put her on the stand, afraid she will do more harm than good. "But," Ellis continued, "Madeleine won't have it. She told me today that she is determined to go on the stand." Jane nodded, confident of Ellis's report, especially given Madeleine's anger. She wanted nothing more than her day in court.

Ellis still lingered, fidgeting with the key. As a constant court-room companion to Madeleine, Ellis was perhaps hurt that she was not included in the evening carriage ride. Jane kept talking, paying dedicated attention to her and feeling her way around Ellis's walls. A crack appeared: a new witness. Jane gently picked at the opening; Ellis released the information, bursting to share and very much excited to be in the know.

"It's a piece of great good luck," Ellis confided. "Mrs. Gist is coming from Lexington to testify." The words tumbled out. Carlisle and Wilson had asked her to appear, but she'd declined. Then today, to their surprise, she telegrammed, saying she will come after all. Miss Ellis was breathless—this will be a major point for Madeleine, a "great card for their side." On Monday, Breckinridge and Charles Stoll had fought Gist's written deposition, arguing point by point what must be excluded from the courtroom. Judge Bradley had agreed, much to Madeleine's disappointment. Miss Ellis dropped her voice and moved even closer. "But now she is coming in person. We cannot let Breckinridge know. We must," Ellis whispered, "keep this a secret. They think they won that battle. They cannot know she is coming."[14]

Jane chatted a few minutes longer; Ellis was proving a useful source. When sufficient time had passed to avoid raising Ellis's suspicion, or hurting her feelings, Jane offered an apologetic excuse as she backed down the stone steps, leaving her afternoon sewing unfinished. She hurried to her typewriter. In her room, she grabbed her notes on the case and skimmed through the details. Stoll's summary made no mention of Gist. Who was she? What would she say? What did she know? The plaintiff's team believed they had an ace in the hole—but in what way?

Jane rolled a piece of paper into the Remington and began to type. "Why have you not told me about her? I find no mention of her at all. Now, who is she?" Jane wrote. Dread crept over her. She warned Stoll. "Your kid-glove handling of Mrs. Blackburn damaged the case. I fear another Kentucky lady coming to the front to testify will do the same." Jane sighed in frustration and wonderment. "What can the women of Kentucky be thinking about when they voluntarily appear in such a suit as this?" Gist could be another Blackburn, Ellis was warning—whatever this testimony was, it was big. She had lost the afternoon with Madeleine but had scored a victory, nonetheless. A messenger ran the letter up to Breckinridge's Q Street headquarters. The lawyers needed to prepare.[15]

Stoll sent a note back later that night, grateful for the heads-up on Gist's arrival but correcting a misidentification. Mrs. Gist was not a second Mrs. Blackburn, and she wasn't a missus. Jane chuckled at her error. Miss Ellis's triumphant air had led her to assume Gist was an elite Kentucky lady. The laughter would be short-lived. Sarah Gist may not have moved in Blackburn's social circles, but she had a few things to say.

The carriage ride and a night's rest had recharged Madeleine, and the next morning, Wednesday, March 14, she and Miss Ellis stepped from the streetcar and walked to the courthouse fighting a cold wind. A gust raised the hem of Madeleine's dress, revealing ready-made patent gaiters worn over her large feet. Miss Ellis wore a velvet casket bonnet edged with a band of pearl gimp around the rim. Madeleine's lawyers had deemed one day in seclusion sufficient to make their point of a mother's heartache. Madeleine and Ellis moved swiftly to the courtroom and out of view of the spectators, necks straining for a view. Madeleine, the newspaper continued to report, was still not beautiful. On this day, her complexion was described as waxlike yet healthy; her cheeks were long, full, and drooping, and she possessed enviably high cheekbones. Her dark-gray eyes gleamed. She breathed, the reporters wrote, as if she had consumption.[16]

Court began promptly at 10:00 a.m. The plaintiff's lawyers returned to the stand Sister Cecelia, who had traveled from Colorado to identify Madeleine and the much-disputed volumes of Washington Irving.

The plaintiff's team had first interviewed Sister Cecelia shortly after the suit was filed, gathering her deposition at St. Joseph's Asylum in Ohio. Madeleine was present. Initially, Sister Cecelia testified of that meeting that she was uncertain if the woman she spoke to in August was familiar. At the asylum, so many unwed girls had passed through the doors, many of them veiled in shame, that the nuns there hardly remembered one from the other. And nearly ten years had passed since Madeleine's first pregnancy. Madeleine, however, had sent the sister a letter, reminding Sister Cecelia of fellow patients, a nurse, and the daily routine of the asylum. It was enough to convince her to talk to the attorneys and, later, to testify, although she had little sympathy for Madeleine's cause. "Why," she asked Madeleine, when giving her deposition in advance of the trial, "did you want to ruin that old man in his old age?" "Why," Madeleine retorted, "did he ruin me in the days of my youth?"

Sister Cecelia shamed Madeleine for bringing disgrace on Breckinridge's daughters. Madeleine shot back. "I am my mother's daughter," she said, "And he did not consider his daughter, which was mine by him."

Madeleine's daughter, Marie Gertrude, was born on May 29, 1885, and baptized on June 1.[17] Breckinridge had forced Madeleine to give up the child. What, Madeleine asked the sisters during her August visit, had happened to her daughter? Marie Gertrude had died one month after birth, in July. Madeleine had not previously known her daughter's fate.

Seven months later, Sister Cecelia sat in the courthouse. The senior sister took the stand bedecked with a stiff black hood and black cape, firm fabric covering her to the throat. She wore a heavy poke bonnet of black crepe. Beneath yards of cloth, the sister had a wide mouth and a strong jaw. Her eyes shone, sedate and stern, her face pallid with a good brow and nose. She had no agenda, no personal mission in agreeing to testify, although her severe manner made clear she disapproved of the proceedings.[18]

The plaintiff's team sought to confirm that Madeleine had been pregnant by Breckinridge and given birth at the asylum, providing evidence to the narrative Madeleine had claimed of seduction, lost youth, and hardship at Breckinridge's hands.

On the stand, Sister Cecelia recalled a woman by the name of Burgoyne, the nom-de-hiding Madeleine claimed, but whether Madeleine and Burgoyne were one and the same, she was uncertain. The Washington Irving books linked Madeleine to the asylum: Cecelia confirmed that the volumes were a gift presented in 1885—Madeleine regifting the Christmas present Rodes had given her. Sister Cecilia had placed the books in the asylum library.

The attorneys squandered time arguing about testimony that would prove to be inconsequential. The spectators grew bored with the attorneys squabbling in legalese. Judge Bradley called an end to the bickering and told the lawyers they had gone astray. There is only one question at hand, Bradley reminded them: Was Miss Pollard in the Norwood Asylum? Sister Cecelia had sat silently, waiting in the witness box, a silhouette in black. With a few more answers, she was released.

The plaintiff's team introduced testimony from three Cincinnati physicians to document Madeleine's first birth and slow recovery. The previous day, Dr. Mary Street's deposition had been read into the record. Thirty typed pages of plaintiff's inquiry took one hour to read aloud; the defense's cross-examination was one hundred pages long.[19] Dr. Street had first met Madeleine in Cincinnati in the spring of 1885. She understood her to be an unfortunate widow, estranged from her husband's family. Street brought Madeleine books as she waited out her pregnancy, alone, in a small, rented room near a mattress shop. She arranged for Madeleine to give birth at Sister Cecelia's St. Joseph's Asylum in

Norwood, and for her postpartum care, Street sent Madeleine to the shared practice of Drs. Belle Buchanan and Kate Perry. During the taking of the deposition, the defense attorneys had grilled Street relentlessly, an experience so harrowing that she broke down. Her husband stopped the proceedings, what Dr. Street later called a persecution.

Similarly, Dr. Kate Perry (now married and known as Cain) was prevented from testifying in Washington by her husband, who strongly objected to such notoriety. Writing to Desha Breckinridge, Dr. Cain, who supported the congressman, indicated her willingness to testify, but, she implied, she could not go against her husband's command. However, in a subversive move, she reminded Breckinridge's son she could be subpoenaed, and she would have to obey.[20]

Dr. Perry gave her deposition in Cincinnati. She knew Madeleine as Louise Wilson when she arrived from the Norwood Asylum, depleted from childbirth and needing a place to recover. She had understood her to be a poor Kentucky girl who had gotten into trouble. Dr. Cain's recollections offered nuggets for both the plaintiff and the defense: she established that Madeleine had been pregnant and was the woman known as Louise Wilson—a point for the plaintiff; she also stated that "Wilson" loathed her unnamed seducer and would never marry him even though, she recalled Louise Wilson saying, he had offered to make things right—one for the defense.

When the bailiff called the next witness, Dr. Belle C. Buchanan, the spectators murmured in surprise as Madeleine's constant companion rose to testify; until this point, many in the courtroom had been uncertain as to who she was. When she took the stand, Madeleine, not wishing to be reminded of her frightening first pregnancy and her lost child, left the courtroom.

Madeleine Pollard was very much alone when she faced her first labor and delivery in 1885. For nineteenth-century women, childbirth was a dreaded event, and women lived with the fear that their lives would end during labor, their child would die, or they would suffer debilitating injuries during delivery.[21] Both ether and chloroform had been available since midcentury, but many physicians hesitated to use the pain-relieving anesthetics. Some feared that the drugs could make women unmanageable—that in the absence of pain, women would rave and be unruly. Others had moral qualms. Birth was supposed to hurt, the ancient consequence of Eve's transgression in the garden of Eden. To remove pain, especially for the unmarried patients at St. Joseph's, was to eliminate a divine consequence for a moral transgression. Some physicians argued that labor pain had a positive outcome. Dr. Charles Meigs believed that birth pain stimulated "motherlove" and was thus an important step in the bonding process between mother and child.[22]

Ideally, a woman delivered in her home surrounded by female family, friends, and neighbors whose support and experience would guide the expectant mother through her trials, as well as provide the practical support of caring for her and her family and of running her household during her recovery. This community of women also provided a voice for the laboring mother. In the presence of a physician, attending women could and did play an active role in the course that labor took and the interventions a physician used or did not.

Madeleine had neither a community nor a voice. Her mother, who had that very spring rushed to Madeleine's sister's side for the birth of her grandchild, believed Madeleine was working in Cincinnati and did not know she was pregnant.[23] And Madeleine could certainly not call on her still-single classmates or favorite female faculty from Cincinnati Wesleyan. Dr. Street believed she was the only female friend Pollard had in Cincinnati. There was no motherly advice, no baby gifts and good wishes, and no praise for fulfilling her female role. Madeleine was shamed, alone, and about to give birth; for nineteenth-century women, this was a very sad and frightening fate. She was twenty-one years old.

Dr. Belle Buchanan had trained at Pulte Medical College in Cincinnati, mastering the homeopathic principles and treatments and graduating in 1883. She practiced first in her hometown of Piqua, Ohio, and in Columbus, before returning to Cincinnati by 1885.[24] Dr. Kate Perry had also trained at Pulte Medical College, and following her 1885 graduation, she and Buchanan went into practice together. While a medical student, Buchanan had also met Dr. Street. The women physicians became friends, and over the next four years, Buchanan and Street saw each other once a week or so. Following Madeleine's confinement at the Norwood Asylum, Dr. Street arranged for her extended recovery under Dr. Buchanan's care. Buchanan treated Madeleine with therapeutic massage and, she testified, "such treatment as any mother would give to a girl."[25]

Buchanan described Madeleine's recovery. Madeleine, she said, had recuperated at Buchanan and Perry's home office between four and six weeks in 1885; it was during strawberry season, Buchanan remembered quite vividly. Madeleine had arrived in a weakened state, within two weeks of having given birth. Buchanan knew that to be true, she answered as the defense lawyers challenged her conclusion, because she was a trained physician and, as a mother, had given birth—she had no need to make a detailed examination. Madeleine's condition was obvious to any mother or doctor. As the attorneys continued to second-guess the treatment Madeleine received, Buchanan grew irritated: "I can't say exactly whether I took a spoon in my right hand and a tumbler in my left hand, or a tumbler in my right hand and a spoon in my left. This was nine years ago, and I do not recall such trifling details."[26]

Lawyers from both sides fired questions. In his cross-examination, Charles Stoll slipped in a reference to Buchanan's divorce from Jeremiah S. Shearer, with whom she had had three children. Buchanan shared that she had lost two of her children and then divorced, returned to the use of her maiden name, and, as a single parent, attended medical school. Stoll's backhanded comment was designed to raise concern about the witness's moral fiber and the competency of a female professional, an attempt to taint her testimony.

Despite the challenges to her virtue and medical expertise, Buchanan kept her cool, sitting in the witness box with aplomb. In a nutshell, she testified that Madeleine Pollard used the alias Louise Wilson and perhaps Burgoyne. She had been pregnant, she had owned books by Washington Irving, and she had been alone.

While Stoll questioned Buchanan, Breckinridge read the newspapers, leaning back in his chair. Finished reading the accounts of his trial, the congressman allowed his eyes to wander around the courtroom, seemingly oblivious to the witness on the stand but, in his disregard for the ongoing legal proceeding, undercutting the importance of the female physician and exhibiting a surfeit of confidence in his innocence.

Jane steeled herself for her nightly battle. Her luck ran bad again— Sister Dorothea met Jane at the door and let her enter but refused to let her upstairs. Stymied and stalling, Jane hovered on the first floor, hoping to pick up more information. Sister Ella filled her in. Madeleine had a hard day, Ella said, worn down by the depositions and Belle Buchanan's testimony about her seclusion in Cincinnati and the birth of her first child. The detailed testimony of such a lonely, frightening, and sad time stirred up old memories. Distressed, Madeleine left court midday, Ella reported. With her testimony completed, Buchanan was leaving this very evening to return home to Cincinnati. Madeleine would surely miss her nightly massages.[27]

Sister Ella reported that Madeleine was also frustrated because it was fairly certain her attorneys would not place her on the stand. Carlisle and Wilson would rest their case shortly. The lawyers had decided that Madeleine would not go into the courtroom in these final days of testimony and instead would wait in Carlisle's office. So Miss Ellis would not be needed as an escort after tomorrow and could get back to her sewing duties at the Home. But Jane could not find Sarah Ellis to confirm this plan. She left with little insight and a lot of frustration.

Jane arrived at her boardinghouse to find a jubilant Dudley Pollard. He was in great spirits but tight-lipped. Every question she asked, he answered, "I do not know." But Jane could see that Dudley was bursting with anticipation. He did not name Gist but told Jane to expect sensational testimony tomorrow. In her nightly letter to Stoll, Jane pondered the possibility of Gist on the stand. And exactly what, Jane wondered, did she have to say?

HEMS TO THE TOPS
OF HER SHOES

There was a calm quiet as the morning commenced.
Madeleine and Miss Ellis were seated and chatted quietly. Attorney Ed Farrell joined Carlisle and Wilson at the plaintiff's table.
Farrell, on behalf of the plaintiff, had taken depositions in Kentucky and, today, came to court to support one of the deponents, a
woman of color, seated now in the front row. The lucky spectators
who grabbed a seat glanced at her, curious about her connection
to the case. Breckinridge chewed on a quill toothpick, masticating
the poor thing for much of the morning. He recognized the woman
but paid her little attention. The bailiff called the first witness of
the day, Sarah Gist. She rose from her front-row seat. Breckinridge
leaned back in the chair, taking an easy attitude and, one reporter
noted, a rather indolent sort of interest in the proceedings.[1]

Gist had given her deposition in Lexington in February 1894,
dutifully answering Attorney Farrell's questions, providing her
recollections of Breckinridge and Madeleine Pollard. A stenographer recorded her words in loops and swirls, which were then rendered into a typewritten deposition. The defense rejected the typed
document. When the laws guiding the taking of depositions were
codified at the end of the eighteenth century, the statute required
a handwritten document. The plaintiff's team protested: the law
was created long before the invention of the typewriter. Whether
typed on a Remington or handwritten with a quill pen dipped in
ink, the plaintiff's team had met the spirit of the requirement in

rendering the oral statement into a permanent, readable form, with the stenographic notes to assure accuracy. Judge Bradley had agreed—the defense argument was ludicrous, but by the letter of the law, Gist's deposition was inadmissible. Smug defense attorneys thought they won a great victory. But now that Madeleine's lawyers had convinced Gist to travel to Washington to testify in person, paying her expenses and a $1.50 per diem for her time, there was no way to silence her. She had arrived in Washington the previous day, and Dudley and Attorney Farrell escorted her from the train station to a boardinghouse run by a Mrs. Richardson, easing her travel and keeping her out of sight of the defense. Now the plaintiff's lawyers were smug, but thanks to Agnes Parker, the plaintiff's surprise witness was not a surprise after all.[2]

Sarah Gist made her way to the witness table and sat down. She was short and described as a light mulatto. Her father was white, and her enslaved mother was mixed race. The *Cincinnati Enquirer* depicted her as "a little Moor out of the Arabian Nights."[3] A reporter described a flat face with a stocky nose, straight mouth, and black eyes and eyelashes. Instead of appearing like a madam of a brothel, a reporter concluded "she might have passed for a good church member," or passed as white. The *Washington Post* said she "had an intelligent and rather pleasant cast of countenance."[4] She wore a black dress, still in deep mourning following her mother's death. Not quite a year had elapsed since Kitty Gist's passing.

As women took the witness stand—and most of Madeleine's witnesses were women—the male attorneys typically began their inquiries with a question designed to establish the witness's place in the social hierarchy, a place earned by family lineage, marriage, or profession. Defense Attorney Thompson had asked Julia Blackburn if she was the widow of the former governor of Kentucky, thereby establishing that she, too, carried clout by way of her excellent marriage to political power. Mary Desha was linked to Breckinridge's wife, her sister, establishing her connections to two esteemed Kentucky families. Belle Buchanan recited her medical education, nature of her practice, and marital history. But Mr. Farrell, for the plaintiff, asked Gist, Black, single, and formerly enslaved, to relay her personal history in detail. Her answer would help these white men of the court establish her place and assess her veracity. On the stand, she told her story.

———

Sarah Gist may well have remembered the auction at the Planter's Hotel in Tuscumbia, Alabama. Seven years old in February 1841, Sarah was old enough to be aware of the press of crowds and the gaze of men; she was certainly old enough to be scared. Her enslaver and father, Andrew Gatewood Gist, formerly of Lexington and in 1841 an Alabama cotton farmer, owed money to several business associates, and the sheriff had forced the sale of real estate and nine enslaved persons to settle the debt.[5]

The 1840 census recorded that Andrew Gist owned thirty-three Black people: thirteen men, seven women, and thirteen children under ten. He was the only white person, male or female, in the household. He fathered children with the enslaved women, including Sarah's mother, Katherine (Kitty), who had been born in Virginia. Of her offspring with Gist, she first gave birth at age twenty-five.[6]

On the steps of the Tuscumbia hotel, Gist sold two fifty-year-old women—Amy and Milly—an eleven-year-old girl named Evaline, thirty-five-year-old Kitty, and Kitty's five children: Elizabeth (age 10), Robert (9), Sarah (7), Nat (5), and Catherine (2). Fifty-three years later, Sarah relayed to the court that the family then went to New Orleans, then Louisville, Jeffersonville (Indiana), and Lexington, where she had lived for twenty-five years or so, interspersed with short stints in Cincinnati and a return to Louisville. Sarah stated her entire family was emancipated in Indiana but elided the specific circumstances and date.

Sarah's family had arrived in Lexington by 1850. In 1862, Sarah and her married sister Elizabeth Obey bought property on East Short Street in the central business district of Lexington. They continued to purchase property, setting up family members in their acquired homes. The source of their funds is unknown.[7]

Sarah's sisters married and had children, and the Gist women continued to live near or with one another. They worked as domestic servants, washerwomen, and tuners of musical instruments. Sarah's brother Nat worked as a delivery man and janitor. They cared for their mother, Kitty, who, like Sarah, enjoyed horseracing. In the summer, Kitty and Sarah watched the races in Lexington, Cincinnati, Chicago, and Louisville's Churchill Downs, the racetrack built on land donated by Julia Churchill Blackburn's brothers.[8]

Sarah owned a frame cottage with two rooms and a kitchen near the city schools. She claimed she had known Breckinridge since she was a little girl, suggesting that Sarah was in Lexington in the 1840s. Around 1874, Sarah offered her rooms for assignations. She was not a madam; she did not run a brothel or have prostitutes for hire (there were plenty of those opportunities elsewhere in Lexington).[9] In 1884, when Breckinridge brought Madeleine to Sarah's door, the furniture was new.

———————

Breckinridge first took twenty-year-old Madeleine to Lexington in August 1884 following their fraught meeting at Mrs. Rose's Cincinnati establishment, where the congressman had tried, but failed, to seduce Madeleine. They boarded the late-afternoon train, arriving in Lexington at dusk. Breckinridge told Madeleine she was too young to stay in a hotel alone, feigning a protective air, but he knew a home where she could stay. He took her to the Broad Street residence of Sarah Gist. Breckinridge knocked several times, but the house was empty. He waited for half an hour, but Gist did not return. The dinner hour approached; he grew impatient. Gist knew he was coming; he had made arrangements earlier

in the week, she claimed. Madeleine thought she might stay with
a nearby friend, but Breckinridge refused that plan. Wait here, he
commanded; Gist should return soon, and later, so would he. He
left, and Madeleine waited alone on a stranger's porch. She stood
in the shadows, afraid of being seen by family or friends, afraid
of having no explanation for her absence from college, fearful of
what was to come.[10]

While Breckinridge dined with his family and dallied at an
evening election parade, Gist returned and took pity on Madeleine,
left on the porch like a forgotten package. She sighed; this one was
young, a schoolgirl, a rose only just in bloom. Gist invited her in.
She fed her. As the evening deepened, they sat in her kitchen. Gist
explained her business. Gist, like Rose in Cincinnati, profited from
the weakness of men. She kept Lexington's secrets; she asked no
questions; she told no tales.

Breckinridge returned. They sat in Gist's front room, making
small talk in a facsimile of polite society, a mirage of husband and
wife reviewing their day. Gist opened the door to the bedroom.
Madeleine crossed the threshold; Breckinridge closed the door. It
was 10:30 p.m. Gist sat up in the front room. A half hour later, the
door opened. Breckinridge embraced Madeleine, kissed her, and
went home to his wife.

Gist glanced through the open door. The bedsheets were rumpled. Madeleine's nightdress was askew.

Gist testified how she had cared for Madeleine over the weekend,
at the congressman's request. Breckinridge visited on Saturday and
Sunday night, each time leaving rumpled sheets and kissing Madeleine goodbye in front of Gist. On Monday morning, Breckinridge
rushed Madeleine out of the house and onto a train to Cincinnati
after he had encountered a worried James Rodes, who had been
searching for his fiancée.

Mr. Farrell asked Sarah how old she believed Madeleine to be
in 1884. "Seventeen or eighteen," she answered. "She had dresses

up to the tops of her shoes—a school dress. . . . Sometimes she wore her hair down her back in a plait [braid]." Women—of course, there weren't many in the courtroom—recognized that girls wore their hair down, but young women of marriageable age wore their hair up. And as young ladies' hair went up, their hems came down until their skirts brushed the floor. Girls' dresses were shorter—a few inches above the floor, covering the ankles and resting on the tops of button-up shoes.[11]

Gist continued her testimony, sharing that Breckinridge had been a frequent customer of her service with Madeleine and others, but Madeleine had come only with him. Together, they visited Gist fifty or sixty times over three to four years.

On cross-examination, Attorney John Shelby, Breckinridge's Lexington law partner, pounced on a contradiction in her recollection of dates. Her discarded deposition had stated that the seduction occurred in late August, but her testimony here put the date in early August. Gist asserted that the early August date was correct. Although she could not read and kept no calendar, she went to the horseraces every August, and she knew Madeleine had come before the race season began. Pressed to explain the difference between the oral and written accounts, Gist stated, "If that is true, then the man writing it down wrote it wrong."[12] The spectators laughed.

She had more to tell. Gist shared how Breckinridge had come to her twice in the past year. First, he asked her in June 1893 to board Madeleine, following Madeleine's miscarriage. Gist declined. She had retired, owned her own home, and had family living with her. Her mother had recently passed. Gist explained to the court that she did not want to be connected to anything unseemly, the insult directed at Breckinridge.

The second visit came in the fall of 1893, after the scandal was national news. Breckinridge returned to Gist's home, suggesting to her that if asked, she would not testify about their previous interactions. She declined again, stating that she had to obey the law. Besides, she informed the congressman, the "three Marys," friends and relatives of Gist who had witnessed Breckinridge's visits, knew all about his history with Madeleine. It was no secret around Lexington.[13]

Gist's testimony hung heavy in the courtroom, overshadowing the witnesses who followed. Kate R. Burt, a clerk in the land office, had boarded at Mrs. Hemingway's house at Thirteenth and F Street.[14] In October 1887, Burt saw Madeleine there with Breckinridge. Madeleine, whom she knew as Mrs. Foster, had just arrived in Washington and was visibly pregnant. Madeleine stayed in a room on the third floor, and on a Sunday morning, Breckinridge had called on her there. Madeleine stayed only ten days at the Hemingway house.

Lucretia Marie Minear, the matron of a fashionable boardinghouse on Lafayette Square, testified that Madeleine had boarded there in 1892 and 1893. Minear had seen Madeleine and Breckinridge walking together in Lafayette Park and had noted when Breckinridge had called on Madeleine at, or returned her to, the boardinghouse.

Calderon Carlisle read the depositions of Mrs. M. A. Ketchum and her sister, Miss Mary G. Hoyt, the owners of the small store and lodging rooms where Madeleine had lived from 1884 to 1887. The audience thinned as men headed for the exit. Breckinridge grew impatient and urged his attorneys to skip over what he saw as trivial details. The depositions painted a portrait of a young, studious woman who took music and drawing lessons and mourned the loss of her Wesleyan education. Ketchum's deposition was interrupted by the midday recess. Madeleine left the court and did not return. Breckinridge was present, and when the afternoon session commenced, Carlisle returned to reading Ketchum and Hoyt's depositions. Neither woman had suspected a thing. The same was true of Major H. B. McClellan, the principal of Sayre Institute, whose deposition testified Madeleine was a good student and no one had thought she was anything but a chaste young woman.

These witnesses established moments and locations of Madeleine's intersections with Breckinridge, for the plaintiff building a case of when and where Breckinridge had means and opportunities for illicit acts. But what both sets of attorneys missed was a narrative centered on Madeleine's growth rather than her fall—how Ketchum, Hoyt, Burt, and Minear's testimony illustrated Madeleine's climb from boarding with two elderly ladies in Lexington to living in increasingly tony neighborhoods in her first five years in Washington—from the working-class boardinghouse Burt had inhabited, to trading teaching for room and board at a convent, to residing at a fashionable residence within sight of the White House.

Jane hurried to the House of Mercy and found Madeleine deep in preparation for the next day's court appearance. She felt triumphant. After days of listening to women relate the successes and failures of her life, Madeleine would take the stand after all. Despite her faint and earlier outbursts, during the most recent sessions, she had remained calm and composed, and Carlisle and Wilson could not deny Madeleine was smart and articulate. She sat in her room and practiced answering the questions she knew her attorneys would pose, adding hand gestures to emphasize important points. Jane, Miss Ellis, and Sister Ella were her captive audience. As Madeleine practiced, Jane saw a well-prepared, well-rehearsed testimony. A flicker of worry crossed her mind.[15]

Madeleine took no chances. She moved her iron-framed bed away from the drafty window to avoid a head cold. The sisters made batches of beef tea to bolster her strength. Miss Ellis doted, running between the kitchen and Madeleine's room. To relax before sleep, the plaintiff soaked in a warm bath. She gargled a medicinal toddy of whiskey, hot water, and lemon, like an actor preparing for the stage. Her voice would be clear and strong. Madeleine's appetite had returned. She ate an orange, a gift from Jane—purloined from her boardinghouse breakfast.

Jane, relieved to be back in Madeleine's orbit, cautiously addressed a delicate subject: Dietz. Did she miss him? Had she wanted him? Madeleine stared at Jane and, after a beat, said, "I would have given my life for my son." It was Breckinridge who did not want the babies, she said. "I love babies and would be so glad to have one that I could always keep with me." A family of her own.

Jane brought the conversation back to one of Madeleine's favorite topics, Judge Bradley.

"You seem to own Judge Bradley," probed Jane. "Isn't he a great help to your side?"

"Undoubtedly," agreed Madeleine, "and he is so kind and nice to me." The jury liked her too. One juror wore a flower in his buttonhole, Madeleine said, as if he were "perfectly irresistible." She entranced the older fellow, and caught up in the plaintiff's charm, he hung on her every word.

But they were rather ordinary men, Madeleine thought. "Isn't it funny," she asked Jane, "to think of such men being called upon to listen to and judge all these little intricate points of the law when most of them cannot half comprehend what it is all about?" Hardly, Madeleine might have offered, a jury of *her* peers.

"Are you scared to sit alone on the witness stand in a courtroom of men?" Jane asked.

"I am not one bit afraid," answered Madeleine. She had wanted this from the moment she decided to sue. Breckinridge's lawyers could ask all the questions they could think of. Madeleine was ready. "I will surprise them all," she said. She ate, she gargled, and she dismissed Jane.

―――――

Jane prepared her evening report. She was back in Madeleine's good graces, and, a win for the sleuth, Madeleine's practice session had revealed the topics the plaintiff's lawyers would cover. Jane passed them along to the defense. As far as she could tell, Madeleine would be the last witness for the plaintiff's case. Miss

Ellis had stated the same. There would be no more surprise visitors from Kentucky dropping bombshells in court. Madeleine expected to be on the stand all day. Jane predicted an excellent performance; when Madeleine finished speaking, Jane wrote, the jury would "think that never was [an] innocent little country girl so wronged before."[16] The newspapers, she feared, would no doubt agree.

For all her cutting comments, Jane understood that tomorrow's court appearance was Madeleine's one chance to be heard, and she would make the most of it. Writing with characteristic sarcasm, Jane advised the attorneys to be sure to order a bouquet for "the star."[17] But in their evening talk, Madeleine had not mentioned fame or fortune as her goal—if anything, she eschewed notoriety and riches. Madeleine spoke to explain her choices; she spoke to vindicate ambitious women; she spoke out on a pervasive double standard. She had owned her moral lapses. When would Breckinridge? She wanted to be heard but not as a disgraced socialite, a dismissed mistress, or a scorned lover. She wanted to be heard as a young, single woman with the odds stacked against her who wanted a share of the privileged life. She wanted to be seen.

Jane longed to watch Stoll cross-examine Madeleine. The two were well-matched in intelligence, and she knew that both would hit their points hard.[18] It would be fun to watch them spar. But more so, she wanted to witness the fruit of her labors—to feel validated for her effort, contribution, and successes. Jane wanted to experience the product of her energy and intellect; she wanted to see that her hard, and invisible, work mattered. But the bailiff controlled admission to the limited seats, the judge prohibited women from listening to such tawdry testimony, and she knew her visibility might compromise her secret identity. Stoll would never allow it. "I wish," Jane wrote, "I could be a man."[19]

11

SO LIKE A WOMAN

Madeleine's moment was here, and she was ready to face it head on. She had a difficult line to walk; she needed to be intelligent but not outshine the men, assertive but not aggressive. She needed to be confident but not dismissive, remain calm but not cold, show emotion but not fall apart. She was a victim but not weak; she needed protection, not patronizing. And if she succeeded, if she could convince the jury that although she had erred, Breckinridge had as well and he deserved his share of the shame, then Madeleine would succeed in this, as she called it, great fight. A loss would vanquish her from polite society. But success—a decision for the plaintiff—could, in the logic of the Gilded Age, restore a limited respectable status. She would always carry the stain of mistress, but a court victory could set her back on the path toward her dreams.

Rested, soothed, and bathed, she wore her dark suit, a neatly fitting coat, a black bonnet, and black silk gloves. Her hair was neatly coiled on the back of her head. Madeleine rose from the attorney's bench and moved to the witness stand. A Bible rested in readiness for her to swear she spoke the truth. Madeleine sat and folded her hands in her lap. Breckinridge was but a few feet away; Madeleine did not bow her head or avert her eyes. Miss Ellis sat in a chair to the right and just beyond the plaintiff, ready with an ample supply of handkerchiefs and smelling salts. Calm and collected on the seventh day of the trial, Madeleine didn't need Ellis's help. Her lawyers exhaled in relief.[1]

Every seat was filled, the largest crowd yet. The men and women relegated to the corridor pressed against the windowpanes, looking across the light well into the courtroom. Several well-known spectators were in attendance: a retired sheriff, the former district commissioner, a prominent minister, and several members of Congress. The murmurs of anticipation quieted as Calderon Carlisle rose from his seat. Today he would establish the foundation of his argument that Breckinridge had breached his promise, beginning with a narrative pitting a naïve young girl without the protection of father and family against a man of prestige, a manipulating, selfish man who cared more for his own pleasure than the dire consequences of his actions.

Madeleine's path to a broken promise began with the death of her father. Carlisle led Madeleine through her early years, painting a portrait of a vulnerable girl who since 1876, at the age of twelve, was passed from aunt to aunt and lacked a permanent home and consistent parent. Although she was well cared for, her youth left her unmoored, even to the extent that she was uncertain of her age. Madeleine said that she believed she had been born in 1864. But, she told the court, her mother later said she had been born in 1866. Ever since, she had used that date in good faith. It was the date on her school records and her civil service papers, Madeleine said, dismissing the air of mystery the defense had attempted to create. "Breckinridge," she continued, looking at the defendant, "ought to know." He had endorsed the latter documents. Breckinridge smiled.[2]

Carlisle skipped ahead to August 1892 to focus on the critical moment when Madeleine returned to Washington from her summer at Bread Loaf. Now he would show the promises this trusting young woman believed. Breckinridge had met her at the rail station. They left in a carriage and, Madeleine said, "He told me he had something to tell me that he thought would please me."

She continued: "He told me that his children were grown, and their plans were set. He had thought it over and had determined to marry me if I would marry him." Issa Desha Breckinridge had been dead for but a month. "And," concluded Madeleine, "I told him I would."

In the months following the proposal, she testified, she had seen the congressman daily; on some days, he visited two or three times. He called on her in Washington and when she traveled to New York, trips he paid for. Yes, she admitted, he supported her.

Breckinridge listened intently, keeping his gaze focused on her gray eyes. But his restlessness betrayed his pretense to calm. He shifted uncomfortably in his seat, first pressing back and then leaning forward. His tell was his beard—he stroked it absentmindedly, a reporter noted, "first with one hand, and then the other."[3]

Carlisle moved to the subsequent declarations of the congressman's intent to marry. On Good Friday, Madeleine asserted, echoing Julia Blackburn's testimony, Breckinridge expressly stated that he sought Blackburn's protection for his fiancée. And on following visits, Madeleine described how Breckinridge had affirmed his marriage pledge but put off naming a specific date, as Blackburn and Major Moore's testimony had shown. Carlisle drew out the crux of his argument: the congressman had promised to marry her, but then he had not. He hedged, suppressed the news of their engagement, stalled, and dithered on a date, but ultimately, he had married someone else.

With the alleged breached promise hanging in the courtroom, Carlisle returned to 1884. "When and where did you first meet the defendant?" he asked. And Madeleine told her version of the fateful meeting on the train to Frankfort, how she was headed to her mother's house to see her dying sister, Rosalie. Breckinridge had approached and pretended to know her, a "mashing dodge," said the *Cincinnati Enquirer*.[4]

"Your face is very familiar; don't I know you?" Madeleine described him saying.

She said she replied, "I don't think you do, but I know you are Mr. Breckinridge."

They only said a few words more, Madeleine testified, but it was enough for him to ask if he could see her at her mother's house. Madeleine replied, "I had no doubt my mother and my aunt would be glad to have him." Such a renowned man, taking time to greet, and visit, a simple schoolgirl.

Breckinridge leaned over and whispered to Butterworth. His attorney made a note.

Three months later, when Rodes pushed for marriage, Madeleine needed help. "How," Carlisle asked, "did you come to discuss your difficulty with Colonel Breckinridge?"

"I had no one to consult with," Madeleine explained, the ghost of a fatherless household hovering. "Then, I remembered Mr. Breckinridge from the train, and I wrote him and asked if Mr. Rodes could make me marry him." Madeleine continued, Breckinridge's eyes still locked on her face.

"A few days later he came to the college. At 2:00 a servant brought his name up to my room and told me he was in the drawing room. I went down. The first comment he made was that he saw I was dressed in deep mourning. Rosalie had died."

They sat in a corner of the drawing room; other students entertained visitors, and a faculty chaperone, Orvon Brown, son of the president, patrolled the room. Carlisle asked how they came to take a carriage ride. Madeleine described what happened next.

"Breckinridge had received my letter and I tried to ask him about Rodes, but he pushed me off. He said he could not talk very well in the noisy parlor and asked where we could go to talk." Madeleine had no answer. "Then he suggested we go out in the evening and he took up a paper and found a concert we could go to. Who, he asked me, do I need for permission? Mr. Brown was nearby; I introduced Mr. Breckinridge who told Mr. Brown that he was an old family friend"—practically her uncle. Brown gave permission.

The carriage arrived at eight. Madeleine described her surprise at a closed carriage on a humid night. She told the court how Breckinridge claimed the night air was bad for his throat. Madeleine described what happened in the carriage: he took liberties, and she resisted. He chided her for being a silly little girl, then apologized for his actions, praised her intellect, and told her how much he had loved and still missed his first wife, who died following childbirth. He seemed charming. Once again, Breckinridge delayed speaking about Rodes. "He said," Madeleine declared, they "could talk of that the next day."

The following day, Breckinridge and Madeleine met at the Cincinnati Public Library, but yet again, Madeleine testified, Breckinridge did not discuss her difficulty. That evening, they were in Lexington at the home of Sarah Gist. They had traveled on the same train. When asked about their conversation, Madeleine explained that the congressman had urged her to leave Cincinnati Wesleyan and enroll at Lexington's Sayre Institute, which she did in the fall of 1884.

Miss Ellis sat back in her chair. Madeleine had kept her voice deliberate and slightly raised so everyone could hear. She spoke without hesitation but took care with each word—deliberate but not defiant.

Carlisle got right to the consequences of this liaison.

"Why," Carlisle asked, "did you leave school and go to Cincinnati in February 1885?"

"Not because I wanted to," Madeleine answered, "but because I had to." She continued, voice quiet but steady. Madeleine explained how Breckinridge had conceived the plan for her to hide in the city, take on a false name, and seek out Dr. Mary Street for care. She did as she was told and found a room over a mattress store. A month later, she went to St. Joseph's Foundling Asylum in Norwood. Her daughter—*their* daughter—was born on May 29. The delivery was difficult, and after a fortnight, Madeleine went to stay with Drs. Perry and Buchanan while she continued to recover. She remained in a third-floor room; she could not manage stairs. Dr. Buchanan provided her care.

"Who furnished the money for your stay at the asylum and in Cincinnati?" Carlisle asked.

Madeleine answered assuredly, "Mr. Breckinridge, of course."

"Miss Pollard," asked Attorney Carlisle, "who was the father of the child you bore on the 29th of May at the foundling asylum?" Spectators had seen the answer in print; an excited frisson anticipated her verbal response.

Again, she replied, "Mr. Breckinridge."

"Had you ever before meeting Mr. Breckinridge, at any time or place, had sexual relations with any man?"

Madeleine waited until the courtroom was utterly still. She raised her voice. Slowly, she answered.

"No, never!"

And since meeting Breckinridge?

"No, never!"

Madeleine became his willing, waiting mistress, and he, her only partner. Madeleine described their relationship. At Ketchum and Hoyt's house, when she lodged on the first floor, Breckinridge would come to her room at night. Later, when Madeleine was on the second floor, they avoided a squeaky staircase and went to Sarah Gist's establishment. As Gist's testimony evidenced, fifty or sixty times they had visited her establishment.

Carlisle asked, "Were you ever at Sarah Gist's house with any other man than Mr. Breckinridge?"

"Certainly not!" she said.

Carlisle painted Breckinridge as a selfish partner. In Washington, Madeleine continued, he visited almost nightly. She moved from Mrs. Hemingway's boardinghouse to the foundling asylum at St. Ann's—in both places ousted because of Breckinridge's too frequent, too visible visits. Madeleine found herself bouncing from place to place, just like after her father's death. In 1894, she was thirty years old and had not had a permanent home since she was twelve. She had spent nine years with Breckinridge.

Breckinridge paid the expenses for each pregnancy, an arrangement he felt entitled him to dictate her movements. With the first, hide in Cincinnati; with the second, stay with the Mc-Kenzies. After her miscarriage, he sent directives: stay in Washington, don't come to Cincinnati, remain in Thomas's home. Without her own financial means, Madeleine had little choice. Breckinridge had orchestrated her life to rely on him. On the stand, she reviewed the letters and telegrams sent between them following the miscarriage—correspondence documenting Madeleine's increasingly desperate attempts to draw her estranged lover closer, Breckinridge pulling away—the published engagement announcement hanging in between.

Madeleine faltered only when Carlisle asked about her request to be sent to a sanatorium, where one could heal in comfort and solitude. "For what purpose?" Carlisle asked. Her eyes filled with tears; Ellis reached for a handkerchief. "I don't like to state these things before so many men," Madeleine whispered. Jeremiah Wilson jumped in. "Never mind," he said. "You needn't answer." Her tears were answer enough.

After testifying for two and a half hours, Madeleine's energy flagged, worn down by the public recitation of the collapse of her future. The judge called a midday recess. Carlisle, Wilson, and Ellis escorted Madeleine back to Carlisle's office. She had done well.

The afternoon crowd was the largest yet as news spread of Madeleine's morning testimony. Every seat was occupied, scores of men were standing, and just as many spectators had been turned away. Breckinridge was the first to enter the room; Madeleine was the last. She retook the stand, refreshed.

Carlisle led his client through Madeleine's engagement announcement and Breckinridge's subsequent denial. She explained that she saw no harm in publishing it, she said, because rumors of their engagement had been in the papers, fodder for one-liners in the society columns. Naturally, she said, she was taken aback to read Breckinridge's denial in the Louisville *Gazette*. Madeleine held in her hand the tiny slip of paper cut from the newspaper and shared with the court how she pasted it at the top of the letter she sent to Breckinridge demanding that he retract his statement and confirm, in writing, their engagement. She had given him a deadline: July 22. It was the last correspondence between them, she said. Breckinridge had failed to respond. She did not contact him again.

"When," Carlisle asked, "for the first time, was a date for your marriage mentioned by Mr. Breckinridge?"

"At the second visit to Major Moore's, on May 17," Madeleine answered. "Mr. Breckinridge set the date as May 31, 1893."

Madeleine knew that was Carlisle's last question. She offered a final comment, spoken in a voice both wistful and firm. Reporters said it was the most dramatic statement yet: "From the time he took me to Sarah Gist's house in August of 1884 to the 17th of May 1893, there had never been a discussion of ending the relations between us." This scandal, this court battle, was on him. Carlisle yielded the floor to the defense's cross-examination. "Gentlemen," he said, addressing Breckinridge's attorneys, "you may take the witness now."

———

Benjamin Butterworth rose from his seat. Carlisle had painted a portrait of a vulnerable, unprotected girl, naïve to the ways of lecherous men, but Butterworth would challenge this view, beginning with the much-discussed question of her age. Madeleine covered familiar ground in describing her youth. She answered in a voice tinged with pique: "As I said this morning, there has been a question about my age, whether I was born in 1864 or 1866. I always gave my age as 17 when I first met Mr. Breckinridge. I did this in the best of faith, believing it to be true." Really, though, the question of whether Madeleine was a girl of seventeen or a young woman of nineteen when she met Breckinridge was moot: the age of consent in Kentucky was twelve.

As for her education, Madeleine described how her father taught her to read and write and to understand the rudiments of arithmetic. She got a laugh when she said her father taught her history. "Of the United States or Kentucky?" Butterworth asked. "Of both," Madeleine replied, "but not as much of the history of Kentucky as Mr. Breckinridge afterward taught me." The spectators laughed out loud at the innuendo, and the constable rapped on the desk to regain order.

Butterworth switched to rapid-fire questions, but Madeleine met his lightning-round challenge. She had read poetry, including Longfellow, much of which she had memorized. She used to sing "The Brook," a piece set to music. She enjoyed *Cotter's Saturday Night* and some Burns. She could recite some of Pope's translation of the *Iliad*. In fact, she had learned some Latin words before she could read. She had read the Bible, too, but, admittedly, not as much as she might have. She slipped in that Breckinridge brought her books from the Congressional Library.

Butterworth dug out details of her childhood but learned little that would help the defense: she was studious and retired. Her siblings were her playmates. Madeleine turned the tables, asking the attorney if he knew the life of an ordinary country girl. "Most certainly," answered Butterworth. "Then you know," Madeleine said, "that she sweeps and dusts and sews and does a thousand things like that. And if she is a good girl, she does them gladly and willingly, Mr. Butterworth." She had been that good girl, but living that life of feminine duty was not enough for Madeleine Pollard.

Butterworth turned to her suitors, reading back to Madeleine passages from her article in the *World*. She laughed when he asked about her first proposal. William Woods, a carpenter, visited Madeleine every Sunday at her aunt's house outside of Lexington. Madeleine accepted his marriage proposal, but when he admitted he could not take her to Europe, she gave back (or threw at him, according to one story) the ring. But of his proposal, she answered, "I had no more to do with that offer than you had, Mr. Butterworth," overriding his implication she had enticed Woods, and other men, to propose, hopping from man to man until she landed a congressman. And when the attorney read from a letter Madeleine had written to her college friend Wessie Brown, she pointed out the absurdity of using it as evidence: "I think it is very queer to introduce under such circumstances an old schoolgirl's letter like that." She wrote the letter in her youth, she explained; it was silly and sentimental.

Thrust and parry, the verbal sparring continued. Butterworth asked about meeting Breckinridge on the train. "I believe you spoke to him on the train," Butterworth opened.

"That is not true, Mr. Butterworth."

"I beg your pardon?"

"I cannot grant it, for it seems so intentional a misstatement. He came across the car to speak to me—and by the way," she continued, adding some parsley, "that's quite a trick of his, to speak to young girls," a move she had discovered since filing the suit when others had dared to speak out.

Butterworth turned to Breckinridge's visit to Cincinnati Wesleyan. Who had planned to attend the concert? Who decided to take a drive instead? Breckinridge, Madeleine insisted, made the plans. Butterworth asked who proposed the carriage ride.

"Certainly not I, Mr. Butterworth," replied Madeleine. "Do you imagine that I got a carriage and took Colonel Breckinridge driving?" Really. What were these lawyers thinking?

It was three o'clock. Judge Bradley adjourned the court, to be reconvened on Monday.

On Connecticut Avenue, Jane paced, waiting for the afternoon papers: the *Evening Star*, the *New York World*, and the *Louisville Courier-Journal*. Worthington had sent Jane a note that morning assuring her that the defense team would go easy on Madeleine today. As for what information Jane could "pump out of her" this afternoon, he said it would be helpful to know if Carlisle and Wilson planned to put her back on the stand. Jane would try. Worthington enclosed ten dollars cash for her room and board, promising to send more in the evening.[5]

Ellis and Madeleine had returned to the House of Mercy. Jane made the short walk from her boardinghouse and slipped upstairs, unimpeded. Madeleine was in a good mood, pleased with her testimony and herself. The lawyers, Madeleine told Jane, had been no match for her, and they even backed off when tears gathered in her eyes. She was glad Butterworth cross-examined her; he was the nicest of the defense team, she thought. Stoll, she told Jane, was perfectly dreadful: "He asks so many questions and in such a way one can never tell what he is driving at." Jane snickered to herself; her favorite employer was verbose.

Madeleine's mood spiraled down; Jane mentioned how Judge Bradley always seemed to rule in her favor. "Oh," said Madeleine, ignoring the implication of unfair rulings, "he told Mr. Carlisle I had such a sweet voice and pleasant manner. He called me lady-like and refined and told Carlisle how well I conducted myself in court."

"That's quite the compliment," offered Jane. "How do you make such a good impression on important men and get them to sympathize with your cause?"

A stony silence followed. Jane sat still. Madeleine answered in an even voice, looking into Jane's eyes: "I don't see how any man could help but feel sympathy for me when he saw me in [that courtroom] in all that sorrow." Jane did not reply.

Madeleine kept her gaze on Jane. "What do you do all day, Aggie?" she asked.

Silence, heart beating against Jane's chest.

"I, I take in typing," said Jane, "and do office tasks for busy men. I have more than enough work to keep me busy. I use a Remington and type away in my room." A room Madeleine had never visited.

Madeleine stared at Jane, considering her answer, and then shared that she, too, could type and did so at her civil service jobs.

Jane took hold of Madeleine's hands, her adversary's smooth skin resting in Jane's rough fingers, calloused from work with needles, fountain pens, and typewriters.

"Your hands, Madeleine, are lovely. Your nails are beautiful. It's fortunate that the typewriter did not break them."

"Oh, I was very careful not to run it fast enough to hurt my fingers. I never do anything that can hurt my nails."

Jane could not say the same. It seemed an opportune moment to leave before Madeleine asked more questions about Jane's daily tasks. She left Madeleine to her bedtime ritual: beef tea and a hot toddy As Jane descended the stairs, she exhaled after what felt like a very close call.

Jane had little to report to Stoll. Sister Dorothea was upset that Miss Ellis's presence in court dragged the Home into the newspapers. Ellis was exhausted by the difficult testimony but determined to save Madeleine's soul. Jane pondered the rumors swirling in the press about Breckinridge and a wedding in New York. She shook her head: "It's probably a newspaper lie and really won't amount to anything."[6]

Jane held the needle firmly as she pushed it through the linen, pulling the thread to the back. While Madeleine spent this Saturday with her attorneys, Jane sat with the House of Mercy residents, sewing the decorative linens the Home sold for a modest income. Stitch by slow stitch, she lingered, waiting for Madeleine's return. The clock approached 6:00 p.m. As the afternoon light faded in the sewing room and the stitches were harder to see, Jane gathered her things. But just as Jane left the Home, Madeleine and Miss Ellis appeared.[7]

"Providence must have sent you," Madeleine said in greeting. "I have an errand for you. It's vital."

Madeleine explained that the *Brooklyn Standard Union* was publishing a bombshell article—"Pollard's Confession!" the advertising screamed. "The article is a miserable lie!" she said. "They claim I am an opium eater!!" But Madeleine had a plan:

Jane would find the article, and then, together, they would craft a response.[8]

Jane hustled along. She tried the newsstands at the Cochran House, Willard's, the Shoreham, and the Arlington, but the newspaper, Jane learned, would not be available until the next morning. She insisted that a news vendor hold one for her, guaranteeing access to Madeleine the next day.

———

Evening fell, and the lights on Connecticut Avenue twinkled. Jane worked her Remington, sharing with Stoll what little, she feared, she had gathered from the plaintiff. She reported how Madeleine studied the court transcripts and that she and her attorneys had spent hours going over her testimony so far. Jane warned the defense team, "I will venture to say you have not thought of a single discrepancy in her story that has not been discovered by her lawyers or herself, and they will be ready for you with a story to cover up her tracks."[9] Be prepared.

She set aside her report and turned to the work piling up in the thick of the trial; determined to contribute, she typed notes and indexed testimony and depositions for Breckinridge and his team. When Jane answered Madeleine's query about how she spent her day, she had not entirely lied. She did do work for men; she just hadn't mentioned that these men were determined to deny Madeleine's claims and achieve a courtroom victory.

Jane's work kept her busy well into the evening. The late-hour quiet gave her a moment to write to her mother, apologizing for her lack of letters. She was hustling, she explained, so busy that she had not even had the time to pick up her mail.

Jane was proud of her work. She shared a story with her mother. The lawyers had asked her to complete a task, and she offered an alternative way to approach the work. Mr. Stoll, she told Mollie, was set on how to do it, so Jane did it his way, and the idea was a failure. Mr. Butterworth said to Stoll, "I told you to let that girl have her way in this thing entirely, that she had more sense than you and I put together! Next time, you listen to her!" Well, concluded Jane, "That goes to the fund for swelling my head. If it was that sort of thing and no setbacks, I should have to buy a new hat."[10]

But there were setbacks: blockades by nuns, nonanswers from Dudley, and a mercurial plaintiff who vacillated between pulling Jane close and pushing her away.

The clock struck half past eleven, and Jane needed sleep. She closed her letter, wished her mother a happy birthday, and sent her a gift of writing paper. This week, Jane hinted, things will hum.

Jane awoke early and hurried to the newsstand for the Sunday *Standard Union*.[11]

The sisters offered no barrier on this morning, curious, perhaps, about the article. In Madeleine's room, Jane sat in the rocking chair as Madeleine ate breakfast, lounging in the bed. Newspapers were piled about. Together, they pored over accounts of Madeleine's testimony in the *World*, *Courier-Journal*, *Herald*, and the *Washington Post*. Despite newspaper jibes of her being waxen, colorless, or too self-possessed, she knew she had done well on the stand; so did the defense. Butterworth admitted she was quick and smart.

Madeleine opened the *Standard Union* and read the article, forcing herself to focus line by line. She knew the author and had trusted her. They had met at Bread Loaf in the summer of 1892 and had become fast friends. Then, Mrs. Bridgeman, the wife of the *Standard Union* managing editor, penned an enthusiastic review of her summer season at the Vermont resort and filled her column with praise for an up-and-coming young author, Madeleine Pollard. But in the wake of the scandal, Bridgeman had a change of heart and, in this column, had withdrawn her friendship. She accused Madeleine of claiming authorship of "Love's Power," a poem by the similarly named Josephine Pollard. Bridgeman said that Madeleine had claimed to be publishing a novel, but she had since learned that was untrue. And worst of all, she claimed Madeleine was an opium eater—an abuser of morphine. In the 1890s opium crisis, the most frequently addicted were leisure-class white women, succumbing to the power of a drug their physicians prescribed. Bridgeman's hurtful charge was an accusation readers could reasonably believe.[12]

Madeleine read the article a second time.

What do you think? asked Jane, eager for a revelation that could blight Madeleine's chances for victory.

It wasn't as bad as Madeleine had feared. "It's not worth answering," Madeleine began. "It is a cowardly lie with just enough truth to make it all the meaner. It is so like a woman to strike when I am down; that is the time they always take and strike the harder because I seem helpless now."

No, she told Jane, she would not engage in a newspaper debate about lies. These were lies put forth to sell newspapers—Mrs. Bridgeman's husband's newspaper.

Nonetheless, Madeleine took a sheet of writing paper and a pen and defended herself to Calderon Carlisle, who was, in her eyes, the person whose opinion mattered most.

She told him that she had never claimed Josephine Pollard's poem as her own—the *Lexington Herald-Leader* had misattributed the poem to her in 1888.[13] As for using morphine, Madeleine blamed Charles Dudley Warner for that unfounded rumor. Of the other accusations, nothing in this article, she wrote, could hurt their case.

She handed the note to Jane to deliver to Carlisle.

Jane proceeded cautiously.

When she returned, Madeleine grilled Jane. Was Mrs. Carlisle slight or stout? What did she wear? What sort of draperies covered the windows? Were the furnishings lovely? Jane disappointed Madeleine; she had not set foot in the house. A young servant in livery answered the door and accepted the letter. When he mentioned he saw the Carlisles coming up the street from church, Jane beat a hasty retreat.

The evening grew late, and Jane left Madeleine to prepare for Monday's court appearance. She would get strength from her beef tea, soothe her voice with her hot toddy, and sleep out of the path of drafts. Jane reported to Stoll that Madeleine had shampooed her hair—in the 1890s, an activity typically undertaken only monthly. "Since the newspapers have spoken of it," Jane observed, "she has taken great pains to have it becomingly arranged."[14]

Pollard v. Breckinridge was not the only case Jane had on her mind. Back in her room, she wrote to Mame. In 1887, Jane's sister had married Al Clayton, a fellow actor, but the marriage quickly soured. Clayton stole and drank up Mame's money, and her in-laws used her labor for their benefit as well. He had all but abandoned Mame yet still demanded her earnings. Jane urged Mame to divorce. She had called in a favor from Stoll, and he had agreed to help. Jane explained, "I have done some pretty hard kind of work for him, and I believe he appreciated it enough to want to do something for me."[15] Mame resisted; Jane reassured her sister: "It's not selfish to want a divorce."[16] And Stoll could help, Jane urged—a less capable lawyer might mishandle the case, leaving Mame with a divorce that was not legal and wasted money. Women had to know how to protect themselves and their hard-earned wages from cheats, scoundrels, and the realities of life.[17]

With Madeleine on the stand, the crowds returned to the courtroom on Monday, pressing against the door-guarding bailiffs in a mass of force and being shoved back only with tremendous effort.[18] At the back of the courtroom, white men stood four deep, hats in hands to keep their bowlers from the crush of onlookers. Sketches of the courtroom show no men of color among the spectators, but the trial did not escape the notice of W. Calvin Chase, the editor of the *Washington Bee*, a weekly Black newspaper. In a Saturday

editorial, Chase suggested that instead of codifying de facto segregation through revisions to the "separate cars" passenger train
laws, if the Kentucky legislature had "gotten up an amendment . . .
regulating the movements of [Breckinridge and Pollard,] the country's nostrils would not now be fumigated with their disgraceful
doings."[19]

The plaintiff's team led the morning's examination, the eighth day
of the trial, March 19. Calderon Carlisle motioned to Madeleine,
and she took the stand. Her freshly washed hair sat in rich coils
upon her neck. The bailiff arranged her chair and placed a glass of
water on the narrow desk that served as the witness stand. George
Townsend, reporting for the *Cincinnati Enquirer*, admired her
self-control. Despite the woman-scorned stereotype, he noticed
that she "is not furious nor angry at any time. She is pleading,
appealing, soft-spoken, and calmly in earnest."[20]

Carlisle posed his questions from his chair, seated at the
plaintiff's table and rarely glancing up from his written notes.
His goal this morning was to document Breckinridge's multiple
attempts to seduce Madeleine. Madeleine described the congressman's failed attempt at Mrs. Rose's Cincinnati assignation house,
after their meeting in the public library, and then their train ride
to Lexington in August 1884. Carlisle concluded with an intimate
inquiry—how long had Madeleine continued her sexual relations
with the congressman following her weekend at Sarah Gist's,
when Breckinridge succeeded in his desire? "Up to the 17th of
May, 1893," Madeleine answered without hesitation. Nine years.
Carlisle turned the witness over to the defense.

Contrary to Carlisle, Benjamin Butterworth was a man in
motion, rocking his chair back on two legs as he questioned the
plaintiff, later standing to continue his cross-examination. Butterworth turned to Madeleine's literary dreams. He appeared gentle
in his approach but spoke with a mocking tinge, an attempt to
undercut her aspirations. Speaking of her childhood, Madeleine

mentioned that she had hoped to be a writer, an ambition she had held from an early age.

"Then it takes a great deal of training to become a writer, does it, Miss Pollard?" asked Butterworth.

"A great deal more than I have, Mr. Butterworth."

"You consider that it demands an immense amount of all-around knowledge then, do you?"

"Yes sir, or a gift from God."

Madeleine spoke about her youthful dreams. She wanted to become a teacher but had to give it up when her life imploded. Butterworth pounced: "You understand the value of character, then, do you, Miss Pollard?"

"Most certainly, Mr. Butterworth, and never to such a degree as now."

When Butterworth read again from the schoolgirl letter Madeleine had written to her Wesleyan friend, she challenged the accuracy of its contents. He offered that perhaps the letter was "a bit of fancy play." Madeleine saw through his implication of a letter full of lies. She didn't miss a beat: "You are saying that, Mr. Butterworth, not I."

A chastened Butterworth returned to her career aspirations and asked about her reading and training for teaching. "No," Madeleine responded, "I hadn't followed any particular reading plan but had access to many books and read often and widely." For example, she said, on the day of the carriage ride, she had been reading a bestselling religious novel, Elizabeth Stuart Phelps's *The Gates Ajar*. "And no," she answered Butterworth before he could insinuate such, "I have never read anything that could not be appropriately put in the hands of a modest young girl."

Jere Wilson objected. "This line of questioning," he argued, "is irrelevant to the issue at hand." On the contrary, Butterworth rebutted, "The matter of the character of the plaintiff is very much in evidence and is the proper subject for question. Throughout her story, this plaintiff has endeavored to surround herself with an atmosphere of absolute purity."

Wilson interrupted Butterworth. "Has she?" he asked, glancing over at Breckinridge.

Butterworth ignored the cut and replied that he had a perfect right to find out the circumstances of her early years and whether she could withstand temptation when it came. Before Wilson could object, Butterworth withdrew the question. He had made his point: character, maturity. Next question.

"When you were at Wesleyan, Miss Pollard, were you competent to care for yourself?" Madeleine said yes, just as Wilson objected: "The question of whether a girl is able to take care of herself and resist temptation depends largely upon the sort of people with whom she is thrown and the character and personality of the man who comes with silver tongue to fill her mind with fair promises."[21]

This time, Judge Bradley interrupted as the spectators laughed at Wilson's sly joke. "I want it understood right here that we are not conducting a show," he lectured. "I am sorry so many people of Washington think it necessary to come here to attend this trial. When they do come here, they must obey the rules of the court, and I will say right here, if I hear any demonstrations of approval or disorder, of snickering laughter, or anything of that sort, I will clear the room. I won't have it."

The room was silent. Chastised spectators looked at their feet. Why *were* they there? Grown men with gray hair jostling each morning to win a seat. To watch a congressman fall—a bit of schadenfreude directed toward the powerful? Or did they delight in a sanctioned bit of porn, the opportunity to vicariously experience the fantasy of keeping a mistress? Madeleine sat, calm, hands folded in her lap. Butterworth let the judge's words sink in and then continued his cross-examination, probing Madeleine's past acquaintances, particularly her friendships with young men.

The defense had yet to enter into the record numerous depositions that would challenge the plaintiff's claim of innocence— statements from men young and old who claimed to have had intimate experience with Madeleine. In due time, the defense would use that evidence, but for now, Butterworth worked to build his case that when Madeleine met Breckinridge, she was no virgin, and therefore, he had not seduced her. He raised an incident from her youth: a mock marriage.

In advance of the trial, rumors had churned in the newspapers that on Christmas morning 1884, Madeleine attended a party at the home of Squire Tinsley, who hosted the festivities with his wife and daughters. Madeleine's uncle George attended, as did Alex Julian, a young blind man. Everyone drank eggnog, and, newspapers alleged, the young people staged a mock marriage between Julian and Madeleine, culminating in the happy couple retiring to Julian's bed. Madeleine confirmed she knew Julian and admitted she wrote of him as a love interest in one of her youthful letters, but, she told the court, Alex was sweet on her sister, not her.

"Did Mr. Julian," Butterworth asked, "ever bear himself as a lover? Did he caress you?"

"Indeed, he did not! He would never dare." And furthermore, added Madeleine, her uncle George would never have allowed it.

"How long," Butterworth asked, "after this party had Julian remained your friend?"

"Well," began Madeleine, "I thought he was still my friend. I have no reason to believe he is not."

More young men, more letters. In one letter, Madeleine had used a Spanish phrase. Butterworth stumbled. "*Kwen saybes?*" he attempted.

"*Quien sabes,*" said Madeleine. "It means *who knows.*"

Butterworth read 1883 letters from the plaintiff to Owen Robinson, who was studying at the Kentucky Military Institute and on whom Madeleine had a crush. Robinson did not return her interest. Butterworth homed in on a March 1883 letter Madeleine had sent Robinson. "I am willing to confess," she had written, "I was guilty of a very unmaidenly bit of conduct, perhaps," referring to a letter she had sent on Valentine's Day, but "even if it was not, it was certainly very silly." When she learned that Robinson was engaged to be married, she reminisced in a letter about good times in sentimental terms: "We are good friends, aren't we, Owen?"

Madeleine sent him a lock of her hair, a keepsake. She signed her letter, "Your truest ami, Mattie Vivian Pollard." Although Butterworth attempted to paint this relationship as evidence of Madeleine's unvirtuous youth, Madeleine on the stand remained firm: there was no engagement, no love affair between them—they were warm, cordial friends.

Benjamin Butterworth continued to grill her in the cross-examination, asking for details on the 1884 rendezvous with Breckinridge in the Cincinnati library and her subsequent visit to the George Street assignation house of Mrs. Rose. She met him at the library, she testified, the day after the carriage ride, hoping, again, he would speak of her contract with James Rodes. When the librarian shushed their conversation, they left the building. Breckinridge suggested stopping at a friend's house. The visit, she noted, was strange: Mrs. Rose did not offer tea or refreshments. Instead, she ushered them to a bedroom. Breckinridge locked the door. Madeleine sadly reported that was when she first learned what service such a house provided. But Madeleine resisted, and despite the intervention of Rose, who urged Madeleine to give in to Breckinridge, on that day, he was unsuccessful.

Butterworth asked how long she and Breckinridge remained at Rose's. "I don't know," she replied, "Perhaps it was two hours, not quite three hours." Madeleine abruptly turned to the defendant: "Colonel Breckinridge, how long was it?" The defendant squirmed and flushed deeply, men snickered, and Madeleine returned to her story. These were the first words she had spoken to Breckinridge since May 17, 1893.

After the midday recess, the crowd filled the courtroom and corridors. Breckinridge arrived first; Madeleine, tired, was late. Her fatigue pulled at her calm demeanor, and she answered Butterworth's questions with growing irritation. As she testified, Breckinridge, with heavy eyes, read his correspondence and jotted notes in response.

Why had she gone down this path? Butterworth asked. What had she hoped to gain after sacrificing her purity? When did she realize her position?

"I have never realized it fully until now when I am an outcast. Since he had made it hard for me to live. I loved him then, and a wish of his was religion to me," she said.[22] Tears gathered. "Some men were simply impossible to resist." And now that Breckinridge had made her life dark and hopeless, she fully realized the disgrace, dishonor, and degradation heaped on her. "In my darkest hours," she added, "death seemed preferable to life." Breckinridge looked up and stared at the plaintiff, listening to every word, hearing her sadness. In his hand, he played with a rubber band.

Butterworth asked about her relationship with Rankin Rossell, the young clerk who had accompanied her to Cincinnati Wesleyan in November 1884. She explained that this had been their first meeting, and because she did not know the city, he guided her to the college. He visited her often, always in the parlor and always in the presence of a chaperone. He had given her a chaste kiss upon his departure twice but with a chaperone present. They were acquaintances, then friends, and then they were engaged. But now, ten years later, Madeleine knew that Rossell claimed that he took more liberties with her than an innocent kiss. Before Butterworth could challenge her, Madeleine lobbed an accusation, suggesting that Rossell's racy deposition was given in exchange for a government job in Breckinridge's district.

"Then you mean he has prevaricated?" asked a surprised Butterworth.

"I mean," Madeleine responded, stretching out her final word, "that he has lied."

Butterworth had been leading up to a point that would set up the defense's argument. He lobbed questions about Madeleine's relationships with Rodes, Rossell, and Breckinridge in the late summer of 1884. "Then am I to understand," Butterworth asked as if it had just occurred to him, "that while you were receiving visits and letters from Mr. Rodes, who had offered you marriage, you were actually engaged to Rossell and being kept by Mr. Breckinridge?"

"Yes, Mr. Butterworth, as bad as that sounds, that was the precise state of the case."

Butterworth shifted to Madeleine's first pregnancy. She repeated how Breckinridge took charge, issuing commands. Above all, he had said, hide your identity and mine. And so, she did, Madeleine testified, calling herself "Mrs. Burgoyne" at the foundling asylum and "Louise Wilson" for her postpartum care. She told Butterworth she wrote to Breckinridge at a post office box, addressing the letters to "Margaret Dillon," a fake name to protect the then-new congressman's identity. Madeleine wore a veil at the asylum—she removed it only in her room with the door locked. "Of course," she added, "a woman in such an asylum is not out of her room very much."

The conversation with the asylum sisters at the deposition had been heated. Remembering the nuns' caustic accusations brought tears to Madeleine's eyes. Madeleine looked directly at the jury. She had brought the suit forward, she said, to seek vindication for the principle of the double standard. "I was fighting for a greater and noble principle," she said, "whether a man has the right to do as he chooses and suffer none of the consequences of his act, while the woman must be bowed down with her shame. I believe the time will come when there will be a change of feeling on this point, and there will be equal retribution for men and women." Madeleine addressed the jury. "I believe these men will help me."

The spectators murmured in surprise. Caught in Madeleine's spell, the jurors looked at each other, the spectators, and finally the plaintiff.

"Then this is your motive in bringing this suit," asked Butterworth, "this striving for a higher plane of morality or something?"

"I do not understand," answered Madeleine precisely, "that I must answer any questions as to my reasons for bringing this suit." Butterworth let it drop.

The afternoon wore on, and Bridgeman's article had yet to be addressed. Madeleine grew testy. Butterworth asked a question, Wilson objected, and Bradley opined that the question was not proper. Madeleine sniffed from the stand, "And I do not see its importance."

Madeleine continued her life story. Her mother knew nothing about her difficulties. Madeleine's mother, sister, and brother-in-law had visited her in Lexington once, late in the summer of 1885. Butterworth asked if she had confided her secret. "No," answered Madeleine, "I did not. I told her nothing."

At Breckinridge's request, Madeleine said, she left Lexington in the fall of 1887 and moved to Washington, where she had her second child. Madeleine described her travels and took the bull by the horns. "I called on Mrs. Bridgeman," Madeleine said, "the woman who wrote that article in the *Brooklyn Standard Union* you are about to read."

"Well," huffed Butterworth, miffed at being outmaneuvered. "Is it true?"

"I am sorry to say that it is not. It has been colored. I am not an opium eater, and I never claimed to have written Miss Josephine Pollard's poems."

Judge Bradley interrupted, anticipating that Butterworth was gearing up to read the entire article to the court and that Jere Wilson would object. "These things are all collateral matter," the judge said.

And to Bradley's surprise, Wilson said he would not object. "Let them read all of the article. They are bound by her answers, and there are more things in it that we would like to have read."

Butterworth began to read from the *Standard Union*, pausing for the plaintiff's explanations. He read of her friendships with noted literary men, laying groundwork for the defense to portray her as an adventuress targeting the wealthy and famous. But Madeleine denied being intimately acquainted with James Russell Lowell or William Dean Howells. Butterworth read a little more, then stopped. Why had Wilson not objected? What was the plaintiff's team up to? He set the paper down.

It was close to three o'clock. Butterworth asked Madeleine to describe her return to Washington in August 1892. She repeated what she had testified to previously. Breckinridge met her at the station, and they drove into the country. They would marry, he promised. And that evening, they visited an assignation house on Eighth Street. With that sad image, the court adjourned for the day.

————

At 7:00 p.m., an angry Sister Dorothea opened the door and lit into Jane. There would be no shared confidences tonight; the matron was on a rant. "I will not have you coming up to see Miss Pollard against my express wishes and better judgment," the matron said, voice raised, keys jangling. It had been a bad day for Dorothea: a resident had scaled the back fence and escaped, the newspapers continued to mention the House of Mercy with each reference to Miss Ellis, and here again was Miss Parker, who simply would not listen to her warning to stay away from Madeleine Pollard. And when Madeleine had returned from court today, Attorney Carlisle had sent orders with Miss Ellis: Madeleine was not to talk to anyone, even the sisters, and no one was to mention the trial. Since when did Mr. Carlisle dictate the rules in her Home? Dorothea stared at Jane, awaiting an explanation for her presence.[23]

"I overheard men talking in a streetcar," Jane said. "They had information about Mr. Breckinridge that Madeleine should know." Jane's tall tale made Dorothea all the angrier. "What," she said, "could you have heard, I would like to know, that would be worse than this woman has already said herself?" Jane resumed her strategy: soothe and sympathize, agreeing with the matron's frustrations and hurts, offering platitudes that it would be over soon, all the while backing across the entryway and toward the staircase. The matron's ire weakened, and despite, or to spite, Carlisle's rules, Dorothea waved Jane up the stairs.

Madeleine was in a friendly mood, pleased with her day rebuffing Butterworth's cross-examination, and delighted that Jane offered oranges. As she peeled one for Madeleine, Jane retold her story of men on a Georgetown streetcar, this time constructing bits of conversation to entice Madeleine to correct her or fill in gaps. Jane was fishing for the name of Madeleine's financial supporter, how much she was paid for her *New York World* article, and which witnesses for the plaintiff were waiting in the wing. The first two lures were designed to show Madeleine begged money from the wealthy and then made more off her own shame; the last bit of bait sought Carlisle and Wilson's strategy for after the cross-examination.

Jane's story failed: Madeleine gave up no benefactor's name, swore she turned down payment for her essay, and told Jane she must have heard wrong—there were no more witnesses. "But," Madeleine added, "it was so sweet of you to take so much interest in me and my affairs."[24] Madeleine pressed two favors on the thoughtful Agnes Parker—to buy some flaxseed to soothe a boil on Madeleine's arm and to find out Breckinridge's new address now that he had left the Cochran Hotel. "Of course," Jane agreed, and both Madeleine and Miss Ellis thought Jane so thoughtful a girl, but Mr. Carlisle had given an order to keep visitors away, and Ellis ushered Jane out of the room. "Tomorrow morning," Ellis assured Jane as she left, they would have their "claws nicely sharpened for the fight."[25]

Jane shared with Stoll what little she gleaned from Madeleine, writing her nightly report in her room. Madeleine had gushed about Carlisle and the dainty lunch he had provided. Beaten biscuit and cold lamb—Jane really didn't know what to do with that information other than to mock Madeleine's infatuation with the married, and uninterested, attorney. Jane reported that Madeleine had not seen Dudley for over a week; neither had she. As for the plaintiff's strategy, Jane believed Madeleine wept whenever Butterworth got her in a corner to gain time to think out an answer. Yet she had to admit that Madeleine rarely got rattled, and her answers were crafty and clever. Jane, who spoke French, laughed a bit at how Madeleine schooled Butterworth on the Spanish language. She reminded Stoll that Madeleine studied every word of her testimony; her lawyers had trained her well. If the defense was counting on the plaintiff to slip up on the stand, they should rethink that.

As she readied for bed, Jane gave that evening's conversation more thought, troubled by Madeleine's request for the congressman's address—would the plaintiff end their love story in a shooting, or was Dudley going to defend his sister's honor by gunning? And Madeleine's compliment might have worried Jane too; when Madeleine thanked her for taking an interest in her, it sounded less like praise and more like a criticism of Jane's absence at the trial.

———————

For a third day, Madeleine testified. Butterworth stood to continue the cross-examination, choosing, as his first topic, James Rodes. Madeleine confirmed she had written the letters to him that earlier that morning had been read into the record, including ones from New Orleans penned in 1885 during her pregnancy and recovery in Cincinnati.[26]

Butterworth argued that the New Orleans letters proved that Madeleine had not given birth in Cincinnati. She insisted the letters were a deception Breckinridge designed to keep Rodes, and her family, in the dark. She had never been to New Orleans— Breckinridge dictated what to say or typed the letters himself. He posted some letters from trains, which obscured the writer's location and supported the ruse offered Rodes that Madeleine was traveling with an aunt.

Butterworth dismissed her explanation. No, he said, the court would take the written word of the letter over her spoken word as fact. Then, urged Jere Wilson, goading Butterworth from the plaintiff's table, read the entire letter, including the envelopes.

Butterworth did. The cancellation on letters mailed by the Railway Postal Office provided the train number, the date, and the endpoint cities of the route. The postmarked envelopes indicated many of the "New Orleans" letters had been mailed in Kentucky.

The defense moved on, sharing letters Madeleine had written Rodes from 1885 through her move to Washington in 1887. She asked Rodes for money and scolded him when he was late to provide. Madeleine promised pleasant visits if he brought money, cool receptions if he did not. Madeleine explained that Rodes believed she would either marry or pay him back; asking for his continued support kept him from discovering another man provided for her. Her sole purpose, she claimed, was to keep Rodes from asking questions she could not answer.

Butterworth's questions continued, and Madeleine, awash in the deception and confusion of that time, offered detailed explanations. When her answers grew long, Butterworth grew impatient. He asked her to answer yes or no "and not envelop her answers in a fog of phrases."

"Facts are not phrases," muttered Madeleine.

When Madeleine returned for the afternoon session, she was pale, and a weariness hovered around her answers. Still, she weighed each word carefully as the cross-examination dragged on. Many of the spectators failed to return after the morning session, leaving but a small crowd.

Butterworth peppered Madeleine with questions, turning to her civil service employment. Yes, she said, Breckinridge had secured jobs for her at the Agriculture Department and the Census Bureau. No, she had not been writing while in Washington; that was a story Breckinridge created to explain what she did with her day and to provide a cover for other activities one didn't discuss.

"Were you not studying for the stage this time?" asked Butterworth, hoping to prove Madeleine was focused on fame.

"No, sir," Pollard replied with surprise.

"Did you not think of adopting the stage as a profession?"

"Nothing could have been further from my thoughts," Madeleine answered. "The stage does not present itself as a likely place for a plain girl. It is only a place for pretty girls."

In his cross-examination, Butterworth attempted to portray Madeleine as promiscuous and deceptive, lying to get what she wanted, even to her mother. Now he would portray her as dangerous, so unhinged that the congressman could not be held to any promise he had made under the duress of her physical threats.

Butterworth began with Madeleine's anxiety in the spring of 1893. Her smile faded. Madeleine described her growing confusion; she had heard that Breckinridge had attended social events with his cousin Louise Wing, and she knew they had traveled together. How, Madeleine wondered, could such a worldly woman go with such a man? She told Butterworth how she questioned Breckinridge repeatedly until he maligned Mrs. Wing to such an extent that she realized he would not marry that woman.

Madeleine continued: She had gone to New York to meet Breckinridge, but he wasn't there as promised—she found his room empty, except for his traveling bag and pistol. When the congressman eventually returned, Madeleine explained, she was beside herself with anger and worry. She grabbed his pistol; he locked himself in his room. She pounded on a connecting door; he threatened to call the police. Butterworth hammered away at Madeleine, pressing for every detail on her attempt to shoot Breckinridge at the Hoffman House on May 1. He did not notice the council for the plaintiff, Jeremiah Wilson, rise quietly to his feet.

"Your Honor," Wilson began, staring at Butterworth. "I must rise to interfere right here, now that I understand where this line of cross-examination is tending." This inquiry would not do, he said, badgering Miss Pollard about a shooting, implying that such a mortal threat negated any promise that Breckinridge may have made. Wilson continued with a level voice and a level gaze.

Breckinridge's proposal of marriage, Wilson said, and the promise the congressman had made in August 1892 after the death of his second wife, the vow he shared with Mrs. Blackburn on Good Friday 1893, and the wedding plans he confirmed before Police Chief Moore in May of last year would never have come to pass. Breckinridge could not have married Madeleine Pollard on May 31—and not because she threatened his life in a New York City hotel room. He could not marry her because he had already, secretly, married someone else.

12

HAPPIEST WOMAN IN WASHINGTON

A year before Jeremiah Wilson exposed Breckin-
ridge's secret wife in court, the winter season of 1893 was in full
swing, and Washington parlors welcomed Louise Scott Wing to
the whirlwind round of society events. Louise was tall, slender,
and graceful with auburn hair and a keen mind, a near doppel-
gänger to Madeleine Pollard's slight form, beautiful hair, and
quick wit, although Wing was her senior at forty-eight years old.
Louise Wing had come to winter in Washington and stayed the
season with her cousin Carrie Sterling.[1] Wing still had the stylish sense of dress and learned, energetic conversation that had
marked her younger days.[2] She spoke French, played the piano,
and entertained with taste and charm. She was quite bright in both
manner and intellect and quickly became a welcome figure in the
capital's social scene.

Breckinridge was no fan of the endless parties and gatherings that marked the winter social season. Nonetheless, obliga-
tions of family, geography, and social class dictated that he pay a
call on his Kentucky relatives, including his distant cousin Louise.
In Sterling's parlor on Seventeenth Street, Breckinridge and Wing
conversed: a six-month widower and a widow for almost twenty
years. A spark flared as they chatted and dined, and it grew in
the following weeks. Together, the widow and widower attended
gatherings of the Kentucky Washington contingent, hosted by the

wives and women of Bluegrass men serving in Congress or other federal positions. The newly found companionship deepened. By mid-February, Breckinridge and Wing's spark had blossomed into something richer, something very much resembling love. People noticed. People whispered.

"Dear Cousin Willie," Louise dreamily wrote Breckinridge on Valentine's Day. She described for his amusement a dull evening entertaining General John Floyd King, former representative from Louisiana.[3] "Why," she wrote with humor, "did you not give me a clue to this man! A whole day lost out of my life—a day which began so well." And the next morning, she sat alone and played the piano in cousin Carrie's parlor, lost in thought. She played "Warum," a German tune. "I need not tell you [it] means *Why*, and I was making myself dreamy [asking] Why—so many times." Why was Valentine's Day so fair? Why was her evening so dull? And why was she sending this "hurried foolish letter?"[4] Perhaps because she was falling in love.

Louise wrote Breckinridge almost daily, composing her notes on small, ivory-colored cards in a firm hand, the dark ink slanting to the right and her lack of precision reflecting her ebullient mood—dashes connecting sentences, the dot atop an *i* hovering over the following letter or two along, and the crosses of a *t* drifting to the edge of the page. "I am in such a mood this morning," Louise wrote, "like champagne only more real and lasting, I hope."[5] She chided Breckinridge for his busy schedule that led him to break dates: "You must not be so rash in promising me your visits, but do save me next Sunday evening."[6]

Breckinridge was an attentive suitor. He visited and sent flowers. He wrote messages each morning, sending them to Louise via a messenger, who would run the missives of love the few city blocks between their residences. And when he was out of Washington, he sent telegrams. Breckinridge wooed the longtime widow, who was surprised by the intensity of her emotions and elated at this second chance at love. The congressman moved quickly.

In mid-February 1893, Breckinridge proposed marriage. They would become engaged, Breckinridge offered, but they could tell no one. Louise's joy was suddenly tempered, reluctant to hide this happy state. Breckinridge reasoned with her: Only seven months had passed since his wife's death; announcing an engagement so soon would be unseemly. And, he explained to her, he wanted to tell his children in person to prepare them for another woman sitting in their mother's place at the table. She acquiesced; it was the proper thing to do given the recent death of Issa Desha Breckinridge, and she wanted his children to love her. But uncertainty nagged her joy as she pondered her future. "Life has become so suddenly serious, and I am a coward before all this . . . I have been so free and careless and indifferent—you must help me to realize the future," the once independent woman wrote, turning to Breckinridge for direction.[7] They agreed to a clandestine engagement. And just like that, Breckinridge had a second secret.

Despite her misgivings, Wing was thrilled and happily anticipating the marriage and her new social role as Mrs. Congressman Breckinridge. "Please always write the 'Happiest Woman in Washington' in big letters when you write of me," she told her fiancé, receiving each of his daily letters with "such a thrill of new delight."[8] With her fiancé's permission, Louise shared the engagement news with her sister, Ella Green, seeking her counsel, support, and sympathy for the unusual situation. Green pondered the circumstance of such a singular proposal, "bewildered and tearful with such a secret to think over." Eventually, she wrote her future brother-in-law a warm, supportive letter. Breckinridge, she trusted, would give her sister affection and protection with "a name that you have honored as well as your ancestors . . . I thank you for the assurance that Wing shall be happy and content in your care."[9] Still, Louise had trouble sleeping.

———————

While Louise Wing tossed and turned at night, chasing sleep, Madeleine Pollard was also troubled: in March 1893, she became pregnant for the third time, and Breckinridge had yet to name the promised wedding date.

———————

Louise's initial excitement faded, replaced by nagging insecurity. She depended on Breckinridge's letters to buoy her sinking spirits. His missives were a lifeline between the secret she kept at present and the future she grew to fear. "I have a sense of grief," Wing wrote in late March, "mysterious but which gives me strength, and when the morning dawned dark and rainy, I was not dismayed for there were your letters to read and another surely coming by noon."[10] After a sleepless night, Wing complained how "nothing soothed me. It was so long and dark and lonely."[11] In addition to daily letters, Wing and Breckinridge sent each other telegrams. I "am anxious," she wrote when her future husband's daily letters had not arrived; "send me a telegram."[12]

Fear overshadowed Louise's happiness as winter turned to spring, and illness began to structure her day. She was happy when she received letters and fretful when she did not. She worried about being a good companion to Breckinridge and feared his children might disapprove of her. She described herself as haughty, distant, and cold. A doctor prescribed an invigorating tonic to revive her flagging energy. She wanted Breckinridge to make her softer: "Don't stop writing me (or loving me). You are doing more than the Doctor's horrid tonic."[13] For much of April, Breckinridge remained in Kentucky. Louise waited impatiently for his return to Washington to celebrate Easter, and she became upset when he sent her only a one-page note. Fear dogged Louise Wing: "Your letters are the most perfect, the most ardent, and yet, a dread comes that such love will not last. I am very sad today and full of forebodings."[14]

———————

Breckinridge returned to Washington for Easter weekend. On Good Friday, Breckinridge and Madeleine Pollard called on Julia Blackburn and announced their engagement.

As Easter flowers bloomed, Louise withdrew from the social scene. She sat alone in her dressing gown. She could not sleep and had little interest in eating. She was constantly anxious, and she grew depressed. Louise wrote Breckinridge daily. Bitter notes crept onto her pages, but then she would apologize for a letter written when she was "so blue," setting a pattern that followed her vacillating moods—she would lash out and then retract, accuse and then apologize. Her brother, Preston Scott, a Louisville physician, prescribed aggressive bed rest for what he defined as her nervous condition, but Louise hated the treatment. She pleaded with Breckinridge: "Hasten back to me. They are so unkind to me here. . . . They keep me in bed and give me almost nothing to eat and scold me because I was so independent Friday and had a relapse." Since the engagement, Louise and Breckinridge had rarely been together. "When will you come?" she asked, "Can you give me a faint clue?"[15]

A few days later, Breckinridge returned to Washington. He rescued the ailing Louise from her jailer caregivers and her narrow life in her cell-like room. His elixir—a jaunt—offered the nervous woman a freeing vacation with no plan. Breckinridge took her to New York City for two weeks. Louise stayed at the grand Fifth Avenue Hotel, Breckinridge across the street at the famous Hoffman House hotel at Madison Square on Twenty-Fourth Street and Broadway.

Madeleine Pollard arrived in New York on the twenty-ninth. She registered at the Hoffman House, telling the desk clerk she was Sophonisba Breckinridge, the congressman's daughter. The clerk gave Madeleine the room adjoining that of her "father."

On the evening of April 29, Breckinridge knocked on the door of an old friend, Rev. John R. Paxton, a minister who resided on West Forty-Fifth Street. With Wing at his side, Breckinridge asked

him for a favor. Paxton married the couple in his parlor. It was
7:00 p.m. The ceremony was private and efficient. Mrs. Paxton
and a visitor, a Mrs. Collier of Pittsburgh, served as witnesses.
The perfunctory ceremony concluded, Breckinridge filled out the
marriage certificate, inadvertently noting that this was his second
marriage when it was his third. Breckinridge pulled Paxton aside
for a private word. He asked the reverend to keep this marriage
confidential and not file the marriage certificate. And he told his
new wife the same—no one could yet know of this wedding. They
had to think of his children and give them time to get to know
Louise and get used to their father's remarriage. The newly married couple celebrated their union at the Hotel de Logerot on the
corner of Eighteenth and Fifth Avenue. They registered as Mr. and
Mrs. William Campbell.[16] On Monday, May 1, Breckinridge left
his bride at the hotel and stepped out to attend to some business.

Madeleine Pollard was relieved to see Breckinridge return to the
Hoffman House on Monday, May 1. In her adjoining room, she
had listened for his return. She had been lonely and angry; he had
been gone all weekend, setting up a new, lucrative business, he told
her. She had her doubts.

With their jaunt concluded and in such a happy manner, Congressman and Mrs. Louise Wing Breckinridge returned to Washington.
Back in the capital, Louise's balloon of happiness deflated. They
returned to their separate residences and their secret relationship.
Shortly after, Breckinridge left for an extended trip to Lexington
and then to paid speaking engagements in Virginia, Tennessee, and
Missouri. Defeated, self-deprecating, and desperate for an affir-
mation of love and worth from her husband, the lonely wife concluded, "I am too great a millstone about your neck."[17]
    As the weeks passed between their wedding and a longed-for
reunion, Louise's handwriting grew larger and loosened, as if the

pen drew airplane loop-de-loops on the page instead of letters. She filled her correspondence cards front and back, rotated the card, and continued her message, writing crosswise across the letter—a palimpsest of longing and pain. In Washington, Dr. Tabor Johnson attended to the ailing Louise and prescribed a narcotic to help her sleep. If he knew that the congressman had arranged his services for Pollard *and* Wing, both suffering from nervous prostration and claiming an engagement to Breckinridge, Johnson didn't let on.

At the end of May, Louise Wing Breckinridge took a suite of rooms at the Hotel Windsor in Atlantic City to regain her health. She traveled with her close friend Rose Covarrubias, who brought along her young children. The seaside air should prove reviving. The rest cure was reinstated; a new doctor offered massages to improve the flow of blood. A nurse cared for her day and sleepless night. The doctor forbade excitement, eyeing with suspicion the emotional barometer the mail brought. Louise grew cautious about the content of her letters, fearing the doctor would discover her relationship with her daily correspondent. "I can't bear to say you good night," she wrote as she concluded her letter, "but you know I am under the control of a new authority now and am not yet able to write a real letter. I *dare not.*"[18] Was the doctor her new authority? Or was it Breckinridge to whom Louise yielded control, daring not to express her hurt and anger at a marriage in name only? Confined to her bed, and despite the doctor's cautions to avoid emotional stimulation, her letters grew in length—four, seven, twelve pages of worries and fears.

Louise feared the discovery of their secret, but why she worried so about the revelation of her hidden engagement and now lawful marriage is unclear. Worries over social propriety devolved into paranoia. She warned her husband not to name her in his letters. "Be very careful what you write," she warned, "I am simply your cousin now."[19] A few days later, she reiterated her warning: "I trust very few people, and we have not announced the 'engagement.'"[20] By week's end, she suspected someone was opening her mail: "I don't trust those maids. Naturally, they are curious (or may be bribed)."[21]

During the "fatal month" of May, Louise was terrified. Painful memories, the extended separation from Breckinridge, and the daily use of opiates—Louise fell away from stability. When Breckinridge's letters and telegrams failed to arrive, she feared the worst. Preston Scott implored Breckinridge to write to his sister every day. Louise told her absent husband, "I can't live without the telegram, even if you can't write the letter. I have been wild for it all morning." Without news, she imagined his death: "If anything should happen to you, I should not care to live a moment after."[22] "Telegraph me without fail," she urged a few pages later.[23] At night, unable to sleep and dreading the long hours until the next day's mail, she imagined "dreadful things."

Louise vacillated between clinging to Breckinridge and pushing him away: "Now, darling cousin, don't think of me. You belong to your children and your country. I suppose my family will look after me." And then she apologized: "I am so sorry to trouble you, but you need not see me. Just try and forget me and enjoy your life."[24] Louise complained repeatedly of being "tired, so very tired" and "useless, very useless." Her new physician recommended the complete rest cure: all correspondence would go through her nurse; she would remain in bed; there would be no reading, music, or other distraction; and her meals would be spare.[25] In a note to Breckinridge, Louise noted acerbically that while she was entombed in a bed staring at a gray sky and a gray sea, he was in Louisville "meeting friends and relatives. Greeted, Loved. Feted."[26] "Why," she wrote, "can't I be the old Wing of April 29th—ready to face everything?"[27]

When Louise's traveling companion was called back to Washington, she resolved to leave the "gray gloom" of Atlantic City and make the trip home to Louisville despite her continued weakness.

In early June, Congressman Breckinridge gave a speech in Nashville, Tennessee, to benefit a local charity. Generously, he would not accept remuneration. The organizers presented

Breckinridge with a large, beautiful basket of flowers. Breckinridge offered his sincere thanks, noting that, sadly, he had no wife with whom he could share this gift.[28]

In mid-June, Louise Scott Wing Breckinridge returned to Louisville to the home she shared with her brother, Preston. She was eager to rest, see her husband, and end the secrecy.

As Louise was settling in back home, Madeleine Pollard sought an escape from the oppressive Washington heat. Terese Graham Blackburn, Senator Joseph Blackburn's wife, had invited her to join the extended Blackburn family and summer in Virginia. She packed her trunks, anticipating the cooler breezes and convivial hotel life with the senator's family, Julia Churchill Blackburn, and Emily Zane. Before leaving Washington, she completed a lingering task. Eager to end the secrecy and move Breckinridge forward on setting a wedding date, Pollard wrote an engagement announcement and sent it to the *Washington Post* and the *New York Times*. The happy news spread quickly.

On June 24, Breckinridge sent his wife an urgent telegram. When he reached Louisville, he called on her. He did not come to Louisville to publicly announce his marriage and, in one fell swoop, negate Madeleine's claim and give Louise her rightful position. Nor did he come to comfort his depressed wife. Breckinridge came to manage a crisis. He came to deflect Louise's anger and to offer her an excuse about the lovelorn woman who had imagined a relationship where none—he claimed—existed. But Louise, who had harbored her suspicions about Madeleine throughout the spring and had heard the whispers in the parlors, would not listen to his weak explanations. Her anger, frustrations, anxiety, distrust, and perhaps even regret—all the forbidden feelings she could not express fully in her letters—spewed forth. She had no patience for his stories; she would not play the passive, dutiful wife in this scene. All this time, her "nerves" had been blamed for her anxiety and depression. Louise's emotional state sounded less like an illness and more like intuition. At the end of that day, the happiest woman in Washington was the angriest woman in Louisville. Breckinridge spent the night at a hotel.

Two days later, Louise wrote to her husband. She had skipped a day in their daily correspondence and explained that she did not have the time or energy to write to him in the flood of visitors, or so she claimed. She alternated among apology, anger, and truth. She wished she had written at least one line "to tell you I love you just the same . . . and [I] hope today of being more patient and self-controlled." She needed rest after the press of the curious: "Mrs. Cox came for a short time out of pity. What a tiring day, dear sweetheart, and here you too tired to write me last night, as nothing has come yet." The new wife spoke plainly: "Yesterday all faith and courage died within me. Not quite, but nearly."[29] Breckinridge replied to her letter: he forgave her.

As the anniversary of Issa Desha Breckinridge's death approached, Louise knew there was little reason not to announce the truth. Madeleine Pollard, after all, had announced her misguided engagement with propriety, while Louise, Breckinridge's wife, suffered in secret. As Breckinridge rode trains here and there, she endured the unwelcome spotlight. Social calls were torturous as she sat sipping tea, making small talk, and struggling with her secret. Resentment simmered. This moment of congratulations should be hers. She should be greeted, loved, feted. A guest asked where she would winter next year, and Louise almost blurted out her frustration, "God knows!" Anger mixed with angst. She grew suspicious of her visitors and believed friends were spreading rumors. "We can't keep it long," she wrote.[30] She had "tired of all this doubt and mystery and separation."[31] She imagined a future where "we will be happy someday or at peace . . . away from all these things which torture me."[32]

In Virginia, Madeleine Pollard assembled her trousseau.

In the courtroom, a hush fell over the spectators. Madeleine sat silently at the witness stand, stunned by Wilson's words. Wilson turned to Butterworth. "Do you admit the marriage to Mrs. Wing?" Butterworth said nothing. Wilson repeated his question: "I want to know if your position is that Colonel Breckinridge was secretly married on the 29th of April, 1893, to Mrs. Wing?" From reading the newspapers, Jeremiah Wilson said he understood that such a secret marriage was alleged.[33] Since the defense had failed to deny it, he could only assume it was true. Calderon Carlisle joined his colleague, doubling up on the defense lawyers: "I understand that it is admitted. You say that they were secretly married."[34]

"Please forbear using the word 'secretly,'" Butterworth replied. He would take it upon himself, Butterworth said, to advise the plaintiff's counsel as they were walking in darkness and sought the light. He paused. "Mr. Breckinridge," he stated for the record, "was married to Mrs. Wing, April 29, 1893, by the Reverend Doctor Paxton," Butterworth's use of the passive voice removing agency from the congressman as if it were an event that happened without will. Butterworth continued: "But it was not a secret marriage." He turned to the opposing counsel: "Is that the light you wanted?"

Wilson replied, "I have no worries about walking in the darkness," but he did want to know about the marriage records. Why had the marriage not been recorded? The papers reported that the marriage certificate had only now been filed, nearly a year late.[35] What was Breckinridge hiding? What was behind this secret?

"That cuts no figure here," Butterworth shot back, dismissing the issue. "I am not going to be betrayed into talking about foreign matters at this stage. The question is one of shooting."

"No," responded Wilson. "It won't make a particle of difference if she had cut his ears off!" The defense, in asking Madeleine about the hotel threat, was building an argument that any promise Breckinridge had made in front of Major Moore in May would be unenforceable, that her violent threats had caused Breckinridge such duress that he could not be held to a forced promise of a May 31 marriage. But Jeremiah Wilson turned to the court and, with great eloquence, pointed out what was obvious: Breckinridge had violated his contract with Madeleine—the promise of marriage made in August 1892 and made again in Mrs. Blackburn's parlor on Good Friday, 1893, and confirmed in front of Major Moore and Dr. Lincoln. What had or had not happened in a hotel room on May 1, 1893, was moot: whether she had slashed his nose with a knife or shot him with a gun would make no difference. When Breckinridge married Louise Wing in April 1893, he had breached his promise to Madeleine Pollard.

While the lawyers argued, Madeleine had remained in the chair at the witness stand. As tempers cooled, Butterworth turned back to the plaintiff; the admission of the secret marriage led him to redirect his questions about the events of April 1893. Madeleine recited the details of her late April trip to New York—and now, suddenly, eagerly, could fill in the gaps that had so confused her a year before. She could see Breckinridge's unconvincing story of the new business opportunity in a new light. And now she understood his two-day absence when he left her alone in the hotel at the end of April. She didn't trust him then and had told him so when he returned on May 1. "You can imagine he was wild," she told the court. "He had reason to be after having broken his promise to me and just being married, too."[36]

With renewed confidence, Madeleine testified. Her face grew flushed, and her voice rose in excitement. She pounded her fist on the witness box, punctuating her statements. She shook her head in disbelief as she reconsidered the events of 1893, the end of their affair. She leaned forward on the desk, elbows propped at its edge, challenging Butterworth to challenge her.

Madeleine insisted that in her presence, Breckinridge denied he intended to marry Wing, even though when doing so, he was already married. "She was not a woman he wanted to marry," Breckinridge had said to her, and then he reiterated his promise to marry Madeleine. To secure Madeleine's trust, "Willie" discussed their future and where they might live. As Madeleine spoke, Breckinridge fidgeted, and he whispered to his counsel. In considering the potential husband she had lost to the similarly deceived Louise Wing, Madeleine summed up Breckinridge's appeal: "A life with that man could not be delightful for anybody."[37] Breckinridge winced.

Madeleine had scored a victory. On the stand and with the court's complete attention, she relayed the last days of their relationship—letters received and promises made. Once again, he denied his new wife using abusive words, which Madeleine refused to repeat in court. Her smile faded as she relayed their denouement. She had, she admitted, considered suicide. She purchased a revolver when "anonymous letters came to me, telling of his conduct with colored women, and I was heartbroken enough to end my life." The portrait of a Gilded Age racial taboo generated a low murmur in the court and a titter here and there. In multiple states, Kentucky included, laws forbade marriage between the races, and in some states, miscegenation—sexual relations between whites and people of color—was similarly illegal. Moreover, the image of a white, privileged man with Black women resurrected images of white enslavers and their Black enslaved prey. And for Madeleine, it was one thing to be, along with Wing, one of Breckinridge's two partners in the spring of 1893—white, elite—but to be grouped instead as one mistress among Black sexual partners was, in that era, a horrifying fall from grace. With Madeleine's accusation hanging in the air, Breckinridge's face revealed a deep blush. A secret marriage, the prolonged affair, a married man's deceitfully fervent promise to marry his pregnant mistress, lies and misdirection—Breckinridge's behavior had surprised even the most experienced lawyers in the courtroom and, outside of it, Jane.

Madeleine was on a roll, eager to continue this tale of duplicity. Butterworth rose to interrupt, but Breckinridge took hold of his sleeve: "Let her go on. Let her talk," Breckinridge said quietly. And Madeleine did. She recounted their interview with Major

Moore and denied that Breckinridge had tried to end the affair. On the contrary, she stated, "I should like the Court to have heard him plead for me to stay. I made an absolute sacrifice of me and mine. I never pressed a thumbscrew to keep him in my power. He made his promise to marry me. I never released him from that promise. He broke it when he married, yet, in talking to me, he maligned his present wife in an abusive manner, beyond my power or wish to tell you."

Madeleine continued: "On the last day that I talked with him, that 17th day of May 1893, he made me believe he would keep his promise. He talked of our unborn child and what we would name it. I did all that he asked. I gave up my babies because he asked it and for fear their parentage would be known. I saw my last baby lying dead in its coffin, dead because it had not been given a mother's care, and yet I concealed from him my sorrow. What more could a woman do?"

There was no concealing sorrow on this day: Madeleine's final words—"I never let him see me cry over it. I never"—trailed into a sob, choked with grief for her dead children, for her lost youth, for her blighted future. In the stillness of the room, men with moist eyes looked away, and jurors fumbled for handkerchiefs. Madeleine's head rested atop her gloved hands, her sobs echoing off the plaster walls. Butterworth approached Carlisle, sitting at the plaintiff's table, and bent to whisper a few words. Carlisle nodded, rose, and quietly suggested that Butterworth's cross-examination be continued the following day. The plaintiff would not object. The bailiff's voice merged with the sound of weeping. Court adjourned. Breckinridge turned to leave the room, a forced smile on his face. His head hung down, and he held his hat in his hand. A cool breeze waved at his snowy locks. Those he passed followed him with their eyes. He spoke to no one.

———————

Jane intercepted Madeleine at four fifteen that afternoon and knew right away the defense had worked the plaintiff hard. Madeleine,

Jane thought, watching her step off the streetcar at Washington Circle, looked entirely dejected and the most miserable-looking person she had seen in a while. Jane headed toward her, pausing only when she saw Miss Ellis, who reminded Jane of a loyal guard dog who sees danger approaching. Before Jane could say hello, Miss Ellis repeated the orders Carlisle had issued once more: no one was to talk to Madeleine. Not even Carlisle had said a word to her, despite wanting to discuss the day's surprising proceedings. "She must have absolute quiet," Ellis said.[38]

Jane plowed ahead anyway, telling Madeleine that she had not yet found Breckinridge's address. A desultory plaintiff replied that it didn't matter; she had only been curious. With memories now fresh of the losses in her life, Madeleine had little else to say. She and Miss Ellis left Jane in the Circle and headed to the Home.

Jane returned to her room and wrote Worthington. She blamed the defense attorneys for Madeleine's malaise, "for they did use up the lady so tremendously during the day." To that critique, she added a complaint about the short accounts of the proceedings that the defense team shared with her. She read the newspapers "very anxiously," but she was, in her words, impatient to know more.[39]

Jane continued to worry about access to Madeleine at the House of Mercy. Miss Ellis had taken on a gatekeeping role, emboldened by Carlisle's directives to wrap Madeleine in calm and silence. Jane had taken to privately referring to Ellis as the "dragon." Jane had an idea, and in concluding her evening report, she asked Worthington for an extra five dollars above her room and board. Dorothea was under the impression that since leaving the Home, Jane took in businessmen's typing. Jane could try to unlock the House of Mercy door with a five-dollar donation, a gift to repay the sisters for the bed and meals provided the week she spent in residence. Jane didn't know what else to do, she told Worthington: "I am having a perfect circus to get in now at all and sometimes am at my wits' end for an excuse."[40]

Jane rose early on Wednesday, March 21, and headed to the corner of Pennsylvania Avenue and Seventeenth Street. She would attempt to encounter Madeleine in the open, on her way to court. Jane scanned the passing streetcars for her quarry. When she saw Madeleine on the front seat of an approaching car, she slipped in behind her and the ever-present "dragon." "Why Aggie," Madeleine said, "you are more devoted than a lover. I never knew anyone to appear in such an astonishing manner as you do. You must spend all your time waiting around on street corners for me." "No," Jane laughed, hoping it sounded effortless; "I needed to run to Woodward and Lothrop and thought if I came down Pennsylvania Avenue perhaps, I would see you." [41]

Despite her disinterest the day before, today Madeleine asked again for Breckinridge's new address. Jane offered the vague excuse that the clerk at the Cochran Hotel, his former residence, had no forwarding address. Try the post office, Madeleine suggested. "What a good idea," Jane replied, as if she were genuinely stymied. Madeleine kept talking, but Jane's focus had drifted, puzzling over why Madeleine wanted her opponent's location. Madeleine made a joke; Jane failed to respond. The sudden silence snapped Jane back to attention.

"Agnes," Madeleine chided, "you are not as smart as I am." Jane knew it was best to agree. Jane declared, "I never could be. You are an extraordinary woman, and I am simply ordinary." Madeleine agreed.

Jane and Madeleine reviewed the previous day's testimony as the streetcar plodded along on its morning commute. Jane had been wrong—the leaked report of Breckinridge's secret marriage had not been fake news. Madeleine had worried that the revelation could cause a mistrial, but her attorneys assured her a secret marriage was a very good thing for her side. Madeleine claimed that men of the jury and even the judge had tears in their eyes as the impact of the congressman's duplicity sank in. Madeleine was in good spirits. She told Jane she had had her say, and she had said her piece well. "Today," she said, "will likely be my last day on the stand."

With the defense soon to take the witness stand, Jane was desperate to discover how the plaintiff would attack Breckinridge's story. Happenstance meetings on streetcars was not enough for getting the information she needed. Stoll needed. "Madeleine," Jane said as if the idea had just occurred to her, "I will come by this evening with tomatoes and a French dressing." Madeleine's eyes lit up at the mention of a fashionable meal—salad with the latest dressing, markers of meals among the leisured class. "But," Jane said, trying a new strategy to enter the House of Mercy, "in exchange Miss Ellis must persuade Sister Dorothea to let me come to the Home and visit you whenever I like—no more barricades and refusals."

"Oh Agnes," Miss Ellis said, "you are such a sweet girl! I will speak with Dorothea. You should certainly be allowed to come up when Madeleine is able to talk." The dragon had softened.

When Madeleine entered the crowded courtroom that morning, she expected another grueling day under the glare of Benjamin Butterworth's cross-examination, but her spark returned when Butterworth attempted to sow seeds of doubt about her Cincinnati pregnancy. Dr. Street, he said, hadn't recognized her at first. Madeleine replied, "But she would have done so if she had had an opportunity on the redirect examination, and she certainly was ready to say that the picture of Colonel Breckinridge was the picture of the man who called to see me in 1885 at her house and—" Butterworth and Wilson both interrupted her. "Hold on, Miss Pollard," yelled Butterworth before she could speak to evidence not yet admitted in court. "You must not tell anything but what I ask you."[42]

"I truly beg your pardon, Mr. Butterworth," Madeleine apologized, "but my mind is so full of things I want to tell you that

I can't help breaking in." The truth of Breckinridge's secret marriage had set her free.

Butterworth continued with a few more questions about Street and when Madeleine came to use *Breckinridge* as a middle name. With his permission, she testified, she had a card plate crafted in 1889 or 1890 adding that middle name. And then, to her surprise, Butterworth released her. "That is all, Miss Pollard," he said. Astonished at the brevity of his interview, she stood to leave; Carlisle motioned her to remain seated on the witness stand. But not for long. He rose and addressed the court: "If your honor please, counsel for the plaintiff rests their case here."[43]

Madeleine Pollard's ordeal had ended. Calderon Carlisle escorted her to the jurors' door. She had done well in this bastion of law and men, an arena where she, too, claimed the civil right to define and defend herself. Madeleine Pollard had offered her story. Now Breckinridge, with his silver tongue and silvery-white locks, would present his.

13

FRENCH DRESSING

Jane walked with determination to her afternoon meeting. She dressed to blend in and covered her face with a veil. In case anyone was watching, she took a circuitous route. Defense Attorney Enoch Totten's I Street house was not conspicuous, but it was in a busy part of town. With the trial so close to a conclusion, Jane could not afford a mistake. As Breckinridge prepared to take the stand to offer his defense, she tried new strategies to uncover the information that would give the congressman a victory. A veil, an illustrator, and French dressing were her secret weapons.[1]

Jane arrived at four o'clock sharp; she rang the bell and told the servant the coded statement, "Miss Parker wants to meet the engagement she had there at four o'clock."[2] Jane was admitted and waited in the parlor for Charles Stoll. Some discussions could only be held in person. Jane had a scheme for Stoll. It was best that Breckinridge not be present.

Jane had arranged for Stoll to meet a friend, newspaper sketch artist Max De Lippman, who was in town illustrating the trial for the *New York Herald*. Through Max, Jane suggested Stoll might win reporters over to the congressman's side by providing insider information that painted Breckinridge in a better light. Stoll could share information not heard in court with De Lippman, who could then pass it to selected members of the press—leads reporters could follow for hot stories. The source would be unnamed. The jury read the newspapers; some of the spectators did—Jane reasoned that articles

with a positive spin might sway a juror or two, bolster public support, and mitigate Breckinridge's flailing defense.

Stoll was game and made plans to meet with Max. Jane
slipped away from the rendezvous, blending into the workers
walking home and DC residents taking a late afternoon stroll. She
reversed her indirect route, stopping at a newsstand to pick up the
afternoon paper. Jane hurried to her room, reviewed the news of
the court, and wrote her mother a quick note until the dinner bell
interrupted her thoughts. She signed off, grabbed a whisk and a
few groceries, and headed to K Street.[3]

Putting on a disguise and taking winding paths to secret meetings
was standard fare for detectives, but none of the many detectives
Breckinridge had hired had considered cooking for Madeleine.
Unlike her male counterparts, Jane realized that in her isolation,
Madeleine lacked a mainstay of female Victorian life—the bond
between mother and daughter, or sisters, or close female friends,
and what better way for faux friend Jane to provide that caretak-
ing role than to fill a lonely Madeleine's needs with food.

Tomato salad was a strategic choice. Lettuce and vegeta-
ble salads were increasingly popular with the middle class in the
1890s, and a French dressing nodded to a culinary appreciation
among the well-heeled for French food and chefs. Even a recipe as simple as a French dressing—in the 1890s, a vinaigrette
of oil, vinegar, salt, and pepper—signaled to Madeleine that her
new friend recognized her refined palate. The meal was a culinary
compliment.[4]

Jane's refined gift thrilled Madeleine. Jane cut and seeded
the tomatoes, then dressed the salad, entertaining Madeleine and
feeding her many hungers. Jane later wrote to Stoll, "It is astonishing how much more agreeable she is when I take her something
to eat."[5]

Madeleine was agreeable this evening but had no interest
in answering Jane's questions about her past; tonight she was

focused on her future. Madeleine pointed to the mountain of mail piling up in her room, excited by the letters and offers arriving daily. Sympathetic women cheered her on, lonely men offered marriage, and businessmen smelling profit promised lucrative opportunities. A New York show promoter offered Madeleine $3000 for three lectures on "What I Know about Colonel Breckinridge." An opera company would pay $500 a week. Other promoters didn't care if she could sing or act—her name alone would be the draw.

Jane oohed and aahed over the possibilities, hoping to hear a decision on posttrial plans. Madeleine's next step might reveal the rationale behind the lawsuit—Was it money? Fame? Jane suggested she accept both the lecture series and the opera company. "The money," Jane said, "could set you up for life." Madeleine shook her head, momentary thoughts of stardom fading, her mood somber. "I could not sell my shame in that way. I shall never be able to face the public after this trial is over. I could not go on the stage."

Jane returned to her typewriter with little to show for the evening except a handful of letters supporting the most well-known woman in America.

In the fourth week of the trial, on the Thursday after Easter, Madeleine sat in Calderon Carlisle's office. Miss Ellis and Dudley kept her company while the last of the defense's depositions were read into the record. Madeleine had not attended court for much of the week, having had no desire to listen to vile lies. Over the previous weekend, Judge Bradley, in a closed courtroom, had reviewed the defense's depositions gathered in Kentucky and decided which ones could be heard in court. He had announced at the start of Monday's session that some of the depositions that would be heard were, in his mind, indecent. He appealed to the press to suppress the details for the good of public morality.[6]

At 1:45 p.m., Carlisle's clerk raced into the office: Colonel Breckinridge was about to take the stand. Madeleine grabbed her coat and rushed from the room, neglecting to say a word to her brother, Miss Ellis hurrying to keep pace with the plaintiff.

The courtroom was packed—every bench, chair, and floor spot taken. The sultry day raised the humidity, and one reporter made note of the room's pungent odor. The crowd leaned forward, craning heads to lay eyes on Breckinridge. Butterworth commenced the defense, calling the congressman to testify. Breckinridge took his place at the witness stand, his public prominence reiterated in his height looming over the courtroom. He rested his right hand on the witness table and placed his left arm on Judge Bradley's desk, casually leaning as if having bourbon at a bar. His ruddy face was pinker than usual, and it provided a striking contrast to his snow-white hair and beard. Breckinridge had only just begun when Madeleine entered the room with Miss Ellis, their skirts rustling as they walked to the plaintiff's table, the crowd murmuring at their presence. He paused while they took their seats. Madeleine kept her eyes firmly fixed on the man who ruined her life. When she tired, she leaned her head into her hand, but she did not remove her gaze from Breckinridge.[7]

Breckinridge had lived with a secret—this was the tale the eager, gaping men of the packed courtroom came to hear. Benjamin Butterworth asked his client, "When and where did you first meet the plaintiff?" And from here, the congressman told his story, standing at the witness table.

"In the spring of 1884," Breckinridge began, "I took the train between Lexington and Frankfort."

According to him, Madeleine approached him on the train. Later, she invited him to visit the college. She said she needed his help. At the college, he said, she shared that she had given James Rodes "a higher proof than that contract."

He claimed the plaintiff—he would not utter Madeleine's name—suggested continuing their conversation beyond the college, and she picked an entertainment on Vine Street. He did select the carriage but with no thought to whether it was open or closed. During their ride, the windows were open.

Breckinridge waved his hand in a deprecatory gesture to dismiss any suspicion of impropriety, knocking a glass tumbler from the stand. The crash startled the spectators, rapt in attention.

The ride began entirely properly, Breckinridge continued. The plaintiff was a fully grown woman of perfectly proper manners, very deferential. And then . . .

"She removed her hat and placed it on the front seat. I made no declarations of love. What occurred next, occurred naturally. I put my arm around her and drew her to me, across my lap, in one motion." The courtroom was silent. Breckinridge continued: "I was a man with passion, she was a woman with passion, and I took liberties with her person; without any protestation on my part or her part, without any seduction on the part of either, she was willing and complacent; no outcry, and no protest." "This was just a case of illicit love," he said. "I am a man, she a woman; human, both of us."

As the carriage returned to the college, he continued, hardly a word was spoken. Under the gaslight, Breckinridge put a ten-dollar bill in an envelope. She refused to take it. He insisted. He put the envelope in her hand, closed her fingers around it, and bid her goodnight.

With this part of the story told, the day's testimony came to an end. Breckinridge had stood the entire time. Madeleine waited with her attorneys until the crowd had thinned and Breckinridge had left the courtroom. With head slightly bowed, she exited, ignoring the curious as they gawked and gazed.

———————

Jane did not witness Madeleine's return to the House of Mercy, but Miss Ellis and Dorothea later described the ensuing scene. Madeleine had stormed through the door, livid. To her ears, Madeleine had heard nothing but lies.[8]

Dorothea told Jane how Madeleine yelled and ranted "like a crazy person." Miss Ellis and Dorothea struggled to get her to her room, and it took several of the sisters to put her into bed and hold her there as she thrashed and whipped her head around in a fit of temper. The matron called for a traditional treatment—the nuns placed Madeleine's feet in scalding water and applied mustard plasters to her neck. Her fit subsided. Dorothea sent a note to the attorneys. When Carlisle and Wilson learned of the attack, they worried.

It was just as well that Jane could not see Madeleine. She was to meet Stoll at 9:00 p.m. in Dupont Circle.[9] Stoll arrived on time. They made sure they were not being watched. He shared that Jane's plan had worked—Jane's sketch artist friend had helped Breckinridge get some positive press. Stoll was tickled to death. Jane later crowed to her mother, "We are deep, dark schemers, we people. Max was all my idea. You see, your family have some good ideas now and then."[10]

————————

On his second day on the stand, Breckinridge continued his tale, again ignoring a seat in favor of standing.[11] He had arrived in court with an injury, and as he testified, a bandaged finger remained nervously active, toying with his spectacles case or running through his hair. Breckinridge spoke firmly and carefully, pausing after each word. He testified without hesitation or break, Butterworth getting in a question only by interrupting him when he missed a planned point or a bit of elaboration was needed, and then only a handful of times. If anyone could tell a convincing tale, it was Breckinridge, the famed silver-tongued orator.

He picked up his testimony with the August 1884 train ride from Cincinnati to Lexington. Madeleine's presence on the train surprised the congressman. On the journey, the plaintiff suggested Sarah Gist's house, a place, Breckinridge said, she knew from visits with James Rodes. As Madeleine had testified, she waited on the porch while Breckinridge ate dinner with his family.

When he returned to Gist's, Breckinridge said, the plaintiff neither resisted nor protested. "She was a fully developed young woman with nothing to indicate that she was not experienced in the relations of the sexes." Less than an hour after his arrival, he left. He saw her again on Saturday and Sunday. "At no time then, or until this suit," Breckinridge insisted, "did the plaintiff say I seduced her."

He went on. "On Monday, election day, I encountered James Rodes at the polling place." Rodes indicated that not only did he want to marry Madeleine, but, as a respectable man, he *should* marry her. "He asked me what he should do."

Madeleine interrupted from the plaintiff's table: "Oh, I say he never did." Wilson urged restraint, whispering to her, "You will have your chance by and by." Madeleine cried out, "He isn't telling the truth about anything!" Judge Bradley warned her: keep quiet or leave.

Breckinridge described a sporadic relationship, meeting occasionally or by happenstance. After their initial trysts in the fall of 1884, he did not recall seeing her again until August 1885 and then not at all in 1886. "In that time," he said, "I did not have any correspondence with the plaintiff." Madeleine whispered to her lawyers that it wasn't so.

In the summer of 1887, Breckinridge said, Madeleine told him she was going to Washington. He did everything possible to prevent it. He told her that the city was no place for a young woman. And he wanted to avoid a scandal.

Breckinridge recalled the unpleasant conversation. Madeleine announced she was pregnant. He refused to give her money; he doubted he was the father. He told the court, "We had only resumed our relations for two months!" Then, he claimed, Madeleine revealed, two years after the fact, that she had been pregnant in 1885. He was the father. She had miscarried; her mother had cared for her. Breckinridge said he had no idea.

Madeleine's shoulders shook; Ellis struggled to prevent an outcry.

Breckinridge said, "I had told her that to come to Washington would be disastrous to both her and me. She came anyway in September 1887."

Breckinridge continued. He had little contact with Madeleine until well into the spring of 1888. He learned she had moved to the Academy of the Visitation on Massachusetts Avenue. She wrote that she was in bad health. Breckinridge had sent money whenever she needed it.

She had told him her second pregnancy had also ended in miscarriage. Breckinridge paid the bills, but he didn't trust Dr. Parsons. He felt her charges were high. When he received a second bill, he grew concerned and insisted they meet. Breckinridge worried she knew the true nature of his relationship with Madeleine. He reasoned, "If she were a legitimate physician, she would be bound to keep our secret; if she attempted blackmail, I decided I would rather face it head-on." They met, and Parsons received Breckinridge's approval. But, he asserted, "When I met Parsons, she never mentioned a living child. I did not know that the plaintiff had ever given birth to a living child until I heard Dr. Parsons' testimony in this courtroom." As to paternity, "considering the timing of our encounters," he claimed, "this child could not have been mine." At the plaintiff's table, Madeleine clenched her fists.

Breckinridge claimed their problems really began when Madeleine came to Washington against his will. He knew this relationship could end only in scandal and told her so. Madeleine stalked him, interrupting his work at the Capitol, refusing to leave, and demanding money. Breckinridge grew very angry and spoke harshly to her. "I knew," he said to the court, "that I had few alternatives: submit to her will or destroy my family."

"She would agree to go away but would then return. I was willing to support any endeavor." Madeleine went to Cambridge, Massachusetts, but returned against his wishes. When she spent the summer at Bread Loaf, they had agreed that the affair was over, but she returned to Washington after a few weeks. Breckinridge countered Madeleine's testimony: "I did not propose marriage in a carriage ride. If it had not been for the death of my wife, our relationship would have ended then."

The court remained enthralled, and Breckinridge continued his story after the noon recess.

Breckinridge had urged her to take the civil service exam, and he helped her get civil service jobs. He brought her reading material from the Congressional Library. "She was," he said, "a woman of decided intellect."

In the fall of 1892, Madeleine was offered a chance to study in Germany. She asked Breckinridge for a monthly stipend and traveling expenses and wanted to go as his fiancée. Breckinridge said, "This was the first time the possibility of marriage was ever raised. I told her that I would find the money to send her abroad, but under no circumstances could she call herself my fiancée. She then refused to go." He told her again that their relationship could never end in marriage, only scandal.

That winter, they fought frequently. Nonetheless, on the stand, Breckinridge said, "From January to March 1893, I saw the plaintiff on average five times a week, sometimes three or four times daily."

In late February, he said, the plaintiff came to him in distress. Mrs. Fillette concluded the plaintiff was an adventuress and had told Mrs. Blackburn. Madeleine demanded that Breckinridge tell Blackburn that their relations were proper so that she would stand by her. Breckinridge refused.

He shared how the plaintiff threatened suicide several times and threatened to kill him too. Madeleine told Blackburn that she was engaged and then demanded he confirm it. Breckinridge described how they agreed that he would pretend there was an engagement if Madeleine promised to leave Washington. He had no choice but to do as she demanded, he explained. It was this or risk Madeleine causing a scene or worse. Breckinridge claimed he made this deal to protect his loved ones. Madeleine held all the power in this ill-fated relationship. He never intended to marry her, but by using her sexual influence, which disreputable women have over men, Madeleine held a "terrorizing influence over him" and made him fall into her nefarious plan. Breckinridge argued he was the victim here, not Madeleine Pollard.

The testimony gripped the spectators as the defendant described the collapse of his long affair with Madeleine. His description of the Good Friday visit to Mrs. Blackburn's mirrored Madeleine's and Blackburn's testimonies. Breckinridge described how after the short conversation with Blackburn, he walked the plaintiff to her house without a word. He said, "I put the key in the front door and told her that she must leave Washington or I would tell Mrs. Blackburn the true nature of our relationship. She agreed to go as soon as she could."

"On May 1 in New York City," he said, "I was surprised to find the plaintiff at the Hoffman House in an adjoining room."

He confirmed that Madeleine's account was accurate. He had been absent for two days, she was angry, and they argued. "I replied," he said, "perhaps more rudely than needed." Breckinridge retreated to his room, Madeleine pulled a gun, and he closed the adjoining door, locked the latch, and pushed the electric call button.

"The bellboy," he said, "arrived in response to my bell. I opened the door. I asked for a pitcher of ice water. I don't know if he saw how excited I was; I don't know if I was as cool as I might have been."

The spectators laughed.

Breckinridge countered some of the details of Madeleine's version. He denied stating, at the conclusion of their fight, that he would marry Madeleine; he denied disparaging his new wife. He admitted to the court that he married Louise Wing on April 29 while Madeleine waited at the hotel, stating it as if a wedding was an afterthought.

His account of the second visit to Major Moore's office mirrored Madeleine's and Moore's descriptions. "Yes," Breckinridge had said to the plaintiff in Moore's presence, "I will marry you on the last day of the month if God don't interpose."

"A few days later, she attempted to shoot me at the home of Mrs. Thomas. I escaped injury." And with that dramatic scene, the court adjourned.

When Jane arrived at the House of Mercy, Madeleine was in bed but in a surprisingly cheerful mood. She assessed her adversary's defense. He put out nothing but a string of lies, sniffed the plaintiff. "He did not dare look me in the face once." Madeleine took that as a triumph.[12]

She grew wistful: "I have lost all the old feeling for Col. Breckinridge, that sort of going out to him with my whole heart and soul whenever I saw him, that answering of my heart to his whenever I looked into his eyes—that is all gone." The lawyers need not fear any more outbursts; she had "not a particle of feeling for him left."

Jane had asked Stoll what information would be helpful, and he urged her to question Madeleine about the letter she wrote in 1884, asking for Breckinridge's help with Rodes. The defense believed the letter proved that she initiated the intimate relationship with the congressman that summer. Suspecting that Breckinridge's testimony might have riled up Madeleine, Stoll urged Jane to exploit her nervous condition to get answers. It was the advice Jane had previously offered to him.[13]

Jane asked. Madeleine claimed the letter was a forgery, and she railed against those who would not simply take her word as truth. "*I* said *I* did not write that letter," Madeleine reiterated, in her anger revealing the plaintiff's strategy. The defense had brought in a handwriting expert to claim she had written the letter; the plaintiff planned to bring one in to prove she hadn't. It was a stalemate. But Madeleine knew whether or not she wrote it would not mean much; the letter had little bearing on the events that followed, and asking a lawyer for help was not a crime.[14]

Jane and Madeleine had fallen into an evening routine. Madeleine read aloud newspaper articles that praised her. Her face would become radiant, delighted to see her former lover on the losing end. Then Madeleine would report on her latest offers. A Cincinnati theater manager had made an offer, but the attorneys forbid her from accepting. Jere Wilson offered advice: "He said that I had better things in store for me; that I was a lady in spite of the past and that I must not do anything that would cause the world to treat me otherwise."[15] As one of her many correspondents wrote, "You are not 'ruined,' but *hindered*."[16] Her attorney had an optimistic prediction. "He said," Madeleine shared with Jane, "that I would have plenty of the good things in life without exhibiting myself." Jane pressed for details. Had she settled on a plan?

"I haven't made up my mind yet," Madeleine said. The sole decision, she laughed, was to leave the House of Mercy as soon as the trial had ended. Win or lose, she would not need the protective shield the institution provided. If Wilson and Carlisle suggested she stay, she would know they were not true friends. She laughed at her joke.

Jane asked if Madeleine would be at the next court session. Madeleine said, "I wouldn't miss being there for anything in the world." Second only to the empowering feeling of herself testifying was the pleasure of watching Breckinridge dig himself into a hole.

———————

Stoll had another scheme, and only Jane had the knowledge to make it work. He proposed they write a book together, exposing the "real" Madeleine Pollard—a behind-the-curtain look at the plaintiff when she was not performing in court, an exposure of the woman described in the depositions Judge Bradley had dismissed. Jane's insights from her time with Madeleine at the House of Mercy would be invaluable. Such a book, Stoll explained, could swing public sympathy to Breckinridge. "I realize," Stoll apologized, "that this work will delay your return to Maine by a month or more, but in the end," he said, "the compensation could be generous, as much as $1000 for each of us."[17] Jane agreed.

Thinking about it later, Jane realized the scheme was just desperate enough to signal what she had not wanted to believe: Stoll thought Breckinridge might lose, and he was already planning the next steps—a retrial, an appeal, a public relations boost for his reelection campaign. But she knew it too. Madeleine was outsmarting them all.

On the weekend, as March ended and April began, Jane wrote a long letter to her mother. She and Max had spent a day together at Mount Vernon, giving Jane a chance to pass along items about Madeleine that he could share with reporters. If she had qualms about the book project, concerns about publicly exposing Madeleine's private moments, Max would be a good confidant—but she didn't tell her mother any of that.[18]

Jane did tell Mollie that there was more money to be made. She explained that she and Stoll were going to work together on a project, details left unsaid, and they would split the profits. She warned her mother, "This is a great secret, but I think I will have to tell you this much in order for you to understand why I cannot come right home."[19]

Even more gold was on the horizon. She told Mollie that Stoll was contemplating running for governor of Kentucky, and if he did, he wanted Jane to help run his campaign. Jane's future was beginning to look as bright as Madeleine's. She closed her letter: "I can't stop for any more today as I must attend to business even on Sunday. I must file up my wits and go upon the warpath."[20] Jane headed to the House of Mercy.

Later Sunday evening, Jane returned to her desk and typed her report. Madeleine remained confident of victory. Her rebuttal witnesses, she had told Jane, would make the day. Jane reported a victory—she had learned who would appear: Martha McClellan Brown, the vice president of Cincinnati Wesleyan College; Madeleine's Pittsburgh cousin, now a respected doctor; and her aunt Lou Keene and another cousin, who would document young Mattie's residence at their homes at the times when the defense's dirty depositions alleged Madeleine had frequented a brothel in another town. Indeed, Madeleine's witnesses were so strong that she told Jane they were not going to bother to take on the defense's brothel allegations: a rebuttal was not worth the plaintiff's energy.[21]

Jane paused: the witnesses for the plaintiff would appear in person, no dry depositions to be read into the record. Jane shook her head at the defendant's strategy. "Why," she wrote Stoll, "are you not bringing in live witnesses?" Jane asked about evidence she had obtained and shared: "You have let witnesses leave town—one of them a congressman of national reputation. My newspaper friend tells me Madeleine fell for the congressman and tried to snare him, too. There's a letter from her to him—why are you not calling him to the stand?" She went on: "Then, there is the young man from the Elsmere Hotel. I heard she danced with him and, afterward, became very friendly outside." The depositions from intemperate, philandering men, read into the record by monotone lawyers in front of a jury struggling to stay awake, were not helping the case. Jane reported a final blow: Madeleine would be the last person to take the stand, rebutting the congressman's narrative. It was the last voice the jury would hear. And with her magnetic charisma, this would weigh heavily.

"Well, of course," Jane concluded her report, "you no doubt know these stories already."

14

Treacherous Type-Writers, She-Fanatics, and the Short-Haired Women of Boston

Breckinridge was doing himself no favors on the stand, and Jane Tucker was worried. From the bungled cross-examination of Julia Churchill Blackburn at the start of the trial to the congressman's increasingly testy assertions of victimhood, the defense had not put forth a cogent argument. Realizing the trial was coming to an end, she doubled down on her talks with Sister Dorothea and Madeleine, who was still undecided about her future plans. There were a few surprises left, and in the remaining days, the balance of the trial would be tipped by women witnesses, one who would make Jane furious and another who would put her in danger.

As he continued his testimony, Breckinridge related his take on the end of the affair and his responsibilities toward his unborn child. The second visit to Major Moore in May 1893 had marked the end of Breckinridge and Madeleine's time together, although neither one knew that at the time. During that visit, Breckinridge said from the witness stand, "I told her, 'You know I never seduced you. I took liberties with you the first time I ever saw you, and I slept with you the next night, with your full consent.'"[1] Breckinridge recalled: Madeleine had tried to press her own demands in front of Moore, but after this statement, she said nothing and took out her pistol, looked at Moore and me, and then put it away.

I suggested she give it to Major Moore, and she did. We left his office; Madeleine left for New York shortly after.

The affair, despite all the threats with guns, had not ended with a bang but with a whimper.

While the congressman droned on, Wilson and Carlisle fiddled with an ominous bundle of papers, folding, refolding, and shuffling the contents. The *Enquirer* reporter watched. The attorneys were careful to shield the documents from prying eyes. Something explosive, the reporter suspected, was hidden within.

———————

"I left Washington for Lexington the next day," Breckinridge testified, "secure that the plaintiff had gone to New York and our relationship was over. All that was left was the child." The plaintiff, he claimed, "wanted to get rid of the child, but I told her no," his accusation of an act thought unwomanly in the Gilded Age hovering in the air. Breckinridge painted himself as the true parent, claiming he could tell if the child was his at birth; if it was, he planned to give it all the advantages possible to a child born out of wedlock.

Those advantages, coming from a man who doubted the paternity of the child, the fidelity of his mistress, and the professionalism of Madeleine's female physician, one would imagine, would be pretty few.

Breckinridge described the exchange of letters and telegrams in the early summer. In June, he learned Madeleine had announced the engagement. He denied it. He asked Major Moore to prevent Madeleine from coming to Lexington or going to the Washington press, but Moore couldn't find her. He had sent one hundred dollars for Madeleine's care. Moore sent it back. Breckinridge arrived in Washington with his new wife on August 6. "I learned when the suit was entered that she had miscarried, and this relieved me of any obligation to contribute to her support."

His cool dismissal of his mistress ended the congressman's defense and the morning session of court.

In the afternoon session, Jeremiah Wilson began the cross-examination. Breckinridge glared at Madeleine from the stand. He admitted he had no excuse for his actions. "The hell that I have undergone in ten years has been no more than I deserved," he told Wilson. "Only one other form of hell could be equal to it, and that would be to marry the woman."² Madeleine did not flinch.

The cross-examination went over old stories. Jeremiah Wilson reviewed the high points of the ill-fated romance: Madeleine's initial request for help with James Rodes's contract, the 1884 carriage ride, and Sarah Gist's assignation house. Breckinridge denied there was ever talk of marriage, denied their engagement, denied he forced her to give up children. On and on—if Madeleine testified it was black, Breckinridge said it was white.

And then the tension in the courtroom went up a notch. Wilson paused and then asked the congressman if he had a sister in Lexington named Louise. "No," replied Breckinridge; he had no sister named Louise.

"Do you know a woman in Washington by the name of Louise Lowell?" Wilson asked.

Breckinridge puzzled over the odd question. No, he responded, he knew no such person.

Wilson prompted his memory: Did he recall a type-writer (typist) set up in the corridor of the House of Representatives, near the rooms for the Committee on Printing and the Committee on Post Offices?

"There had always been a woman there," Breckinridge recalled, answering slowly, "but," he continued, he did not remember her name. "If she was brought to court," he said, "I might recognize her."

Wilson pounced: "You claimed you wrote no letters to Miss Pollard in 1886, but didn't you take in February of 1886 a hand-written letter beginning 'My Dear Sister Louise' and ask Miss Lowell to type it?"

Breckinridge grew cautious.

"Since I have no recollection of a woman named Louise Lowell," Breckinridge answered, visibly rankled, "I cannot remember having sent any letter to her." He added, thinking out loud, "Of course, I have a very large correspondence. I have a sister-in-law named Louise, the wife of General Breckinridge, but since she is called Lou in the family, I don't think I could have written in that way. Let me see the letter," he demanded.

Wilson deflected the request with a cool response—"That will come out in time"—and then continued, poking the bear, "Now, to refresh your memory, did you not, in that communication, refer to the disparity of ages between yourself and your dear sister Louise?"

Breckinridge's attorneys stood and demanded the letter, protesting this line of questioning, multiple attorneys speaking at once.

Wilson continued, "Now, to further refresh your memory, did you not say how anxious you were to get back and meet your dear sister once more?"

"I have not the faintest recollection of any such letter, and I don't care to discuss it." Breckinridge continued, throwing down a challenge to the plaintiff's team, "If you will bring the Lowell woman here, if there is such a person, and let me see whether I have ever known her or whether her testimony is a fabrication like that of Sarah Gist, I can tell you."

Wilson did not take the bait. He then asked the nettled Breckinridge if, after two or three months of correspondence, he cautioned his dear sister Louise not to leave the letters around in case curious people searched bureau drawers.

"I never, under any circumstances, wrote any such letter," answered Breckinridge, hitting the witness stand sharply to emphasize each word, "and if any such letter is in existence, it is a forgery, and if notes of any such, they are a forgery." And again Breckinridge offered to provide an identification, calling what he thought was Wilson's bluff: "I can only say if you bring the lady here, I can tell you whether she ever did any work for me. Several women or females have done typewriting in Washington, but I do not remember this particular one."

Breckinridge was not one to remember the name of casual employees. Earlier in the trial, he had asked Jane to quiz Madeleine on potential witnesses from New York City. He explained how "I cannot recall them at all, and if I ever knew them I have forgotten them, or they may be persons I know very well, but whose names I have no special interest in knowing, like clerks in hotels."[3]

He would come to remember Louise Lowell.

Wilson asked his final question of the day, clueing in Breckinridge as to what Lowell had to offer: "Did you not bring to her in the spring of 1886 a package of a dozen envelopes, somewhat yellowed by age and of different dates, and have her address them to Miss Madeleine Pollard, No. 76 Upper Street, Lexington, Kentucky?"

Breckinridge was emphatic: "I never, under any circumstances, had any such envelopes addressed, and I do not care who the woman is who says so!"[4]

Jane was not the only woman on an undercover mission. After court adjourned that day, with the specter of the mysterious Louise Lowell looming over the case, Sarah Ellis and Madeleine undertook a secret task at the behest of Calderon Carlisle and Jeremiah Wilson. From the courthouse, Ellis and Madeleine hopped onto the F Street streetcar; coincidentally, Breckinridge had boarded the same car and stood on the rear platform. Madeleine attempted to pass by him, his bulk crowding the aisle. She was so close she brushed his arm as she squeezed by. She refused to look at him; if he saw her, he ignored her. One would think they were perfect strangers.

The awkward encounter between plaintiff and defendant was momentarily disquieting, but it did not delay the mission. Madeleine and Ellis made their way to the home of Dr. Mary Parsons to ask for her help with a mutual acquaintance. Parsons agreed to the task and promised to make a report to Mr. Carlisle, in person, the next morning at nine.[5]

That evening at the House of Mercy, Madeleine told Jane all about her secret meeting with Dr. Parsons. Jane listened, agog at what she was hearing as Madeleine shared her adventure. Dr. Parsons had been so friendly to her, enthused Madeleine, joyful at being welcomed in a fine home instead of shunned. In addition to her help with the acquaintance, Madeleine reported, the doctor offered to appear in court for rebuttal. Parsons was quite indignant at Breckinridge's lies and his suspicion of her medical legitimacy. Jane nodded encouragement as Madeleine continued. Parsons, she told Jane, had copies of advertisements from 1888 when she had sought a wet nurse to help Madeleine postdelivery—documentation to support Dietz's birth and Madeleine's ill health and sorrow.[6]

Jane did not have to fake interest in Madeleine's conversation this night. Madeleine continued to offer gold. Parsons revealed additional intelligence: Mrs. Eva Thomas, with whom Madeleine had lived in the spring of 1892 and in whose home she had miscarried her third pregnancy, was in Florida, address unknown. But the Thomas cook, still in Washington, had information to share.

Jane offered admiring comments on Madeleine's great adventure, praising her cleverness and bravery. Flush with the success of her mission, Madeleine asked Jane to deliver a message to Attorney Carlisle's home straightaway. Jane was all too happy to do so—and she did, taking a detour first to copy the contents of Madeleine's note.[7] She wrote quickly, loops and swirls recording the plaintiff's plot, and for safety's sake, folded the paper and hid it. Jane then dropped Madeleine's missive at Carlisle's home, cautiously certain that a servant, and not Carlisle, would answer the door. Nonetheless, she moved quickly away from the attorney's residence and headed directly to Q Street to make her evening report to Stoll and Breckinridge in person. This news was big. It was worth the risk of being spotted.[8]

The Q Street brownstone hummed with the sound of men talking as they reviewed Breckinridge's testimony and strategized for the continued cross-examination. The butler showed Jane to the parlor. Tables were piled with transcripts and copies of depositions; newspapers were open to recaps of the day in court; half-sipped glasses of bourbon were likely in hand. The congressman, Stoll, Butterworth, Desha, and Breckinridge's Lexington law partner, John Shelby, listened as Jane skimmed over the usual evening routine of Madeleine reading aloud positive newspaper accounts and letters that praised her bravery or offered her jobs. Jane hurried to two crucial revelations.

First, Jane revealed the location of Mrs. Eva Thomas, solving the mysterious disappearance of a potentially key witness. Thomas's Black cook, though, did not have the same luxury to leave town and winter incognito in Southern climes, out of the reach of attorneys. Jane told the defense team that the plaintiff's team would call the cook, Mary Yancy, as a rebuttal witness. Yancy had seen Breckinridge's numerous visits to Madeleine at Thomas's home and remembered clearly the affectionate lunches and the flowers, candy, and gifts the congressman had brought.[9]

Jane then pulled out her shorthand copy of Madeleine's note to Carlisle. Jane explained: the plaintiff's team was going to call Mary McKenzie to the stand in rebuttal. Breckinridge interrupted Jane—he denied ever having visited Madeleine at McKenzie's home while she recovered from childbirth. "This would come to nothing," he opined, dismissing her report. "There's more," Jane said, reclaiming the floor. She had the attention of all the men in the room. Jane said her piece: the plaintiff's team was coaching witnesses. Dr. Parsons was with McKenzie that very evening. They were telling McKenzie what to say. A stunned silence filled the room.[10]

As the men argued about what Mary McKenzie might say on the stand, Jane slipped from the room and headed for the door. Louise Wing Breckinridge padded after her, reaching for her hand. "Miss Parker," she began, holding Jane's ink-smudged hand in her soft, cool one, "I have been so anxious to know you and to tell you how thoroughly we all appreciate what you have done for us all." Sophonisba was nearby, nodding and cordial.

Jane felt sorry for Louise Breckinridge. Louise had imagined in her new life in Washington she would enjoy entertaining dinner guests as a congressman's wife, not giving over her quarters each night to lawyers reviewing the sordid and obscene. And, Jane thought, as Madeleine had said earlier on the stand, living with Breckinridge could not be easy. Louise had received numerous letters, some kind and some caustic, urging her to divorce. But she refused. Louise told Jane, "You are helping to vindicate a good man, and you will always have our deepest love and gratitude for the brave efforts you have made to help us."[11]

———————

The courtroom filled quickly on Tuesday, and curious spectators eyed a new woman seated at the plaintiff's table. Breckinridge prepared to take the stand and continue the cross-examination, but Jere Wilson—with a twinkle in his eye, recorded a reporter—announced new, surprise evidence: letters from Breckinridge to Madeleine Pollard that countered the congressman's claim that he did not write her in 1886 and 1887. The defense immediately objected, setting off a considerable legal squabble. Bradley consulted law books and rendered his decision: although the plaintiff had rested her case, the law allowed such evidence to be introduced for the purpose of including it in the cross-examination of Breckinridge's prior claims. Wilson smiled; Butterworth grumbled.[12]

Breckinridge remained at the defense table, and Jere Wilson called Louise Lowell.

When Louise Lowell sat in the witness chair, she all but disappeared. She wore a reddish-brown bonnet, drab gloves, and a dark-green dress with a narrow gilt braid covered by a cape. A dotted veil dropped from her hat, covering her graying dark hair. Her forehead betrayed lines of worry. Jeremiah Wilson had promised a sensation, and Lowell's testimony delivered.When Jane read in the newspaper what had transpired in court, she was horrified. Lowell, in her eyes, was a traitor to the stenographic arts.[13]

Born in Maine, Lowell arrived in Washington in 1881 and found a position as a type-writer and clerk for the Treasury Department, earning $900 annually. A single woman, she shifted to self-employment as a stenographer in 1884, living in and working from her brother's home, an ideal arrangement while helping care for her brother's children. Their poor mother had been deemed insane. Before coming to Washington, Lowell made clear, "I had not been compelled to work for anyone," emphasizing her point with a toss of her head.[14]

In 1886, she was a stenographer and type-writer for members of the House of Representatives, one of several women who set up a typewriting service in the halls of the Capitol. Lowell testified that she typed for Breckinridge from February 1886 until she left the Capitol in 1890. She had no difficulty deciphering his scratchy handwriting; she typed letters, speeches, or other documents from his manuscript drafts, returning to him the manuscript original with the typed copies.

Lowell kept her records in small memorandum books. For each client, she recorded the amount of work completed, the name of the party, and the charge. She never recorded the substance of any document "so that no Congressman need waste worry for fear that the ledger will rise up to get them into trouble."[15] Her little red memorandum book for the Forty-Ninth Congress indicated she typed for Breckinridge fifteen or sixteen times, but she was certain her book did not show all her work. She recalled that she had worked for the congressman nearly every week.

Lowell described how she had typed letters to "My Dear Sister Louise" and addressed envelopes to Miss Pollard in Lexington. She pulled out the memo book and handed it to Attorney Wilson. She had recorded the congressman's name and the charges for each task. Typically, she did not record to whom letters were written or the addresses typed on envelopes, except for Madeleine's address, which she had written on the flyleaf.

Wilson passed the memorandum book to Breckinridge. He examined it seated at the defense table, coat rumpled around his rotund frame. "Why," Wilson asked Lowell, "did you make this note of the Lexington address?" Lowell had a feeling, she said, that she would be hearing more of Miss Pollard. The clandestine correspondence seemed unusual "coming from an old man," she said, and that had impressed her memory. "Woman-like," one reporter noted, "she made a memorandum of it."[16]

The envelopes were particularly curious, Lowell recalled. Sometimes the congressman brought just one envelope to be addressed; at another time, Breckinridge brought a package containing not quite a dozen small white envelopes, yellowed with age. Lowell told the court they were not envelopes typically used in business. She addressed them and returned them to Breckinridge.

Madeleine confirmed that she had received typewritten letters from Breckinridge while Congress was in session in 1886–87. The letters began sweetly: "My dear sister Louise," "My dear spitfire," or "My dear sweetheart." The congressman had signed each letter with a soft, lead pencil. She destroyed them after reading them.

Breckinridge, back on the stand, denied writing letters to Madeleine, having Lowell type them, and having packages of envelopes addressed—yellowed, white, or otherwise. He had never used any such endearments as Madeleine had claimed. As for the charming letters to his "spitfire" that prompted Louise Lowell, "woman-like," to record Madeleine's Lexington address, Breckinridge denied it all: Madeleine and Louise Lowell were wrong. Or lying.

While Breckinridge faced Lowell in court, Jane had spent the afternoon with Sister Dorothea and the House of Mercy ledger book. Jane's pen scratched along the account pages, entering income and expenses in neat, orderly rows. "Sister Dorothea," Jane asked, "I see that your meal expenses have risen, but sewing income has declined." Jane knew she poked at a sore point, and she got the desired response: Sister Dorothea unleashed her pent-up anger.[17]

The trial was to blame. "Oh yes," Jane agreed, nodding to keep the words flowing. "It was doubtless very kind of you to allow Miss Ellis to go to court with Miss Pollard" even though the Home was criticized for supporting Madeleine in this way.

"I know," Dorothea said wearily. Madeleine had imposed on the sisters since they first met her in September. Dorothea's keys rattled. "Mr. Carlisle asked me to allow Miss Ellis to go down with Madeleine for a few days until he could find a substitute. I thought the girl was really ill then, for she did impose upon me at first with her pretended sickness, and I felt I could not do less than to send some woman with her when she was liable to faint at any moment and to need a woman's care. They have kept on from day to day, and each time I protest, they tell me it will be for only a few days longer."

Jane lobbed another arrow. "How much did Miss Pollard pay the Home for Miss Ellis's time?"

"She has never paid us a cent, and I do not believe she ever will do so or pay Miss Ellis either." Dorothea took a breath. "The Home has paid Miss Ellis her regular monthly salary of $15 just the same, but by reason of Miss Ellis's absence, we have lost what the sewing room would have earned. I have several orders now waiting for her return to her duties and could have more work if we could do it. We have earned but twenty-five cents this month."

Jane made appreciative nods and sympathetic noises.

Dorothea looked around to make sure they were alone, no curious nuns or eavesdropping girls hovering nearby. She dropped her voice. "I have not told you of the trouble we have had here over this. It is a long story. I tried to put a stop to Sarah Ellis's going down there anymore, and she threatened to leave if I did not allow her to do so. It ended in our going to the bishop. There have been strange things going on here lately. I never saw anyone so infatuated as Sarah Ellis seems to be with Madeleine; she seems to be completely dominated."

Magnetism, thought Jane.

Dorothea was on a roll. It was bad enough that Madeleine's attorneys did not respond to her pleas, but to be challenged by Sarah Ellis? To face the humiliation of appearing before the bishop, as if she were unable to manage the Home—it was galling. And then there was Madeleine—demanding extra meals, acting as if she were superior, treating the girls unkindly. She was a fallen woman! "She has no gratitude for what we have done for her. . . . She never speaks to me unless she is obliged to do so and has never said a kind word of appreciation to me since she has been in the house." The keys quieted. Dorothea was spent.

———————————

Jane left the exhausted matron and headed to the newsstand to buy the day's papers. In the boardinghouse, Jane reviewed Louise Lowell's testimony, anger growing. To Jane, a fellow stenographer, Lowell's explanation didn't ring true, and her conduct went against the foundation of the profession—discretion. That Lowell had volunteered to testify—she had contacted the plaintiff's attorneys at the behest of a friend—was even more appalling. Jane wrote to Stoll to share her experienced opinion.[18]

First, Jane wrote, it made no sense that Breckinridge, who had personally told her he was a good typist but had lousy handwriting, would handwrite letters and then hand them to Lowell to be typed. Why not simply type them himself? It was an absurd transaction!

But more importantly, she continued, what right had Lowell to share the contents of his private letters on the witness stand and to divulge his secrets, any more than a doctor, lawyer, or priest in the confessional would have shared secrets entrusted to them? Hickox's *Correspondent's Manual for Stenography* was precise: any secrets the stenographer learns must be kept secret "and, under no circumstances, should their contents be made known."[19] And if Jane agreed that Breckinridge's envelope scheme seemed odd, she would have praised Lowell for doing the difficult but correct thing in her awkward position. *The Stenographer's Guide* advised women on how to deal with men—typically the very ignorant or the very learned, the guide noted—who thought they knew best: "If the employer prefers an inaccurate form and insists upon it, submit gracefully."[20] That includes using old, yellowed envelopes. Still, Jane was horrified that Lowell would reveal such secrets publicly. "If there is a Type-writers Association or Union in Washington," she told Stoll, "I hope they will take up this matter, for her conduct is a stigma on every woman type-writer in the country."[21]

Madeleine and Miss Ellis hurried to the courthouse. It was Wednesday, April 4, and Breckinridge was back on the stand for the plaintiff's cross-examination. Jeremiah Wilson grilled the congressman, who vacillated between admitting a promise of marriage and denying the same. Of the Good Friday engagement announcement in Mrs. Blackburn's parlor, he confessed, "Such a scene did happen, and it was a superb piece of acting."[22]

"You were honestly trying to deceive Mrs. Blackburn?" Wilson asked.

"Yes," sighed Breckinridge, "I was honestly trying to deceive her. I, therefore, do not blame Mrs. Blackburn for feeling some acerbity about the case." But he did blame Madeleine. In that parlor, he was only trying to carry out his agreement: he would lie; she would leave.

Around and around, Jeremiah Wilson chased Breckinridge, questioning how he communicated by secret messages in the newspaper's personal pages, the difference between love and lust, and his interactions with James Rodes, of whom, the congressman said, "she bled him for three years and [threw] him away like a sucked orange."

Breckinridge spoke contrary views: on the one hand, he stated that he could not marry the plaintiff because she had, unmarried, slept with him and, therefore, could not be trusted as a wife. On the other hand, he noted that she "had associated with the best families of Kentucky, had lived in houses of the highest respectability, and was a brilliant young woman." He claimed the affair wasn't just about sex: "She was a young woman of colloquial talents, sprightly, and interesting."

Wilson turned to the early winter of 1888. He asked the congressman if he had ever visited Madeleine at Mary McKenzie's home on Second Street.

"No, I did not. I never did." And Breckinridge continued with a surprise of his own: "I know that is the place the plaintiff and Dr. Parsons have located as the house where the child was born. I know there is a woman of that name who will be called upon to swear that I was there. I know that certain persons have been sent there to train her as to what she will testify. I never was there. It is false."

Wilson was taken aback. "You say certain persons have been there to train her? Has anyone been there on your behalf?" Wilson and Carlisle were stumped; how did Breckinridge know of their plan? Charles Stoll, smirking at the defendant's table, later reported to Jane that the congressman's statement "fell like a bombshell into the midst of the enemy's camp, and without a word passing between them, it was evident each was asking the other, 'How in thunder did they find that out?'"[23]

Breckinridge had thrown the plaintiff's team into confusion. He answered Wilson's question: "I sent my son there because I had heard she was to be called to testify and that she had been seen by another witness, in this case, regarding her testimony." Stoll later described to Jane the fruits of her undercover labor: "The incident was amusing and was enjoyed by Colonel Breckinridge quite as much as it was by the rest of us."[24]

In a letter to her mother, Jane described how the colonel made a "big sensation, [I] tell you on that point, for they can't to this day imagine how he found it out. I can't either—ha ha."[25]

The court adjourned early. A smug Charles Stoll gathered his papers and prepared to leave, but a sudden thought stopped him. The defense had surprised the plaintiff's team with their knowledge of coaching the witness, and Wilson and Carlisle would no doubt be chewing over how the defense found out. They would suspect a leak—only Madeleine, Dr. Parsons, Sarah Ellis, and the attorneys had known. They might trace the leak back to the young woman who knocked on Carlisle's door and delivered Madeleine's note. Jane could be in danger.

He sat back down. He needed to warn her. "If Miss Pollard is at all suspicious of you," he wrote, "she will think you must have given these facts to someone connected with us. When you see her this evening, be extremely cautious." Stoll implored Jane, "Take no chances. We all feel anxious about the consequences to you should she suspect you."[26]

Stoll called for a messenger to deliver the note to Connecticut Avenue, immediately. Jane read the hurried note. It was not like Stoll to send emergency messages midday. Earlier, she had cautioned Mame to keep quiet about her work for Stoll and the congressman: "I cannot tell you all about it now until it is all over, but I am confident that the people involved in this case would not hesitate to cut my throat did they know I was in [Breckinridge's] employ." Jane recalled Madeleine's finger-crushing wrath: "I have been so darned clever in my work that I think a woman concerned in it would just hunt me up at the ends of the earth and kill me."[27]

Jane would still go to the Home this evening, not that Stoll had even suggested she skip the nightly visit, but, she replied to the worried attorney with sarcastic bravado, "if you don't hear from me by half past nine, send out for my remains."[28]

———

Jane found Madeleine in a happy frame of mind, less concerned with the congressman's small victory and more cheerful at Breckinridge's struggles on the stand: "Jere Wilson certainly went after him." Madeleine smiled, sharing the day's cross-examination with Jane. Miss Ellis slipped into the room. She had enjoyed Judge Bradley chiding the spectators, who laughed and leered in court.

"Aggie," Ellis said, "he told the spectators they were like buzzards sitting on a fence watching a dying horse, hoping to get a piece of carrion."[29]

"They deserved it!" Madeleine jumped in. "What a nasty thing this trial would have been without Judge Bradley. He is such a refined, high-minded man. He could not stand all the filth the defense brought up."

"Well," harumphed Miss Ellis, "it is getting harder and harder for me to keep my seat in court and listen to the defendant. I shall have to get up there and just tell him what I think of him!"

"Oh, Aggie," Madeleine sighed, "going to court every day is so exciting. When this trial is over, I'll miss it greatly." Miss Ellis agreed—going to court beat sewing linens with disinterested girls and was worth the battles with Sister Dorothea and the bishop. Madeleine and Ellis sounded like two nostalgic schoolgirls about to leave high school behind. The trial had become Madeleine's life; Madeleine had become Sarah's. When the trial ended, Madeleine laughed, "I believe we will keep right on going from force of habit." Sarah Ellis laughed too.

Jane so wished she could be in that courtroom.

Madeleine had news to pass along. Mary McKenzie's son had died. She had written a sympathy note in Carlisle's office but could not attend the funeral. Madeleine looked at Jane, an idea forming. She asked Jane to attend in her place. Jane declined but offered to buy flowers for McKenzie. Roses, Madeleine said; they are the correct flowers for funerals. She wrote down the address for Jane. Ask for Wesley McKenzie, she said.

Jane tucked the directions in her bag—but she had no intention of delivering flowers, already thinking of the excuse she would send Madeleine tomorrow, bowing out of this task.[30] But this evening, Jane saw that Madeleine had more to share.

Madeleine drew closer to Jane.

"Aggie, I will tell you a great secret, but you must promise not to even think it aloud. It is going to be a great surprise to the defendant."

Jane drew closer. Madeleine whispered, "Wesley McKenzie will appear in court. He will say he saw the congressman visit me at their house. But," Madeleine paused, "Colonel Breckinridge never met him. He will never suspect for a moment that we have anyone who will testify to his calls there."

Madeleine reminded Jane—Breckinridge and his lawyers cannot know.

Jane drew closer still. "I promise."

Martha McClellan Brown, former vice president of Cincinnati Wesleyan Female College, was more than simply peeved; she was angry. The defense team had brought Rankin Roselle, Madeleine's former Cincinnati boyfriend, to testify in court. Roselle described how Madeleine sat on his lap and enjoyed caresses in the college visitors' parlor, stuttering out his tale with poor grammar and admitting to bouts of intoxication. With Madeleine sitting just feet away from the witness stand, Roselle got nervous and began to finger his collar as if it were shrinking and pinching his neck. He brought no slam-dunk story to court, just two tintypes of Madeleine while she was at Cincinnati Wesleyan, photographs of a young schoolgirl with her hair down and shoe tops visible.[31]

Roselle's testimony may have fizzled in court, but Cincinnati residents, college alumnae, and former Cincinnati Wesleyan faculty and staff were up in arms at his claims of two-hour necking sessions in the college parlor and his portrait of a lax morality among the students and faculty. From Ohio, Martha McClellan Brown attacked Roselle's fabulations in an open letter published in the *Cincinnati Enquirer*. "The whole situation as he describes it . . . is so ridiculously absurd and literally impossible," she wrote.[32] And then she got on a train to Washington.

Martha McClellan Brown took the stand on Thursday, April 5, the twentieth day of the trial.[33] The defense had rested earlier that morning; the courtroom now belonged to the plaintiff, to bring witnesses for rebuttal—testimony that would challenge statements Breckinridge had made in his defense. Calderon Carlisle called Brown. As with many of the women witnesses, Carlisle questioned her history. An educated woman, Brown graduated from Pittsburgh Female College in 1862. She had enrolled after she married in 1858, an unusual chronology for the Victorian era. The Browns joined Cincinnati Wesleyan College in 1882. Her husband was the school's president. She had been vice president and a professor of art, literature, and philosophy from 1882 to 1892, when the school closed. Of late, she lectured for women's causes. She had known Madeleine since she entered as a student on November 20, 1883.

Brown described the college rules: gentlemen were restricted to visits on Friday evenings between eight and ten in the parlor, library, and reception room. There were usually from fifteen to thirty or forty visitors, and people passed from room to room. Even the semblance of privacy or secrecy was impossible. She pointed out that no young man was permitted a visit of more than an hour. Not even engaged women were allowed to see their fiancés other than Friday evenings.

Countering the defense's narrative, Brown had no criticism of Madeleine's male visitors. James Rodes, Brown recalled, visited several times. He appeared to be an honest gentleman with reverential respect for women. His conduct with Miss Pollard, Brown stated, was unobjectionable. As for Roselle, she last saw him at the literary society debate, the night Pollard won, a particularly noteworthy accomplishment. When Brown attempted to elaborate on Pollard's charming character and intellectual gifts, the congressman's lawyers interrupted with a steady stream of objections—letting the assumption hover that the Browns had admitted a less than virtuous girl into their school. Dismissed, Brown left the stand frustrated and deeply annoyed.

Brown defended her school. That evening, in her room at the Riggs House hotel, she drafted a letter to the editor. Her anger filled three sheets of hotel stationery. Every student seeking admission, she wrote, needed reliable references, and Brown examined the personality of each applicant. Pollard was no exception to these rules. She had studied Madeleine's habits and tendencies of mind, her disposition and feelings, her language and facial expressions, her moods—her whole personality. "This bright, young, unsophisticated country girl could not have deceived me had she tried," she noted. She was "scrutinized," wrote Brown.[34]

Brown rose to her task, words and sentences crossed out as a better phrase came to mind; afterthoughts crept up the sides of the paper. "It is false," Brown wrote, "whoever tells it that she was not then a true, pure young and unsuspecting country girl. She was attractive because of her simplicity and great hopefulness, little dreaming of what she had to overcome to attain the goal of her ambition and little suspecting that kindliness might [become] wickedness." Brown offered this assessment: "Everybody admires a simple-minded girl who is not bound by the conventionalities which crush the individuality out of so many people. And all teachers admire a diligent worker as a student. And these traits marked Miss Pollard's career of only nine months at Wesleyan."[35] Brown made it crystal clear: it was not the college that set Madeleine on the road to this courtroom.

Breckinridge, in turn, was furious at Brown's attack on Roselle. Responding that evening to a supporter's letter, the congressman defended Roselle's "perfectly simple and truthful story." In his letter, Breckinridge extended his ire to "all these ladies who attend conventions, deliver speeches and shriek for all sorts of things which they call reform [who then] comes upon the stand and swears to what she knows is untrue, and in favor of a prostitute and against a man who is honest and clean."[36]

By the end of the trial, Breckinridge would expand his wrath to all the professional women who testified: "[The plaintiff] secured the testimony of women doctors who are abortionists, women type-writers who are treacherous; women procurists combined with ladies to make a case which each knew was untrue." Lambasting Louise Lowell and the female physicians, he continued his rant: "Every working woman in America has been injured by this trial. Men who have confidential communications will hesitate to trust female type-writers; and the principal advantage of permitting women to enter the ranks of [the medical] profession seems to be to give to a wanton a better opportunity to hide her shame, and yet to use those female physicians on the witness stand to secure her revenge, or to rob."[37] A supporter agreed and told Breckinridge, "Your case was tried by the newspapers, and the short-haired women of Boston, and that highly perfumed flock of purists that gather at Willards to regulate society and politics." The women's cause was "anti-democratic," the supporter opined, led by "that Willard Hotel gang of powdered, broken down, she fanatics."[38]

On the final day of testimony, Carlisle called Madeleine to the stand to rebut Breckinridge's description of the carriage ride and the accusations of prostitution and assignations in the racy depositions. She responded "no" and "never" to a multitude of questions, denying any and all improper actions until, she made clear, the moment Breckinridge took her arm and walked her through Sarah Gist's gate.[39]

And with that, the case was closed. The attorneys would draw up their instructions for the jury and present them to Bradley for his approval the next day, a Saturday.

And then all that remained were the closing statements. There was little else that Jane could do now, too late for a smoking gun, a big reveal, or a sudden change of heart from the plaintiff. Madeleine's great fight was nearing the end.

On Saturday night, April 7, Jane was surprised to find Madeleine in a cross mood. Dudley vexed her, she said; he had so little pluck. "He is such a quiet, mild sort of person that he ought to wear a *blue necktie*," referring to the Gilded Age practice of linking blue, an emblem of the Virgin Mary, to girls and pink—akin to the strong color red—to boys.[40]

Dudley had asked Madeleine if he should come up on Sunday to take her out for a walk, and, annoyed, she dismissed him. Now, she admitted to Jane, she felt badly for her temper. Madeleine sighed. "He ought to have been the girl and I the boy. He could have done a great deal with those pretty eyes of his if he had only been a girl." And if Madeleine had been a boy, her plain physical features and abundant ambition would have presented no barrier to success in the world.

Jane had brought tomatoes and made a French dressing. The food soothed Madeleine's pique. As she ate Jane's salad, Madeleine opened her heart.

"As soon as I know the verdict, I am leaving this Home," she said. "I am going to pack my trunk a day or two ahead. The day the verdict is announced, I can leave. And I will. I have arranged to go immediately to the Providence Hospital." The sisters would provide room, board, nursing, and healing massages for ten dollars a week.

"Please, Aggie, visit me often."

Madeleine had decided to accept the ten-thousand-dollar book deal: five thousand in advance and five thousand as a royalty on the completed book. Her attorneys approved. She would write an introduction and, from the stenographic notes of the testimony, write a digest of the case. Law libraries around the country would buy the book. Her photograph would be in the front of the volume, and she was thinking of putting Breckinridge's in the back. She joked: That puts the entire book in between. That should be safe. It would be no problem finding a photographer. Several had offered generous payments for the sole right to market her photo.[41]

Jane was astounded. The $10,000 book payment was outrageous—a US congressman, like Breckinridge, made $5,000 a year. Jane's salary of $15 a week grossed $720 annually. But the project gave Jane an idea, a way to stay connected after the verdict.

"Madeleine," Jane said, "I can help you! We'll work together. What fun we'll have."

Madeleine agreed. "Aggie, you will do my typewriting, and I'll pay you when I get my money."

Jane brought up the McKenzies. Wesley McKenzie did not testify—the big surprise the plaintiff's team had planned came to naught when he insisted Breckinridge had a black beard.[42]

As for Mary McKenzie, she electrified the courtroom. Despite her son's funeral, Mary McKenzie took the stand and did as Wilson and Carlisle, through Parsons, had asked: she identified Madeleine, whom she knew as "Mrs. Hall," as the pregnant woman who had stayed at her home in 1888 and confirmed that, with Dr. Parsons, she took Madeleine's baby to the foundling asylum the night it was born. As to Breckinridge, McKenzie testified that "Mr. Hall" had visited Madeleine, but she did not see him then. But, she added, here now in court, "I recognize him from the child." She had no doubt. He was the father.

Jane might have rolled her eyes or shook her head—or tried very hard not to. "But Madeleine," she said, "it's rather absurd to say that a person could be recognized from a baby who had been seen for the last time when only six hours old, and this, too, six years ago. Little babies never look like anything."

The friendly spirit of French dressing faded.

"Aggie, you are mistaken," Madeleine said evenly. Besides, McKenzie was not the only one to see the similarity. "Dietz looked so much like Colonel Breckinridge that Mrs. Parsons said when she entered the courtroom she knew Desha was the colonel's son from his likeness to that baby."

Jane, with no fondness for children and never having given birth, thought it wise not to argue with Madeleine the mother. She packed up her whisk and took her leave for the evening.

———————

With the testimony concluded, Madeleine had no homework—no transcripts to read, questions to anticipate, or answers to practice.

The coming week would be left to closing statements: Calderon Carlisle and Jere Wilson for Madeleine, Benjamin Butterworth and Phil Thompson for Breckinridge. She would likely have her verdict in one week.

On Sunday afternoon, April 8, Martha McClellan Brown took the opportunity to reconnect with her now famous, or infamous, former student. She was not there to reminisce; she wanted something from her. Brown was desperate for Madeleine to lecture for women's rights. It was Madeleine's duty to expose Breckinridge, Brown said, and American women should gather around Pollard in her quest.[43] In the lecture field, Brown enthused, Madeleine could make a million dollars. Madeleine declined. After the trial, she explained, she had no interest in facing the public, and as for money, despite her interest in big book deals, she wanted only enough to pay her debts.

Madeleine did not have an active interest in the women's rights movement, despite her protest against the sexual double standard. She joked with Jane that after the trial, she would become "strong minded," cut off her hair, and become a literary woman. Jane advised against cutting her hair—Madeleine's best feature—arguing that a woman should look womanly. Madeleine offered a compromise: she'd keep her beautiful hair, but she would still become literary.[44]

Where Madeleine seemed uninterested in the cause, Jane was more hostile. On a tour of the White House, her party came upon a group of "old hens there, some woman's rights gang . . . awful queer looking lot."[45] Yet, in letters to Mame, Jane advocated for divorce from lousy husbands, protections from lawyers and those who would cheat naïve women, and the availability of life insurance for women to protect themselves in the future. She was also determined to find information on birth control for her sister-in-law, who did not want more children, despite restrictive Comstock Laws that forbid distributing such "obscene" material through the US mail. And Jane's constant complaints about single women's challenges in the working world signal her concerns regarding labor. These progressive issues found advocates in suffragists and women's rights activists, fighting for a voice in the male-dominated government that ran their country and for policies and laws that supported a woman's ability to govern her own life. But perhaps Jane had not yet made the intellectual leap from the personal to the political.

15

The Eve of My Waterloo

Monday's *Evening Star* summarized the week to come: "Lawyers Now Talk."[1] It had been one month and one day since the plaintiff and defense teams had made their opening statements; now the final week of the trial was underway, and Madeleine's future hung in the balance. First, for the plaintiff, Calderon Carlisle would offer his closing statement. Then, for the defendant, Phil Thompson would speak, followed by Benjamin Butterworth. Jeremiah Wilson, for the plaintiff, would speak last. Bradley urged the attorneys to be brief; he had hoped to finish this trial by Saturday.

On Monday evening, Jane found Madeleine and Miss Ellis reading the newspapers. They were thrilled with the *Evening News* headline "Breckinridge in Tatters." If they had also read the Black paper, *The Washington Bee*, Madeleine would have been pleased. Editor W. Calvin Chase firmly placed the blame on the congressman. This was not a case of a woman taking him down; Breckinridge had done this to himself: "He has dragged the honorable name which he bears in the dust and blackened his own character beyond expurgation . . . and will never be able to outlive the shame which he has brought upon himself."[2] In a pointed commentary, Chase addressed Breckinridge's masculine, racial privilege: a Black congressman would "have long since been expelled from Congress, and a note of sympathy tendered Miss Pollard. But being a white man, his corrupt doings are overlooked, and in vindication

246

of his immoral connection with the woman, he will be returned to Congress by a large majority, and this is the example the superior race is setting for the Negro to follow after."[3]

Madeleine was subdued but in good spirits. She described the day in court. There was quite a large audience for Carlisle's closing statement, and he held everyone's attention. "It was such a strange feeling," Madeleine said to Jane, "to sit there and hear him describe my life. Aggie, he did not spare me, he never has or excused me for my part in this sin. He simply held up my life as it really was. . . . Oh!" Madeleine gushed. "He is just the sweetest thing I ever saw. How I do envy his wife!"[4]

Carlisle had spoken plainly and directly to the jury, Madeleine said, telling them what he would prove and then doing so with the testimony heard as evidence. His goal was to illustrate Madeleine's good character. He made an argument, not an oration, at times waving his hand to dismiss rumors or disagreeable stories lobbed by the defense, at other times holding a pencil to his chin as if in thought or conversation, man to man. Madeleine told Jane, "He just talks to that jury as if he was sitting here talking to us."[5]

His argument was straightforward: Breckinridge was a privileged, powerful man who took advantage of a humble young woman without the protection of father or family. Carlisle lambasted the men and women who offered crude accounts as testimony. He cited Breckinridge's statements that Madeleine was a perfectly proper woman when he met her, as well as his praise for her intellect, voracious reading, and engaging conversation. Carlisle pointed out the chronological and geographical flaws in Breckinridge's deponents' testimony that claimed Madeleine had lived in a Lexington brothel when her aunt's testimony placed her residence five miles outside the city or that Madeleine had been a frequent visitor at a house of ill repute in Kentucky, when her well-regarded cousin's testimony confirmed in those years she lived in Pennsylvania. Testimony from William Wood and Alex Julian noted that Madeleine was a proper girl. Rankin Roselle's attempt at besmirching Madeleine backfired when he showed the court photographs of a schoolgirl, not a young woman, with her long hair down and her short hemmed dresses—a visage confirmed by Sarah Gist.

Carlisle covered ten years of the ill-fated relationship, begun when Madeleine was twenty and Breckinridge was forty-seven. Madeleine's fatal error was trusting Breckinridge: from the carriage ride when Breckinridge, a practiced orator, took liberties and then chided, cajoled, and enticed her with compliments and eloquence, he entrapped a naïve young Madeleine with false promises. Carlisle praised Madeleine's performance on the stand, under the severest strain. There were, he argued, only two explanations for her endurance: either she was long practiced and experienced in public life and trials in court, or she was telling the absolute truth.

"The jury," Madeleine told Jane as she finished her description of the day in court, "hung on his words."[6] As did Madeleine.

Jane had little to report. She had questioned Madeleine on a Christmas card found inside the much-discussed Washington Irving volumes, Sister Cecelia's travel expenses, and whether it was difficult to convince her former landlady, Mrs. Minear, to testify. But all this was moot, and Jane knew it. Still, she tried. Reading the *Evening Star*, she saw that coastal Maine was in the second day of a punishing blizzard; drifts were five feet deep.[7]

On Tuesday, Madeleine, looking cheerful and healthy, sat next to Jere Wilson. The audience was modest; lawyers summarizing the case were not as interesting as Madeleine or Breckinridge testifying. Miss Ellis sat nearby. Yesterday, three registered letters had been delivered to the courthouse addressed to Madeleine. Right away Madeleine knew they were from autograph fiends. She had passed them to Ellis, who signed for her. Madeleine worried that if someone got her signature, it might get forged.[8]

Carlisle completed his argument, reviewing key testimony that showed the relationship's imbalanced power: "When you consider the character of witnesses on both sides, when you think of this man with power, socially, politically and otherwise, who acquired domination over this unfortunate girl, who ruined her life, you cannot but believe that he promised to make good to her the ruin of her life; you cannot, with the thought of the mothers and daughters in the land, refuse to make the only possible reparation to this unfortunate plaintiff."[9] This wasn't just about Madeleine; Carlisle asked the jury to protect all American daughters from duplicitous, hypocritical men using their power, and power of persuasion, to ruin young women.

Madeleine left the courtroom. She had no desire to hear the defense attorneys portray in black terms her errors, mistakes, and heartaches. Madeleine would wait out the remaining days in Calderon Carlisle's office, Miss Ellis at her side.

———

Phil Thompson began his closing argument. He blamed the plaintiff for dragging this sordid case into court. She was a bawd and a wanton living an evil life who, in suing Breckinridge, "brought into Court this mass of filth spreading it through the newspapers before the daughters of the family."[10] The motive? Pure revenge.

Madeleine, Thompson argued, was interested in two things: money and schooling, and, he stated, marriage was the connection between those goals. She had a "mania," he claimed, for education and for travel to Europe, a "regular fever." She would have married Kentucky carpenter William Woods, he said, if he had had the money to take her to Europe. She "went at Rodes booted and spurred . . . telling him he could not come and see her unless he put it up." She was, in his argument, "the most skillful adventuress who ever made a track through a courtroom."[11] Once Issa Desha

249

Breckinridge died, Madeleine made her move on the man she had strung along for years. It was not the fulfillment of a long promise to marry; it was the fruition of her ambitious plot.

Thompson criticized Madeleine for failing to know her firstborn had died. "Oh, inhuman woman! . . . Inhuman monster!"[12] The plaintiff was no mother—she shed "crocodile tears" in court over children she had forgotten.

He had little trust in any woman's testimony. Miss Pollard lied. He didn't trust female physicians.[13] He criticized Louise Lowell's recordkeeping after finding his own name in her memorandum book but not recalling having had any work done by the "old lady" (Lowell was forty-four). Mrs. Blackburn was a lovely "old lady" but getting on in years. "She's no longer a maiden gay," Thompson added. He was quick to state that she would never lie, but, Thompson suggested, she thought Breckinridge had imposed on her and "wanted to put it to Colonel Breckinridge as hard as she could." He continued gratuitously, "I don't blame her; I admire her spirit. Why, I was afraid she would jump down my throat, frizzes and all when I began to examine her."[14]

Thompson excused Breckinridge's misdeeds—all great men lie and "had their troubles with women." He was no worse than any of us, Thompson assured the jury. Men, good men, "start to have a little fun with a woman and the first thing they know, they have got into eternal hell with her."[15]

With that sentiment, Thompson concluded the day. He would continue his harangue tomorrow.

Madeleine likely learned of the defense's closing statements from Carlisle when he returned to his office. Thompson's portrayal of Madeleine as an arch adventuress hurt her, and later that evening, hurt had morphed to anger. Jane made her way through a cold spring storm to find Madeleine seething. Jennie, one of the resident girls, had the misfortune to bring Madeleine her supper. "Jennie,"

Madeleine barked, "that is the meanest supper you have brought me for some time."[16]

Jennie stuttered an apology and backed out of the room. Jane waited for Madeleine to set the conversational tone.

"Aggie, I am perfectly crushed and broken-hearted over this dreadful argument of Phil Thompson's . . . Oh, Aggie, I cannot live through this last attack: to have suffered so much as I have and then to be abused in this manner is too dreadful!"

"But Madeleine," Jane countered, wondering to herself what on earth Madeleine had expected from her adversary, "you must expect this sort of thing, under the circumstances. I wouldn't pay this any mind. After everything in the newspapers, surely the words of one man you can stand."

A smile flitted across her face. "But I thought his speech might break Dudley's heart."

Miss Ellis came in. Dudley had just called at the Home but would not stay when he learned that Madeleine had already retired. If Thompson's speech had broken his heart, it had been promptly repaired. Ellis reported he was cheerful and bright, and he sent up a bottle of port wine. The time for verdict-changing intel was past, but Jane, detective habits now ingrained, made a mental note of Madeleine's evident fondness for alcohol. There was still a book to write.

Jane opened the *Evening News*. "Madeleine, did you see this article about your becoming a lawyer or an actress?"

Madeleine replied, intrigued. "No, I hadn't but what a pleasant idea," she said. "I know [Jere] Wilson would let me study law in his office. I would like to study in Mr. Carlisle's office, but I suppose that would not do, as we are too near the same age." She imagined this future: "If I went into Judge Wilson's office, the first thing I would do would be to fix the place up. I would make him get a new carpet and clear the dust out. It is such a shabby looking old place. I don't suppose the judge would be able to think when I got through fixing up the place." Jane forced a smile at the joke.

Madeleine looked forward to Wilson's closing argument. His would be the last voice the jury would hear. She looked forward to payback. She told Jane, "He has comforted me all along by saying that he would pay it all back when his turn came, and I think he will. You just look now and see if he don't get even."

Jane asked if going on the stage was still a possibility. Madeleine said, "Oh, there is a good deal of difference between a crushed and broken-hearted woman and an actress." Madeleine closed her eyes and raised her head to the sky in a grief-stricken pose. Cue the spotlight, thought Jane.

As Jane left with another pile of Madeleine's fan mail, Madeleine opened the port wine. "I hope, Madeleine, that wine won't make you sick before morning," Jane said, a sly reference to the overindulgence of eggnog at the mock wedding party. Madeleine glared.

On Wednesday, Phil Thompson concluded his closing remarks, petty and mean, calling Madeleine "a walking arsenal" and worrying that a stray bullet aimed at the congressman might find its way to him.[17] Thompson turned the floor over to his defense colleague, Benjamin Butterworth. The courtroom was crowded with spectators and lawyers to witness his oratory.

Butterworth spoke eloquently of his friendship with Breckinridge, moving the audience to applaud his manly sentiment. At the outburst of approval, Judge Bradley cleared the courtroom of all the spectators except members of the bar and the press.

Butterworth then turned to the character of the plaintiff and gave a "scathing review" of Pollard and her choices, after first apologizing for speaking of a woman in this way. Then he let loose—using decorous words but delivered in a sarcastic and cutting tone. Butterworth blamed Madeleine for her failure to slap Breckinridge when he groped her in the carriage: "The instinct of a virtuous woman would have led her to say, 'Get out, you leper!'"[18] Butterworth chastised Madeleine for meeting Breckinridge the next day, for traveling together to Lexington, for plotting to be in his life knowing he had a wife and children. And he condemned her for giving up and forgetting her children, making a distinction, as Breckinridge had in his criticism of Louise Lowell, between a woman and a female. "A woman," Butterworth stated, "will follow them through the gates of Hell."[19] A female, left unsaid in the courtroom, lacking the expected God-given moral virtues, would not. Madeleine Pollard was a female.

In her room, Jane flitted from one task to another—typing her notes, reviewing testimony, seeking an overlooked lead. Her to-do list ran in a loop in her head. She had not given up hope of finding some piece of information that would tip the scales of justice in Breckinridge's favor, not so much for Breckinridge's sake but for Stoll's. But there was little time now.

In the early evening, Jane found Madeleine once again mulling her posttrial plans. Witnessing her indecision on which of several lucrative offers to take was getting a little old. Although she had declared several days ago that she would write a book, Jane had seen no sign that Madeleine had formally accepted the offer. And now the stage was back on Madeleine's list of possibilities.

"I really do not see what else there is left for me," Madeleine said. "I could never marry after this trial, of course, and while I might write in a little room away from the eyes of the public, and possibly make a living, the chances are that I would have to do without all the luxuries of life." Madeleine sighed. "And, Aggie, I could not live without them."[20]

She turned back to the stage, sharing with Jane a romantic view of stardom, servants, and beauty. Jane channeled Mame to offer a dose of the reality of stage life, telling the starstruck Madeleine that she would have a tiny dressing room, have to follow the same rules as all the actors, and have to wear heavy makeup, even if she thought it bad for her complexion.

Madeleine huffed.

Jane waited as her cautions sank in. Madeleine seemed lost in thought. Finally, she spoke. She would decide within two weeks of the verdict. If she picked the stage, she would go to New York immediately to be trained by Frohman, a well-known manager: "I shall study plays, take fencing and dancing lessons, and fit myself in every way to start out in the fall with one of his companies as the star."

Jane glommed onto her fantasy: "Please, Madeleine, take me along. Could I be your scenery prop? Or super?" Jane's facility with stage language served her well; extending their faux friendship beyond the end of the trial might prove useful as she wrote her own book.

"Perhaps, Aggie." She paused, again lost in thought. "It certainly is a great temptation, Aggie, to a girl as poor as I am and one who is fond of the good things of this world to have so much money offered her."

Butterworth continued his closing on Thursday, April 12, and spoke for the entire day, with just a short recess for lunch. Earlier he had spoken in general terms, laying out the broad strokes of Madeleine Pollard's errors; on this day, he focused intently on the testimony, analyzing each answer, each statement. The strategy of the plaintiff's lawyers, Butterworth argued, was to make this a cautionary tale: "To awaken horror before the public . . . a tale that Colonel Breckinridge had led astray a guiltless little girl and had led her down the path of nine years of immorality to a marriage contract ruthlessly violated."[21]

Butterworth aimed to exchange the jury's sympathy for doubt. In his final sentences, he described Madeleine "as a designing woman, an actress who, on this stage of the courtroom, was preparing herself to go on the stage . . . [she had] brought this suit, not for money, not for revenge, not from hatred, but as an advertisement to aid her in her future career as an actress or a writer of books," a clear callout to Jane's reports on Madeleine's posttrial plans.[22] Butterworth pushed home his point: Madeleine was in it to make a name for herself and claim some gold. Jane would have been so pleased to hear her intel used in court.

At the end of the day, the lawyers, the jury, Judge Bradley, and his officers remained in the courtroom for a group photograph, staking their claim to history and documenting for the future how these men made a name for themselves, connected to the infamous trial.[23] Neither the plaintiff or the defendant was present. There were no women in the scene.

————————

Jane hurried to the House of Mercy, no time to stop for tomatoes. She had read the afternoon paper. Butterworth's closing was brutal. Madeleine greeted her coolly.[24]

This evening, Madeleine railed against the stage.

"I could never endure the publicity of such a life," she exclaimed. With Butterworth's concluding accusation in her mind, she now abhorred the theater. She told Jane, "I have the greatest contempt for that life anyway. I never saw an actress for whom I had a particle of respect, or that I wanted to be like."

She continued her argument: the stage was too degrading for one of such high aspirations. She was confident in her abilities, but she could simply not descend to that level. Jane worried for the man who tried to train her for the theater or anything else for which she was not naturally fitted. He will have a very sorry time, she thought to herself.

"What about the book, Madeleine? When shall we begin our work?"

But Madeleine had had a change of heart. "I think I will soon have money enough without either going on the stage or writing a book, until I feel I can write it comfortably."

Jane's spy radar came on.

"But how? Where will you find such money?"

"Oh, I expect to get back some of the money that I placed in S. V. White's hands last year. I think the stocks will come up, and I shall soon have enough to place me in a position where I will not have to worry about money affairs." Investments following an economic crash? Jane's spy radar turned off. A windfall wasn't likely. S. V. White's bank had failed, and any money invested with him was likely long gone.

Madeleine spoke wistfully of her life in the capital before Breckinridge ruined it all. "I always had my breakfast in bed and the girl would bring me my letters and the morning papers, and I would lie there and read them." Madeleine continued, now speaking hopefully of her future: "It is necessary for me to have an easy life, for I am not strong enough to endure much. Then, I must have a pleasant part of the city to live in. I cannot endure to see poor people and a narrow street with poverty about me. I must have a nice broad street and pleasant surroundings in my life."

Madeleine had not yet made any arrangements for where to live after the trial. "Aggie," she asked, "I wish you would hunt me up a boarding place." Madeleine looked through the newspaper and circled several likely places, handing it to Jane, asking her to visit a property on Jefferson Place, where she had once lived.

"I know all the neighbors there, but, after all, one can be as much alone in a city as one desires," she said, thinking of her posttrial life, "and I do not care if people do watch me every time I go in or out. I shall expect that sort of thing where I live now."

"How much are you willing to pay for board?" Jane asked.

"Fifty dollars a month for Dudley and myself. We want two rooms, and I shall have a caterer serve our meals. But don't engage the rooms for more than a month, as I want to be free to leave at any time. I want so much to go to Vermont, but I am afraid Miss Ellis cannot go with me, and I am sure I would not want to go without her."

The earlier invitation to Jane seemed to have fallen by the wayside.

———————

In her evening report to Stoll, Jane reported Madeleine's indecision. Madeleine had mentioned her hope to have enough money to offer the girls at the House of Mercy a strengthening breakfast:

a decent cup of coffee, bread, an egg, and a banana. She wanted to pay for a year's worth of coal for Mary McKenzie in appreciation for holding her baby boy for six hours. Jane poked Stoll on yet another unfollowed thread in the trial, as Jane saw it, an opportunity lost. "By the way," she wrote "speaking of Dietz, can you tell me what became of him from April 18th—the date the records show he died—until May 3rd when Madeleine claims to have seen his remains at the undertakers?"[25]

Madeleine skipped the last day of the trial as her attorney Jeremiah Wilson completed the plaintiff's closing argument in a crowded, stifling courtroom.[26] His manner was sarcastic, mocking Benjamin Butterworth's dramatic passages, as he himself engaged in drama. "I feel sorry for him," Wilson offered, "because he had such a hard time trying to talk with nothing to talk about." Breckinridge's claim of being under Madeleine's spell did not escape notice: "Wherever Madeleine went that lamb was sure to go."[27] Wilson lambasted Breckinridge as a liar and hypocrite, asking the jury, "How do you know he is not telling this story to deceive you? The probability is that he is doing it."

It was Madeleine who was the victim here: "I want the world to know that whatever slime is on her comes from this defendant. It is the trial of the serpent over her life." Madeleine, Wilson argued, was no different from legions of country boys and girls with "an ambition to get away to what they think is a broader and fuller life."[28] He did praise Breckinridge's facility with words and wished he had that skill to praise and honor Sister Ellis, "the noble Sister from the House of Refuge where Madeleine Pollard was sheltered; who had supported her through her ordeal." The compliment was nice, but Ellis, as Jane had repeatedly pointed out, was not a nun.

Jane was both desperate for the verdict and afraid of the verdict; although she held hope that Breckinridge would prevail, she knew that hope was slim. Tomorrow, Wilson would conclude his closing statement, Bradley would give the jury the charge, and a verdict should be rendered by the evening. Jane visited the House of Mercy; Madeleine was calm and confident.[29]

"This is the eve of my Waterloo, Aggie, and I feel sure of victory. It makes me so happy."

Madeleine was sitting up in her chair, rather than the bed, flushed with excitement and anticipating a visit from Father Huntington, her friend from New York. Her table and bookshelves were bare, closet empty but for one dress. Trunks packed, she was ready to leave the House of Mercy. Jane had brought tomatoes and prepared the dressing. Madeleine ate, Jane thought, like a woman with a very easy conscience.

Madeleine's posttrial plans were taking shape. She said, "You know, Aggie, Miss Ellis is going to keep house for Dudley and me. She will make a good housekeeper, for she used to be one of the maids at Windsor and is, of course, perfectly trained for anything of that kind. One good thing about Miss Ellis is that she is never above her position and always willing to do anything I asked her to do for me. English women of that class are brought up to know their station in life, and they expect to wait on you."

Madeleine, Jane saw, was in a brighter mood than the previous evening, thinking about buying the property on Jefferson Place and already hiring domestic staff.

"I am," Madeleine agreed. "I am on the top of the heap." Jere Wilson's closing argument was "simply grand; . . . It was simply wonderful how powerful his voice was. Everybody listened spellbound, for they say it was the finest speech ever heard." She had waited in Carlisle's office. His clerk ran back and forth with reports. Tonight, she read his speech in the *Evening Star*. When she came to the part where Wilson called her a "repentant woman," she laughed. "That's me, Aggie; I am that repentant woman." They both laughed.

"I do feel excited and anxious now that the time is so near. I am confident of the verdict tomorrow. I will wait in Mr. Carlisle's office. The jury will not be out for more than an hour, if that long, and I shall know the verdict by tomorrow afternoon or early in the evening." Madeleine was ready for her future.

"I am all packed up and shall go at once to the Providence Hospital when I hear it. I am to be under Dr. Tabor Johnson's care while I am there, and I will have a good chance to get rested and strong."

Jane returned to her Connecticut Avenue boardinghouse and typed her notes. There was little to report—two women awaiting the verdict in a trial that could change their lives, that had already changed their lives. There would be no more visits to Madeleine at the House of Mercy, no more pulling of secrets, no more tomato salads. Jane had made snide and snarky comments, had revealed the plaintiff's private thoughts, and had doubted her veracity. She had been Madeleine's faux friend, a frenemy, a fellow woman who strived to bring her down.

Yet Jane had more in common with Madeleine than perhaps she was willing to admit. Although they took different routes, they sought a similar destination: directing their lives in the face of, and despite, the challenges women faced: working-class wages barely sufficient for the needs of life; glass ceilings for women professionals like Mary Parsons and Belle Buchanan, whose expertise was questioned and mocked; rules of etiquette that served as a litmus test on social legitimacy; laws and cultural beliefs that limited women's rights to property, fair wages, ambitions, reproductive health care, education, the vote; and practices like the sexual double standard—collectively denying women a full measure of personhood.

Of Madeleine's plan to rest at the Providence Hospital, Jane was typically sarcastic about Madeleine's ordeal. Nonetheless, she understood something else about the most well-known woman in America: "[The hospital] is a comfortable place to go and hide from newspaper reporters, and the sisters will wait on her and guard her from all intrusion."[30] Including from Jane.

16

The Trouble with All
Detective Stories

Madeleine awoke on Saturday, April 14, ready to face her future. She washed in the cold-water basin and put on her dark dress. Her bags would be picked up shortly. She drank a cup of weak tea and ate breakfast, alone, one last time, in her room.

On her way to the front door, Madeleine walked into Sister Dorothea's office.

"Goodbye, Sister," Madeleine said. "I'm sorry to have been the cause of any unpleasantness here."

Sister Dorothea looked at Madeleine, mutual dislike hovering in the moment.

"Goodbye, Madeleine," said the matron.

Silence followed. Madeleine turned and left. One of the nuns unlocked the heavy front door; it swung open, as if it were lighter this morning—Madeleine's steps were. She stepped out into the sun and headed to Calderon Carlisle's office.[1]

─────────

Madeleine's prediction was accurate: the jury took just over an hour to reach their verdict. At 4:35 p.m., the foreman informed the bailiff they were ready. Twelve white men filed back into the courtroom, their duty done, faces betraying nothing. Attorneys and spectators raced to fill the seats. Breckinridge sat next to Desha and two of his counselors, staring straight ahead. The murmuring of spectators died out quickly. The jury members sat with their coats and hats in hand. Judge Bradley waited for the plaintiff's counsel. Madeleine remained in Calderon Carlisle's office with Miss Ellis, Dudley, and Jeremiah Wilson. Jane paced somewhere in the city, awaiting newspaper extras announcing the news. She had been closer to Madeleine than most but, in this moment, had to wait in anonymity, undercover.

Carlisle hustled into the courtroom, surprised to see the jury seated. Anticipation silenced the large room. Judge Bradley warned the crowd he would not tolerate shouts of approval or cries of disappointment. He nodded to the clerk. The room took a collective breath. The court clerk called out, "Gentlemen of the jury, have you agreed upon a verdict?"

The courtroom was still. Breckinridge leaned forward as if to move his ears that much closer to his future.

"If it pleases the court, we have agreed upon a verdict . . . and find for the plaintiff."

Breckinridge did not move, did not pale nor flush. The foreman announced the damages. Breckinridge missed it. He leaned over to Phil Thompson: "How much?"

Fifteen thousand dollars. Three years' salary for a US congressman.

Breckinridge's attorney jumped to his feet, announcing his intention to file a motion for a new trial. Breckinridge remained seated, silent, staring straight ahead.

The judge thanked the jurors, and the courtroom emptied, reporters running to telegraphs and telephones. From Carlisle's office, Madeleine peered out the window. People spilled from the courthouse. Her heart beat faster. Carlisle hurried across the street to tell his client of victory. Surrounded by friends, Madeleine shed a few tears of joy and shook their hands repeatedly, laughing and smiling as months of tension drained away. "Isn't it good! Isn't it good," Madeleine cried.

Well-wishers and the curious tried to join the party. Dudley closed the office door. The victorious plaintiff declined to speak to the press, anxious to remove herself from public view. Carlisle and

Wilson shook their victorious client's hand as she thanked them profusely, and as they left their office, the attorneys announced to the press that they were satisfied with the verdict: "Our cause was just and our hearts were in it."[2] Madeleine Pollard had been vindicated. As Madeleine had once argued for her college debate team, words mattered.[3]

Breckinridge and his counsel sat quietly, the last to leave the courtroom. They declined to speak to the press and walked across the courthouse square to Benjamin Butterworth's office, where Louise Wing Breckinridge waited with Sophonisba. Butterworth made one point to reporters dogging the men: there was no truth to the rumor that Louise would divorce her husband.[4] Fifteen minutes later, the Breckinridges entered a waiting barouche and drove up F Street, crowded with shoppers and clerks buying the extras—single sheets of newsprint—that already carried the verdict. The carriage stopped at a market. Mrs. Breckinridge leaned out to give her order to a clerk. The congressman stood on the sidewalk, laughing as an eager, oblivious newsboy pushed an extra into his hands, announcing the news of his defeat. He gave the lad a coin and drove home.

Jere Wilson received praise and congratulations for his closing argument. At his home, telegrams and newspaper clippings in English, French, and German covered his desk. An Oklahoma fan sent Wilson a caricature that looked like something you might tack up on a tree if you lost a horse or a kitten or sought a gun-toting varmint. In his parlor, the scent of American Beauty and La France roses filled the room, an enormous, lush arrangement several prominent women—Mary Desha, Louise Lowell, and Alice Elizabeth Waugh, the wife of Indiana congressman Dan Waugh, among them—had sent Wilson in gratitude for his efforts to defeat the double standard. No one sent Madeleine flowers. The next day, Mary Desha published a note in the newspaper to make clear that her gift supported the principle of the case, not the plaintiff personally.[5]

Women did more than send flowers. Since March, representatives from several women's organizations had been meeting quietly at the Willard Hotel, determined to keep their deliberations secret until they had perfected their mission. Members of the Woman's Suffrage Association and Woman's Christian Temperance Union (WCTU) were present, as well as Sarah Doan La Fetra, president of the local WCTU, and Ellen S. Mussey, an attorney well known for her involvement in women's advancement. La Fetra and Mussey served as the meeting leaders. Over thirty women had attended the first gathering. Together, they called themselves the Woman's Protective League (WPL).

The WPL sent Julia Blackburn a note expressing their appreciation for her testimony, and during the trial, representatives had met with Judge Bradley to argue that women should be admitted to the courtroom alongside the men. While that request had only moderate success, Bradley allowing women only when the testimony was not unseemly, the discussion inspired him to encourage reporters to keep sordid details out of the newspapers. No one sent Sarah Gist a note.

Week after week, the WPL worked quietly, completing their task on the day of Madeleine's victory. Ironically, given his antipathy to women's rights activists, Breckinridge had provided the inspiration for the project when in court he testified that affairs such as his damaged the man but destroyed the woman. The WPL sought to equalize that double standard. They sent a list of proposed resolutions to the House of Representatives Committee on the Judiciary. The resolutions called for a morals standard for members of Congress, an investigation and possible impeachment of Breckinridge, and an equalizing of expectations for chastity between the genders. The WPL invited Jeremiah Wilson, Madeleine's attorney, to serve as their organization's counsel.[6]

Madeleine's victory realized, exhaustion followed. With Dudley as her escort, she escaped to the Providence Hospital. Located in a quiet section of Capitol Hill, the Sisters of Charity had prepared the same room Madeleine occupied in August 1893 when she had returned to DC from her summer in Virginia and had filed her now infamous, and successful, lawsuit. She refused visitors and the press. She slept and considered her next steps, making plans with Sarah Ellis and Dudley, the only companions permitted in her room. When an enterprising reporter sent up a note to Madeleine with questions, Dudley Pollard walked to the hospital lobby and spoke on his sister's behalf, denying all reports that she would take to the stage. She wanted rest and quiet and would likely remain in Washington, although, Dudley emphasized, she had no settled plans.[7]

It took Jane Tucker five days to see her.

Jane was not sorry to be turned away from Madeleine on the day of the verdict. On her journey to the hospital, she forced herself to act pleased with the outcome but found it challenging to raise even the ghost of a smile. She didn't like to be on the losing side. When a trio of nuns prevented her visit, she felt relief.[8] Jane thought of the Breckinridges, Stoll, and Butterworth, sitting in the parlor on Q Street; their heartache made her heart heavy too.

Or so she claimed in a letter to Stoll. In a letter to her mother, Jane offered a cutting assessment of what had gone wrong. First, she and Stoll should have been in charge. If they had run the case, they'd be celebrating now. The wrong captains had steered this ship. Second, handling Mrs. Blackburn with kid gloves was a colossal error. Treating her so delicately and deferentially had left the door open for Blackburn to lie. Third, Mr. Butterworth's cross-examination of Madeleine was "absurd." Jane had told the legal team that they needed to make Madeleine mad when she was on the stand: "It was the only way to break her solid wall, to get her furious, and then she [would lose] her self-control."[9] But Shelby, Stoll, and the other attorneys dismissed Jane's advice—and look where they were now.

———

Madeleine granted Jane a visit on April 19, five days after the verdict. Madeleine sat crocheting, sitting up for the first time since her arrival. Magazines were on the table, and a bottle of fortifying port wine, a gift from Dudley, sat nearby.[10]

"Aggie," Madeleine said, "I am so glad you waited. I've been so tired." Jane noted Madeleine used her small voice as if she were ill, although she certainly appeared healthy. Miss Ellis had visited every day. One reporter had been allowed to interview her. Madeleine admitted that the reporter made up most of their conversation, once again spreading lies in the press, using Madeleine to advance her ambitions. And a woman reporter, no less.

Victory had brought a financial award, and Madeleine told Jane she was not disappointed in the amount. "I'm happy having won the victory of the principle," she said. And besides, more offers had come to her.

Madeleine weighed her options once again. Offers for the stage competed with an equal number of letters advising her to avoid the theater. Newspapers printed a statement from Madeleine thanking her supporters and graciously admitting the wisdom of her detractors. Her future, she claimed, could not be "in the din of publicity and sensation," denying that she would take to the stage or the lecture circuit. If she should accept a book offer, she wrote, it would only be to craft a work that emphasizes "the moral of my misguided life and to awaken good sentiments in public, rather than keep alive bad sensations."[11] Nonetheless, she told Jane, her future would come down to a matter of money: "I must do something to earn my living, and I do not see that there is anything left for me."

Jane suggested she flip a coin and let fate decide her future: actor or author?

Madeleine scurried around her room and found a copper-colored one-cent coin. The penny flip favored the book. Madeleine tried again with a quarter. This time, the fates presented the stage as her future. She seemed pleased with the quarter's answer—the image of Miss Liberty in her Phrygian cap, wearing a laurel wreath, had pointed Madeleine forward.

Miss Liberty misled Madeleine. In August, when rumors hinted that she would take the stage, the theater community pounced.

"For the past ten years," the *Brooklyn Daily Eagle* reported, "the stage has been afflicted with persons who had no right to appear there." Offering a long list of those whose claim to acting chops was notoriety, the article complained of the "dramatic exploitation of undramatic people for commercial purposes." Acting was a skill that took training, and to be thrust on the stage without years of experience would be a disservice to Madeleine and would draw an audience of prurient gawkers. Unless Madeleine had "the voice, the figure, the intuition, the memory, the inventiveness, [and] the power of mimicry, she had best make bonnets or engage in domestic service."[12]

Actors argued that flash-in-the-pan "stars" put legitimate performers out of work and that the sensational salaries offered the momentarily famous, like Madeleine, lowered wages for the rest of the cast and crew. Further, numerous actors were out of work; sensational solo spectacles would increase unemployment. Seeking to rectify "the accession to the ranks of actors . . . prize fighters, freaks, and other monstrosities" and to "elevate" the stage, five hundred New York actors, musical artists, song and dance men, and others formed the Actors Protective Union, No. 1, of the City of New York. Restrictive clauses, including prerequisites of inherent genius and five years' work on stage prior to required union membership, should keep out "the Madeline Pollards."[13] If Madeleine followed the coin-flip fate, she would have a very difficult time.

At five o'clock, a nun appeared with Madeleine's supper and told Jane to leave. As Jane started down the hallway, Madeleine called out, "Aggie, do come back soon. We can plan our trip to New York."

Jane did not see Madeleine again until May 26. After a three-week stay at the hospital, Madeleine rented a room in a small brick cottage on K Street, near the House of Mercy—the house she had spied on their carriage ride. She had the front room on the second story. The room had plain whitewashed walls and not much for decoration. Inexpensive furniture provided a place to sit and a table at which to eat or write. Hannah, a live-in servant, provided Madeleine's meals, shooed away the press, and acted as a gatekeeper to those attempting to visit. The rent was twenty-five dollars a month.[14]

When Jane visited Madeleine's new home at 5:00 p.m., the latter was just getting dressed. She had spent the day reading in bed, finding the mattress more comfortable than the hard, cheap chairs. Since moving in, Madeleine had designed a self-taught course in English literature to prepare for further study abroad. She had no plans to teach; she would read and study. A generous friend provided funds so Madeleine could rest and read the entire year—but who, she did not reveal. Writing a book was no longer a part of her plan.

Madeleine read more than the classics of English literature. She had kept up with those making a quick buck piggybacking onto her fame by publishing books related to the trial. She had read part of Fayette Lexington's *The Celebrated Case of Col. W. C. P. Breckinridge and Madeline Pollard*. "It is simply a copy of the newspaper reports of the trial. It is very poor at that, and, so far as I have read it, I have not been able to discover one original idea in it."[15] Jane asked if she was the author of *A Marriage above Zero*, a much-discussed novel whose heroine fell for a married politician and talented speech-maker called "The Orator."[16] Madeleine strenuously denied that popular rumor, although she had read the book and gave Jane her review. She thought the author had spoken to someone she had known in her youth. The heroine, Madeleine thought, bore quite a similarity to her youthful days. The author, Nevada McNeill, had contacted Madeleine asking for a review and a statement confirming her authorship. Madeleine ignored McNeill. Her requests, she told Jane, were just an advertising scheme.

She spent her days reading and chatting with Miss Ellis, who visited each evening after completing her duties at the House of Mercy. Jane was not sure why Ellis remained so dedicated. Sister Dorothea thought Madeleine would use and discard her, but

Sarah stayed steadfast. Some evenings, Madeleine and Sarah went riding in an open carriage, but in bad weather, they stayed in the room and talked. Madeleine was indebted to Ellis as a chaperone and companion. She noted, "I could not go anywhere without her, Agnes; you have no idea how devoted she has been."[17]

Despite having pled poverty, Madeleine had ordered expensive dresses from a local seamstress. Miss Coffey charged from twenty to forty dollars per dress.[18] Madeleine's street gown would be blue and trimmed with white ribbons; she would wear it with a blue hat topped with white lilacs. A second dress would be of green lawn. She would order more clothes if she went ahead with tentative plans to summer in Bristol, Rhode Island, not far from Newport. Madeleine's New York City friend, Father Huntington, had personally invited her to enjoy a summer by the sea with members of the "400." Jane wondered who was paying for all of this. It certainly was not Breckinridge. He was broke.

Breckinridge had finally spoken directly to his constituents. He wept, he admitted he sinned, he apologized, and then he asked for their votes. Madeleine was unimpressed. She had witnessed ten years of Kentucky politics. "I think they will return him. His friends are powerful enough to do that. But I don't care if he does return . . . I know he is dead, practically, in Congress. After this trial, he will never amount to anything here in Washington."[19] She was right.

As Jane left Madeleine's plain white room in a little cottage, she paused to look at a bouquet. A young Washington girl had sent the flowers to Madeleine; she had sent flowers at several points during the trial. She was so devoted, Madeleine recalled, and hasn't forgotten me.

Madeleine seemed to land on her feet. She professed to have no funds, yet she found sympathetic—and frustratingly anonymous—benefactors who provided housing, fine clothing, and travel. Society had exiled her, but a few tenaciously loyal followers still called her a friend. She admitted to what at the time had been unforgivable sins and endured heartbreaking personal losses yet lived a life in quiet contentment. She wanted to make a name for herself yet turned down offers of the stage, book deals, and business opportunities. Jane descended the stairs and stepped outside. Madeleine was as great a mystery now as when they first met.

From the K Street cottage, Jane walked past the House of Mercy, the brass doorplate catching the last of the day's sun. She made her way toward Dupont Circle and Breckinridge's rented house just one block beyond. Jane never saw Madeleine again.

———

Following the verdict, Jane moved into the Q Street residence housing the Breckinridges to save the financially strapped congressman her boardinghouse rent. Breckinridge had only days to request a retrial, alleging that Judge Bradley had ruled incorrectly on material challenged in court, thus negating the validity of the verdict. The work was urgent, and she was swamped as she typed documents. "Business before everything just now," she reported to her mother.[20]

Louise and Nisba welcomed Jane's presence in their home and enjoyed her company, although Louise was quite ill from the strain of the trial and its unsavory revelations, and Louise's care, in turn, exhausted Nisba. Both had received cruel letters from anonymous authors denigrating Breckinridge, accusing the women of looking the other way, or demanding Louise divorce her new husband if she had any moral fiber. As a favor to Jane, Mollie Tucker wrote some kind words to Louise, sympathizing with her plight and finding something positive to say about Louise's disgraced husband. Her mother did so for Jane's sake and because she pitied the third Mrs. Breckinridge but admitted that, given the unseemly circumstances, "it was not an easy thing to do."[21]

The women doted on Jane, and the household butler filled her every need. Jane later joked that she would have to dress up the Tucker family dog, Bosen, as a butler as she realized she now couldn't live without one. While Madeleine ordered summer dresses for the Rhode Island shore, Jane upgraded her wardrobe, too, buying a black India silk dress. "I needed a best dress so much and have such good 'prospects' I felt that I could afford it . . . when you are visiting the quality, you have to try to look a little respectable."[22]

Despite the plaintiff's victory, the defense team praised Jane's skill, cleverness, and bravery. One lawyer called Jane the best stenographer he had ever seen. Breckinridge's associates promised positions in Louisville and Lexington. She took great satisfaction from how these influential men valued her work.

Her head was swelling, but her pocketbook was empty. Jane had not been paid in full, and she could no longer afford to buy things on hopes of good "prospects." She had hesitated to ask Breckinridge for her pay in the immediate wake of the verdict, but several weeks had now passed, and Jane needed the money. Since January, when Jane left Maine, Stoll had advanced her $253.50 for expenses; Breckinridge owed her an additional $191.00, mostly her salary. She wrote Breckinridge on May 28 from New York, where she was working on the book project, offering to take the balance owed or a part thereof. She directed Breckinridge, "Send it in my own name, Jane Tucker, as it might be easier to cash a check."[23]

The money did not come. Sophonisba, attending to her father's Washington correspondence while he was in Kentucky, had seen Jane's letter requesting payment. On June 2, having not received a check, Jane had sent a follow-up note, explaining that without the congressman's payment, she would have no money from her present work until the end of June. Sophonisba wrote her father and urged him to send whatever he could spare: "She was very faithful and helpful that last week here [in Washington], & I can't bear to [think] of her out of money in New York." Nisba apologized to her father for asking on Jane's behalf. Aware of her father's financial woes yet anxious about the debt to Jane, she told him to take some of the funds from her monthly allotment. She could forgo new clothes.[24] Nisba assured him that this letter was of her own doing—Jane had not asked her to intervene.

From May to early June, Jane worked diligently recounting the story of her detective work and the "real" Madeleine Pollard, or so author Agnes Parker's words claimed.

Jane and Stoll worked together, first in Washington and then in Kentucky at Stoll's Lexington home. Jane built her tale around the daily reports, highlighting her interactions with Madeleine. Stoll added thinly disguised legal points, rehashing evidence Judge Bradley had dismissed during the trial. Dozens of Madeleine's purloined letters were included. Jane added commentary on her adversary's mood, emotions, dining, and future dreams—observations frequently snarky and often heavy-handed as if trying to lead a witness to a specific conclusion.

Jane finished the manuscript in early June and bid the Stolls goodbye. She carried her typed pages to New York City, where Max De Lippman connected Jane with the editor of the book publishing firm G. W. Dillingham. The editor gave a cursory glance to the first few pages, then settled back in his chair and kept reading. He was hooked.

The editor moved fast. He knew Pollard and Tucker's story would be a nine-day wonder—the talk of the town until some other scandal grabbed the limelight. If Dillingham was to make money, they had to hustle and minimize expenses to maximize profits. The manuscript was quickly typeset. Jane remained in New York for several days, likely to proofread the printed pages. There were no illustrations or fancy decorations. The book did not have hardcovers bound in cloth as a more well-regarded work would; this sensational tale was finished with green paper covers. It would be inexpensive, enticing, and easy to fold into a pocket to pull out and read on the subway, a train, or elsewhere. Like many other capture-the-moment tales, *The Real Madeleine Pollard* was a fragile and ephemeral work. Only one actual copy survives to the present day.[25]

Just shy of a month after her last conversation with Jane, Madeleine Pollard learned the depth of Aggie Parker's duplicity. Dillingham released on June 24 *The Real Madeleine Pollard: A*

Diary of Ten Weeks Association with the Plaintiff in the Famous Breckinridge-Pollard Suit, one year and one day from the publication of Madeleine Pollard's engagement announcement. The *New York Herald, Washington Post, San Francisco Examiner*, and *Atlanta Constitution* each published two full-page spreads, six columns per page highlighting the derring-do of the "girl spy" and illustrated with sketches from the courtroom and the House of Mercy. The greatly condensed narrative made a good read featuring the most exciting scenes from Agnes Parker's book. Mame's theater colleague Jim Kelly commented that the newspaper piece contained "lots of sensation and [was] a good readable article."[26] The book was less successful, and Jane, as Agnes Parker, was taken to task.

The *Herald* editors offered praise for the story, one, they said, that was "of more absorbing interest" than any spy-type story the popular author Wilkie Collins wrote. Parker's skills, although a "novice at detective work," were considerable, yet her "astuteness [was] worthy of a better cause." Her mission, they wrote, "was an unfortunate one," "a pitiful business," and "a humiliating occupation for a woman of intelligence or with a lively sense of honor." It was, they concluded, a task decidedly "unfeminine," and unfortunately, they tsk-tsked, Agnes Parker had acted in unfeminine ways: she "ingenuously admits that she found her 'many inventions' came to her quite easily after a time—a deplorable admission for a young woman to make." There was nothing, the editors stated, to admire about Agnes Parker's character.[27]

The *Washington Post* called Jane's work "a strange book" that crossed between fiction and fact: "It is easier to think that the author invented the tale and cunningly presented it rather than to believe that she actually played the remarkable and questionable detective part that she owns up to."[28]

Additional reviews were similarly unkind. The *Times-Picayune* of New Orleans deemed the book "nauseating from a moral, social and literary standpoint." The reviewer concluded that the author was just out for the money "and does not know how to put what she knows in a readable shape." In short, "there is absolutely nothing in it worth reading."[29] The book review editor of Chicago's *Inter Ocean* called Jane's effort "a weak, trashy book from the pen of a woman, or rather a female" with a "virus in her veins."[30]

Dorothea must have been horrified, finding herself and the House of Mercy in print. Keys shaking in anger, she would have realized she looked like a fool. Agnes Parker had lied to her and bragged that she was good at it. Madeleine Pollard had not been the only contaminant in her Home.

Madeleine would have shared Dorothea's wrath. She would have yelled, shook, and cried. Sarah Ellis must have struggled to soothe Madeleine. Agnes Parker—Aggie—*was* Nellie Bly, stealing her secrets and writing them up all along. Yet another false friend—and a woman at that.

Jane faced disappointment too. The lengthy book extract in the *Herald* and elsewhere had failed to stimulate book sales. With the most dramatic scenes revealed in the newspaper, there was little motivation to read the entire book, especially with such poor reviews and, moreover, since the trial outcome was well known. The mystery of this detective's case had already been solved. Reviewers' sharp criticism of Jane's unwomanly behavior may have weakened sales to more conservative homes where young ladies were expected to be truthful and abhor falsity in word and deed. And it wasn't a very good read. Jim Kelley offered his assessment in a letter to Mame. Jane was a "Jim Lulu!" for her undercover exploits, but her book was found wanting: "Too much sameness and repetition, the trouble with all detective stories."[31]

Although in June, Kelly thought the book would "sell like hotcakes for the next three or five months to come," it didn't.[32] Stores lowered the price from fifty cents to thirty-eight.[33] In July, he reassessed: "Sorry Jane's book is a disappointment, but [I] hardly thought it would be a big seller at this late date. It has gotten out of the minds of the people and the people of modern times 'let bygones be bygones.'"[34]

Jane's family was equally unenthusiastic. When Jane returned to Maine and sat down with her family to tell her tales, they were horrified at the true nature of her Washington work. Her parents and conservative brother, Bill, had little interest in Jane sharing her adventures at the dinner table and even less support for her public rendition. Only Mame was supportive. Jane told her sister, "I'm what I am and can't change my skin . . . and we will stick to each other even if the others don't approve of what we do."[35] And to add insult to the mounting injury, Breckinridge never paid Jane, and Stoll did not help her retrieve the funds, despite Jane's repeated requests to both men for payment. And even with the Kentucky lawyers' high praise, none offered Jane a job, and *The Real Madeleine Pollard* flopped. Instead of being set for life, she was back in the same place she had been in January: in debt, out of work, and with no prospects.

In November, Charles Stoll sent Jane a notarized statement authenticating her work as Agnes Parker, undercover detective. Perhaps Jane wanted to leverage her unusual experience into a job, or perhaps she wanted to document her authorship of *The Real Madeleine Pollard*. She had remained in Wiscasset, getting the family home ready for winter, sewing garments on a new machine, and seeking work. Local politics (or perhaps her facility with lying) kept her from a job in the Wiscasset railroad office. As December approached, she apologized in advance to her sister and friends: she had no money for holiday gifts. At least her mother charged her only three dollars a week for room and board.[36]

Jane had no audience for her tales, but that did not stop her quest for adventure. On a beautiful fall day, her mother and cousin Dick took a day trip to Monhegan Island, eight miles off the Maine coast. They would be gone all day. Jane hurried down to the shore of the Sheepscot River to meet Nat Gordon, a diver from Portland. Gordon was well known in the state for his work helping to lay an underwater waterpipe from Bath to Woolwich.[37] He had a free day. Jane may have liberated a pair of pants from her father. Surely a floor-length skirt would be cumbersome for the activity she had in mind. They rowed up the river to Clarke's Point near the Maine Central Bridge. Gordon dove first. When he emerged, he helped Jane into the apparatus, screwing in place a big brass helmet. Ensconced in a diving suit, Jane dropped to the bottom of the river, twenty feet below the surface. She walked underwater for fifteen minutes. Later, she would tell a reporter the initial sensation was "something terrible."[38] Gordon said Jane was only the second woman to go diving and that she showed "more nerve and courage than any man he ever saw go down for the first time."[39]

When she started her aquatic adventure, no one was in sight, but while she was underwater, a boat with Wiscasset residents approached to watch the unusual scene. Jane ascended, got back into Gordon's boat, and he removed her helmet. The observers saw that the diver was Jane. Her shipmates said, "The expression of surprise and horror on [Jane's neighbors] faces was the funniest thing" they ever saw.[40] There would be articles in the newspaper soon. The whole town would talk about it. Her mother was going to be mad. Dick would be aghast. Jane must have smiled.

EPILOGUE

Following the 1894 trial, Breckinridge lost his bid for reelection, failing even to become his party's nominee. Women in his district, supported in spirit by women across the country, pressured men to vote for his opponent. Women threatened to boycott businesses that supported the congressman; a group of women insisted that the University of Kentucky fire a faculty member who campaigned for Breckinridge.[1] As Jane had suggested to her mother, "Women may not be able to make stump speeches in an election but I will bet they can do just as much . . . out of sight as if they could come out openly and help a candidate."[2] Breckinridge did not hold office again. He returned to his law practice and later worked with his son, Desha, editing the *Lexington Herald* until his death.[3]

By the time of Breckinridge's 1904 death, breach of promise law was fading. Only a handful of cases had come to court in the decade that followed his own. Inevitably, the Breckinridge-Pollard suit became a touchstone in reference to these "heartbalm" attempts well into the twentieth century, but by the 1920s, the law was little used. Changing sexual mores and increased opportunities for women to support themselves made it less destructive to experiment sexually before marriage and less tragic to be jilted.

Louise Wing remained with Breckinridge until his death, a faithful, although desperately unhappy, wife. Her struggles with mental illness continued. She never forged a connection with her

stepchildren, and she refused to undertake extended psychological treatment or go to a sanitarium. After her husband's death,
Louise, who was not included in Breckinridge's will, lived with
her sister Etta Mitchell in Buffalo, New York. Despite an estrange-
ment between Wing and the surviving Breckinridge progeny, in
1918, she offered family furniture and other items to the Breckinridge daughters.[4] Louise Scott Wing Breckinridge died in 1920
from complications following an extended case of influenza. She is
buried in the Scott family plot in Frankfort, Kentucky.[5]

   After the trial, both Breckinridge and Desha insisted an
exhausted Nisba leave the family home and attend to her own
intellectual and personal needs. Nisba continued her education at
the University of Chicago, where she was the first woman to earn
a PhD in political science and economics and the first woman to
be admitted to the Kentucky Bar. Among many other accomplishments, she was a scholar, author, educator, and administrator at
the University of Chicago.[6] Her correspondence with Jane seems
to have ended in 1894, when the woman she knew as Agnes Parker
and Miss Johnson returned to Maine and to life as Jane Tucker.

   When Jane Tucker learned of Breckinridge's death, she wrote
her mother: "Breckinridge is dead. Pollard probably killed him."
She rather unkindly opined that his relations were surely "glad to
plant him, everyone," alluding to the fact that his name retained
a pervasive link to scandal.[7] Obituaries praised his Civil War service, congressional accomplishments, and contributions to Lexington but did not fail to reference the public scandal that he always
feared would come. Breckinridge was buried in the family plot in
the Lexington Cemetery. Sophonisba donated his papers to the
Library of Congress, establishing the core of what would become
a collection of over eight hundred boxes of material from the
extended Breckinridge family, men and women who contributed
to American politics and society across two centuries.[8]

   After the failure of *The Real Madeleine Pollard* and the lack
of payment for her detective work, plucky Jane continued her
adventures. Her father's death in 1895 prompted an exhausted

and heartbroken Jane to travel with her mother out West. The fresh air and majestic mountains of Colorado reinvigorated her. Mollie Tucker told Mame how outdoor life was what Jane needed: "To cure Jane we came West." She gained weight, slept well, and had a bicycle suit made. Mollie described how Jane was "riding a wheel for all she is worth. She learned to do so sooner than anybody here . . . and is as fearless and graceful at that. . . . It is doing her good, too."[9]

Settling back in Boston, Jane continued to plug away for self-support and remained free with her opinions. For a time, she worked for a progressive reformer, Mary Morton Kehew, president of the Women's Educational and Industrial Union, an advocate for working women, and a suffragist. Jane complained in letters home about the long hours and Kehew, who was "very good hearted" but was "most trying to anybody working for her."[10] In the late 1890s, in addition to working for Kehew, Jane developed a cosmetics line called Rose Leaf Balm, mixing preparations in her kitchen and experimenting on herself. When one creation burned her face, she walked around Boston thickly veiled, reminiscing that her disguise reminded her of her Washington days.[11] She sold her preparations directly to Boston stores and beyond, a hustling skill that served her well in later jobs as a traveling salesperson for Gossard's, a New York corset company; Vantine's, an importer of Japanese goods; and, later, McCall Patterns. While at Gossard's, true to form, Jane was not shy in sharing her views on how to make a better corset, forcing one aggrieved supervisor to write, "Your energy and determination in the matter of improving our corset is commendable . . . but you have not always been right."[12]

Always in motion, Jane traveled the United States. In 1905, she passed through Lexington and visited Charles Stoll. His wife, Mary Ellen ("Nellie"), whom Jane had liked for her sharp condemnation of Breckinridge's actions, had died in August 1904. Stoll had retired from all his Kentucky businesses. From this visit, Jane concluded that "the mix-up with that trial froze him out," and now, she could see, he was not in good health or spirits: "He looked bum & and was terribl[y] stupid & prosy."[13] Nonetheless, Stoll remarried in 1906 and had decades of life yet to live. The Stolls moved to Mississippi and then to Tennessee. In an irony of history, his daughter Florence married a man named Pollard (no relation) in 1911. Charles Stoll died in Tennessee in 1948 at the age of ninety.[14]

Jane's McCall's sales route took her to Montana and Wyoming. For a short time, she planned to buy land, build a cabin, and settle in the West, where the sky was big. But Mame Tucker had died in 1899, leaving Jane the lone surviving Tucker daughter.[15] When Mollie became ill, the family claim grabbed hold once more, pulling Jane back to Wiscasset to manage summer boarders, can squab, and hold together the aging family homestead. Mollie Tucker died in 1922, and Jane inherited Castle Tucker; she lived there for the rest of her life. She was active in the Maine Democratic Party and, in 1925, compiled a fundraising cookbook to support candidates for state offices.[16] Women across Maine contributed recipes. Jane supplied recipes for Grandmother Tucker's Melted Butter Cake and Creamed Salt Fish, among others. She never married. Those who knew Jane described her as a Wiscasset "presence." She died in 1964 at ninety-eight years old and is buried with her family in a cemetery not far from the Sheepscot River as it makes its way to the sea past the glacier-carved peninsulas and islands that mark Maine's coast. When the wind is right, you can smell the salt air.

As for her days as Agnes Parker, with Jane's death, one of the most exciting events in her life was lost to history, left to vague stories of her once having been a Pinkerton. No copy of *The Real Madeleine Pollard* survives at Castle Tucker or in the Historic New England archive. Her obituary did not mention her book or her stint as an undercover detective. Indeed, the headline read "Miss Jane Tucker, Sea Captain's Daughter, Dies."[17]

Madeleine Pollard is also buried near the sea. The press during and immediately after the trial hounded her, but by the fall of 1894, newspapers had moved on to other scandals. The name *Madeleine Pollard* became a punch line in jokes, a character in short stories, the subject of an operetta, and the moniker for several horses, a zinc mine, a Maine cow, a Kentucky mule, and a Berkshire pig.[18]

Breckinridge, in tremendous debt, never paid Madeleine a dime of the civil damages awarded her by the court; like Jane, Madeleine had no monetary reward for her considerable effort. Nonetheless. Madeleine did not take to the stage or write a book. She lived briefly with Dudley and tried to find work in New York, but her celebrity was a detriment, with potential supervisors fearing her fame would present a distraction.[19] Nearly one hundred years later, Monica Lewinsky faced the same situation when potential employers feared her celebrity would overshadow her work. Of the dilemma of being known only through the media circus that followed revelation of her relationship with then-president Bill Clinton, Lewinsky said, "I was seen by many but known by few."[20] The same was true of Madeleine.[21]

Likely both seeking escape from such notoriety and moving toward her long-held dream, Madeleine traveled to London with the support of an unidentified woman. After a brief return to the United States in 1896, by 1897, she had taken up residence in London as an American expatriate. Shortly thereafter, Madeleine met a wealthy, young Irish widow, Violet Emily Hassard, who had lost her husband to typhoid in 1892. Both women lived in the Kensington and Chelsea area of London, and their paths crossed. By the turn of the century, they were constant companions, sharing living quarters and traveling together. In 1901, they shared a home in Oxford; in 1911, they lived in the Old Cottage on Tennyson Road in Bognor, Sussex.[22] Around the end of World War I, Madeleine and Hassard rented a flat on the top floor of Lawrence Mansions, a brick-fronted apartment building in artsy Chelsea, just one block from the Thames and the treelined walking path along the embankment. Madeleine had indeed found the pleasant surroundings and broad streets of her aspirations. In 1932, they installed a telephone. Madeleine and Hassard lived there together for nearly thirty years.[23]

Madeleine dreamed of a life of intellectual stimulation surrounded by art, literature, and culture, and she seems finally to have achieved it, not through dependence on a man but with the support of women. With a base in London, she and Hassard traveled throughout Europe and into Egypt. Madeleine lived for a while in Paris, studying French. She spent a semester at Oxford. She traveled to the United States every few years, staying with Margaret Thorne Tjader in New York City or at Tjader's ocean-view summer home, Vikingsborg, in Connecticut. Madeleine had met Tjader in 1894. Tjader, wealthy wife of explorer, big game hunter, and preacher Richard Tjader, is likely Madeleine's post-trial benefactress. Together, the Tjaders founded the Church of the Strangers in New York City, in which Father Huntington (who counseled Madeleine in Washington and served as a reference on her 1923 passport application) was involved, as well as an evangelizing International Union Mission, which both Hassard and Madeleine supported. Madeleine's name runs throughout Tjader's twentieth-century correspondence with references to "our old friend" and seeing Madeleine in Paris, among others.[24] In 1928, Tjader and Madeleine crossed the Atlantic together on the SS *Paris*, first class.[25]

In the 1920s, Madeleine, nearing her sixties, enrolled in classes at Columbia University, staying in Tjader's city apartment. She appears in the 1920 census in Tjader's household under yet another variation of her name: Urquhart Pollard. The 1919/20 Columbia student roster lists her as Pollard M. Urquart; a subsequent enrollment in 1924–25 is under the name Madeleine Pollard. This unusual addition had been in play for at least a decade; the UK 1910 census records Madeleine Urquart Pollard. The origin and reason behind the name Urquart/Urquhart is unknown.

At Columbia, Madeleine fulfilled a lifelong dream and studied literature. Her faculty included Dorothy Scarborough, who taught creative writing and with whom she corresponded after her time at university.[26] It does not appear Madeleine ever returned to Kentucky. Her mother, Nannie, and sister, Mamie, both died in 1920. Dudley remained in New York, married, and had three sons, including a set of twins. Descendants of Dudley Pollard report that the scandal and resulting national notoriety tore apart the Pollard family; none of Dudley's offspring met Madeleine; she was not at her brother's funeral in 1940.[27]

Madeleine continued her European and transatlantic travels through the 1930s until the approaching war ended her journeys. In 1938, she wrote her will. She noted the possibility that she and Violet would die at the same time, "bearing in mind the times in which we are living."[28]

In the spring of 1940, Madeleine and Hassard still lived in their Chelsea flat. By November, they were gone.

Chelsea was hard hit in the London Blitz as German bombers followed the glint of the moon reflecting on the Thames to navigate in their nighttime bomb-dropping runs. Daylight raids and dogfights in the sky above added additional danger, as did unexploded bombs sitting half buried in London streets or gardens. Sandbags, razor wire, and piles of brick, wood, and glass from demolished buildings abounded. Chelsea was the third most heavily bombed London borough.[29] But residents were prepared. A practice raid in 1939 brought accolades for Chelsea locals who headed to shelters in the mock attack.[30] Air raid wardens patrolled the streets, and a system of colors and whistles alerted everyone to potential danger. They kept calm and carried on.

When bombs did explode, the destruction was brutal. In Madeleine's neighborhood, residents took shelter in the crypt of the Most Holy Redeemer Church. Once the siren sounded, Madeleine and Hassard, nearly eighty years old and living on the top floor of Lawrence Mansions, had seven to ten minutes to get to the shelter before the bombs fell. They navigated down three flights of stairs, then walked up Lordship Place, and then turned left on Cheyne Row and walked to the church. Google maps tells us that it is 417 feet from the front door of Lawrence Mansions to the church and, walking, would take you two minutes. The calculation does not take into account the stairs, the darkness of air raid protections, the gunfire of antiaircraft, the bombs falling elsewhere in the city, and two frightened, elderly women moving carefully in a crowd of hurrying, scared people.

On the night of September 14, 1940, the church crypt sheltered 80–100 people, mostly older women and children.[31] They felt safe underground until a high explosive bomb tore through a stained-glass window, crashed through the stone church floor, and exploded in the crypt below. Chaos ensued as the church floor fell in from above and stone pillars crumbled. A pile of coke, stored in the crypt for winter heating, ignited, and thick black smoke filled the room. A heavy woman, unconscious, blocked the narrow stairway, trapping the living in the dark and smoking ruins. Neighborhood patrols arrived and attempted to douse the flames. When the smoke cleared, responders saw carnage of blood and severed limbs. Nineteen people had been killed and scores more injured, overwhelming the system to transport the wounded to hospitals and the dead to morgues, travel complicated by wreckage-filled streets. Thirteen of the dead spent the night in the church garden.

The church was just one of many businesses, homes, and other properties bombed that night; thirty-seven incidents were recorded in Chelsea on September 14. Kitty-corner to Lawrence Mansions, directly in view of Madeleine and Hassard's rear-facing flat, a high explosive bomb obliterated a townhouse, killing two people and leaving only a crater in the ground.[32] Piles of debris filled the streets. The next evening, bombs hit Buckingham Palace. The queen refused to leave. In Chelsea and throughout London, no one had wanted to live in the top-floor flats since the Blitz began.[33]

We don't know for certain where Madeleine and Hassard sheltered on September 14, but we know they left Chelsea shortly afterward. In the aftermath of the devastation at the church, the king and queen visited the site to memorialize the dead and commend the rescuers. Air Raid Patrol volunteer and diarist Josephine

Oakman recalled the flight of Chelsea residents, noting that in October 1940, the streets were clogged with wagons and vans hauling away the possessions of residents in "great numbers."[34] Madeleine and Hassard seemed to be among them. The fall 1940 phonebook, published in November, no longer included a listing for Hassard and Madeleine.[35]

Madeleine and Hassard took refuge in Streatham, south of London across the Thames, staying in a small, rented house on Madeira Road for at least three years.[36] Records are spotty—a war was on—but they reappear in 1945 in the home of Hassard's sister-in-law, Catherine Hassard, and Catherine's sister, Jane Tonge. Catherine Hassard had lived in the Devon village of Lynmouth since the 1920s, purchasing a stone house known as Cliff House, perched on a steep hill overlooking the East Lyn River as it flows out to Lynmouth Bay and the Bristol Channel. Exmoor National Park surrounds the area. Wales is to the north across the channel; Ireland is to the west.

Catherine Hassard welcomed her brother's widow and Madeleine Pollard to sit out the remainder of the war in relative safety. The longtime friends were in failing health. In June 1945, Violet Hassard died in Catherine's home. She was buried in an ancient cemetery, tight with generations of graves, at Countisbury Hill, a mile as the crow flies from Cliff House. Violet Hassard left her entire estate to Madeleine, her "old and dearest friend."[37] Madeleine Pollard, in a month's time, would be a very wealthy woman.

In August, Catherine Hassard died, and Jane Tonge laid her to rest in the Countisbury Hill cemetery. Obituaries praised her generosity to the town. A large, ornate cross decorates Catherine Hassard's grave.

In December 1945, Madeleine fell ill and entered Cottage Hospital across the river valley in Lynton. The small stone hospital, still a medical facility today, looks like a gnome's home with its red sloping roof and quaint appearance. In her final days, alone in the hospital as her heart failed, did she think of Breckinridge's lies, Jane Tucker's betrayal, and the heartbreak both had caused her?

Or was her heart full with satisfaction about the life she had built for herself? A life she enjoyed for fifty years after the trial that gave her a victory but did not define her life. Having lived from the Civil War through the end of World War II, Madeleine Pollard died on December 9, 1945.[38]

I began this project with a simple question that few had bothered to ask in the 1890s or beyond: What happened to Madeleine Pollard? As I climbed the steep hill to Cliff House, leg muscles screaming, and walked Lynton's narrow streets, I found my answer: she lived a great life. I had traveled to Devon to find her burial place and see her gravestone. Philosophers say that we all die twice: the physical death of our bodies and then a second death the last time anyone speaks our name. I was curious—What name would mark her resting place? Reading her gravestone, what inscription would I utter?

At the town hall, arriving before it opened for the day's business, I encountered the mayor, who unlocked the building and proudly gave an unscheduled tour. In the town office, I found Madeleine Pollard's name carefully penned in an oversized leather-bound book recording Lynton deaths. She was buried in the town cemetery. The plot map was tacked up on the back of a supply cabinet door. I looked for Madeleine. She was nineteen rows from the Lych Gate at the cemetery entrance and then four graves to the right. I walked to the cemetery and found her in the shadow of a craggy hill, just a few hundred yards from the sea. Only the most recent graves had been mown; the rest of the cemetery was a field of knee-high grass, pleasing the goats that roam free in this lovely part of England.

What happened to her? Along my research journey, I had found another equally intriguing woman, Jane Tucker—and when I followed the archival trails of the women of the trial, I saw dozens of fascinating stories of women, white and Black, elite and working class, ambitious or not, all just trying to find their ways around the barriers that constrained female lives in order to claim their small part of that elusive American dream—that is, to live the lives they wanted to live, under their own direction.

I had found the end of Madeleine's story and had just one more question—her final words, the name she would take for eternity. Nineteen rows up, four graves over. Madeleine is buried in an unmarked grave.

ACKNOWLEDGMENTS

The short version is simply this: I could not have completed this project alone.

I am so appreciative of individuals who shared their expertise and showed me history. In Lexington, Kentucky, I'm grateful to the late Thomas Grunwald for his tour of the Sayre School and to Mark Coyne and Yvonne Giles for introducing me to African Cemetery No. 2, the resting place of Sarah Gist. In Washington, librarian Letty Limbach walked me through the DC Court of Appeals, Historic Courthouse, and in London, Steve Hunnisett of Blitzwalkers provided a custom walking tour of Chelsea during World War II.

Generous scholars shared their research with me, providing moments with Madeleine Pollard that would otherwise have gone unseen. Thank you, Dr. David Stameshkin, Dr. Rose Neal, and Dr. Syliva Grider. I thank Dr. James Klotter for our conversation on the Pollard case and a special thanks to Caprice Woodburn for answering my shot-in-the-dark Facebook message and sharing Pollard family history.

Newspapers articles were rarely signed by their authors in 1894. I want to recognize the labor of the reporters who sat in the courtroom day after day and provided such rich material for my own account. I thank them for their writing and acknowledge my debt in borrowing and sharing the words they wrote with a new audience of readers.

I am very grateful for research funding from the Kentucky Historical Society, Sisters in Crime, and from the University of New England (UNE) in the form of the Ludcke Chair of Arts and Sciences, two Office of Sponsored Research mini-grants, and three sabbaticals. To those organizations that provided time, space, and encouragement to write, I thank the Key West Literary Seminar Writers in Residence program, the Pattison Residency in Creative Arts, and the Maine Writers and Publishers Alliance for the SLICE fellowship.

The endnotes identify the numerous archives and libraries in which I found traces of Madeleine and Jane, and I thank most sincerely the staff of those institutions, big and small. In addition, I am grateful to librarians and archivists who searched records on my behalf, sometimes with little (or nothing) to find. These include the collections of Tiffany & Co.; the Episcopal Archdioceses of Maryland, Washington, DC, and New York; the Rosemount Center/House of Mercy; Columbia University; Trinity College (Connecticut); Cincinnati Public Library; and the Archives of Ohio United Methodism at Ohio Wesleyan University. I thank Wayne Kempton, Episcopal archdiocese of New York, for providing the enhanced image of the House of Mercy, and the office of Senator Susan Collins (Maine) for assistance in gaining access to records in the State Department. I am especially grateful to Lorna Condon and the archives staff at Historic New England for shifting their doubt that Jane was a girl spy into full-fledged support of this project.

I am indebted to several research assistants, including UNE undergraduate students Kris McLaughlin, Korin Nickerson Fisher, Kelsey Heck, and Sujin An, and independent researchers Michael Thomas and Jessica Riley. A special shoutout to the UNE interlibrary loan librarians, who can find, and borrow, the most obscure article, microfilm roll, or out-of-print book. Elaine Brouillette deserves a special thanks for managing budgets, grant purchases, myriad forms, and travel arrangements; for pep talks and doughnuts; and for always doing today's work today.

Many wise writers and readers reviewed my work, and I owe them so much for their time (and time again) and cogent critiques.

My thinking and writing are stronger for their efforts. Thank you, Jennifer Lunden, Jennifer Tuttle, Libby Bischoff, Pamela Toler, Theresa Kaminski, Rebecca Noel, Sunny Stalter-Pierce, Patti Rutka, Candace Kanes, Etta Madden, Shirley Wajda, David Kuchta, Joan Dempsey, and anonymous peer reviewers. I'm very grateful for the sweeping editorial review of Celia Johnson and the good advice of fellow writers Summer Brennan, Matthew Goodman, Laurie Gwen Shapiro, and Joshua Bodwell, all of whom offered wisdom at fraught moments.

For shepherding the manuscript from draft to publication, I thank editor Natalie O'Neal and the entire staff of the University Press of Kentucky.

This project took much longer than anticipated, and the steadfast support of friends, family, and colleagues kept me moving forward. I thank the members of the Ukulele Strummers of Southern Maine, my friends in the Friends of the Library, Terri Vanderlinde, Jennifer Tuttle, Candace Kanes, Barbara Murphy, Todd and Sharon Pattison, Bella Boo, Ali and Beth Ahmida, and my online writing group, whose daily check-ins on writing and life provided sustenance (encouragement, guilt) to keep at it: Thank you Sunny, Jess, Pamela, Theresa, Becky, Lourdes, and Scottie.

I began this project on June 1, 2008. I saw a copy of *The Celebrated Trial* at an antiquarian book fair and was intrigued by the topic. A little research that evening told me Madeleine Pollard's story had yet to be told. I looked online to order the 1894 book—of three available copies, one was for sale in Maine, where I live. The seller: DeWolfe & Wood Books—my rare-bookseller husband's business, one mile from our home. Scott brought the book home that evening, setting in motion a project that he supported and endured, ups and downs, steadfastly by my side. To my husband—my favorite purveyor of books and old paper, travel partner, decipherer of scratchy manuscript, sounding board, provider of chocolate, and companion in life—there are not words enough to express how lucky I am to have you at my side.

A Note on Sources

The tale of the detective Jane Tucker and her quarry, Madeleine Pollard, would seem to be the product of a novelist's vibrant imagination, but it is a true story, and the rendition here is based on extensive historical research. Jane Tucker's book, *The Real Madeleine Pollard*, gives us our best source on the details of her undercover work. Yet despite reliance on her daily reports in crafting her book, Jane confused dates and recorded events out of order. We know she fabricated scenes, and the book was not a memoir but rather, with her employer, written with a specific political agenda in mind.

Jane's correspondence to her mother and sister help confirm some of her activities. In these letters, Jane shared her opinions on Madeleine, the attorneys, and the trial, yet, frustratingly, she did not disclose specifics of her spying, maintaining the utmost secrecy about her mission and leaving her family to believe she worked as a stenographer. Similarly, Breckinridge's copious letters to constituents, family, and friends and Madeleine Pollard's autobiographical essay in the *New York World* hew to an agenda, the congressman arguing his innocence and Madeleine depicting his guilt.

The court records of the trial would be a valuable source but while the National Archives has an acid-free box whose label promises the trial transcript, depositions, and other materials, the only item in the archival container is a file card with one sentence typed on it: "Do not remove this card." The trial records are missing, leading the researcher to rely on newspapers.

Evocative and colorful, the newspaper accounts were rich with details on the sights and sounds of the trial. But from inattention or mishearing, reporters sometimes got things wrong: Did Madeleine stay with Mrs. Hemming or Mrs. Emmons? Was the assignation house on Eighth Street or A Street? Cultural norms led reporters to censure material deemed unseemly or considered trivial, including the details of testimony by working-class and Black women. Political bias impacted how editors framed coverage, with several papers decidedly pro-Pollard or team Breckinridge right from the start.

The onus, then, is on the historian to corroborate or fill in details using other means. And thus, like Jane, I worked as a detective, seeking out clues from disparate sources, building timelines, weighing words, comparing facts. Navigating among the biases and the agendas and the attempts to catch the public eye, I read between, around, and underneath the lines to find Jane and Madeleine's amazing story.

Notes

Abbreviations

Archives and Family Papers

BFP   Breckinridge Family Papers, MSS 13698, Manuscript Division, Library of Congress

LOC   Library of Congress, Manuscript Division, Washington, DC

NARA   National Archives and Records Administration, Washington, DC

TFP   Tucker Family Papers, MS 033, Historic New England, Boston

Newspapers

CE   *Cincinnati Enquirer*

CJ   *Courier-Journal* (Louisville, KY)

ES   *Evening Star* (Washington, DC)

NYT   *New York Times*

WP   *Washington Post*

Books

RMP   Agnes Parker [Jane Armstrong Tucker], *The Real Madeleine Pollard*, 1894

MPvB   *The Celebrated Trial: Madeline Pollard vs. Breckinridge*, 1894

Frequent Correspondents

CS   Charles Stoll

JAT   Jane Armstrong Tucker

LW   Louise Scott Wing Breckinridge

MAT   Mary (Mollie) Geraldine Armstrong Tucker

MMT   Mary (Mame) Mellus Tucker Clayton

MP   Madeleine Pollard

WCPB   William C. P. Breckinridge

Prologue

1. MAT to MMT, January 17, 1894, TFP.

2. On Jane's life in Boston, see her letters to family from 1887 to 1893, TFP.

3. Joanne Meyerowitz, *Women Adrift: Independent Wage Earners in Chicago, 1880–1930* (Chicago: University of Chicago Press, 1988), xvii–xxiii. On work in Boston, see Sarah Deutsch, *Women and the City: Gender, Space, and Power in Boston, 1870–1940* (New York: Oxford University Press, 2000).

4. JAT to MAT, December 26, 1893, TFP.

5. The term *salesman's sample* is used in the antiquarian book trade to describe a specific historical book form. Although the majority of salesmen were men, women, too, sold books (and other items) door to door. See flyer seeking "lady agents," stored with a copy of *The Celebrated Trial*, Box 343.1 p772c c.3, Kentucky Historical Society, Frankfort. See also "Agents Wanted," *CE*, April 19, 1894.

6. The limited literature on the scandal includes James C. Klotter, *The Breckinridges of Kentucky* (Lexington: University Press of Kentucky, 1986), 161–170; J. Klotter, "Sex, Scandal, and Suffrage in the Gilded Age," *Historian* 42 (February 1980): 225–243; Paul E. Fuller, "An Early Venture of Kentucky Women in Politics: The Breckinridge Congressional Campaign of 1894," *Filson Club History Quarterly* 63 (April 1989): 224–242; Elizabeth DeWolfe, "'Not Ruined, but Hindered': Rethinking Scandal, Re-examining Transatlantic Sources, and Recovering Madeleine Pollard," *Legacy: A Journal of American Women Writers* 31 (2014): 300–310; E. DeWolfe, "More Than a Congressman's Mistress: Ambition and Scandal in the Life of Madeleine Pollard," *The Register of the Kentucky Historical Society* 115 (Sumer 2017): 313–348; and Patricia Miller, *Bringing Down the Colonel* (New York: Sarah Crichton Books, 2018).

7. The phrase *girl spy* is found in "Miss Pollard as She Is," *New York Herald*, June 24, 1894.

8. CS to WCPB, January 16, 1894, Box 788, BFP.

9. Agnes Parker, *The Real Madeleine Pollard: A Diary of Ten Weeks' Intimate Association with the Plaintiff in the Famous Breckinridge-Pollard Suit* (New York: G. W. Dillingham, 1894).

10. JAT to WCPB, May 28, 1894, Box 791, and Sophonisba Breckinridge to WCPB, June 2, 1894, Box 791, BFP.

11. JAT, Invoice, ca. May 28, 1894, Box 812, BFP. Jane included her invoice in her May 28 letter to WCPB, but the two documents had been separated at some point.

12. On how I untangled Parker's aliases, see Elizabeth A. DeWolfe, "Agnes Parker, Miss Johnson, Jane Tucker, and Me," in *Paper Trails: The Social Life of Archives and Collections*, ed. Andrew W. M. Smith (London: UCL Press, 2021), https://ucldigitalpress.co.uk/BOOC/Article/3/102/.

13. On nineteenth-century women spies and detectives, see Karen Abbott, *Liar, Temptress, Soldier, Spy: Four Women Undercover in the Civil War* (New York: Harper, 2014); Kathleen De Grave, *Swindler, Spy, Rebel: The Confidence Woman in Nineteenth-Century America* (Columbia: University of Missouri Press, 1995); Chris Enss, *The Pinks* (Guilford, CT: Twodot, 2017); Erika Janik, *Pistols and Petticoats: 175 Years of Lady Detectives in Fact and Fiction* (Boston: Beacon Press, 2016); S. Paul O'Hara, *Inventing the Pinkertons, or, Spies, Sleuths, Mercenaries, and Thugs* (Baltimore: Johns Hopkins University Press, 2016).

14. On how reading could suggest escape *to* a different future as well as an escape *from* unpleasant circumstances, see Barbara Sicherman, "Reading and Ambition: M. Cary Thomas and Female Heroism," *American Quarterly* 45 (March 1993): 73–103, https://doi.org/10.2307/2713053.

1. Hastily, Jane

1. "Historical/Biographical Note," Tucker Family Papers, Historic New England, accessed March 15, 2024, https://www.historicnewengland.org /explore/collections-access/gusn/187787/.

2. Joann Dalton, "Patience Stapleton: A Forgotten Frontier Writer," *Colorado Magazine* 53, no. 3 (1976): 261–276. See also "Stapleton," *Author* 1, no. 11 (November 15, 1889): 173–174.

3. JAT, Diary, January 9, 1881, TFP.

4. JAT, Diary, May 19, 1881, TFP.

5. *Catalog 1882–1883*, St. Joseph's Academy (Emmitsburg, MD), TFP.

6. JAT, Diary, January 9, 1881, TFP.

7. JAT, "Autobiography," in Composition Book, November 1882, St. Joseph's Academy, TFP.

8. JAT, Diary, May 4, 1881, TFP.

9. JAT, Diary, 1881, passim, TFP.

10. Otto Penzler, ed., *The Big Book of Female Detectives* (New York: Vintage Crime/Black Lizard, 2018), xiii. On detective fiction, see also Erika Janik, *Pistols and Petticoats: 175 Years of Lady Detectives in Fact and Fiction* (Boston: Beacon Press, 2016); Catherine Ross Nickerson, *The Web of Iniquity: Early Detective Fiction by American Women* (Durham, NC: Duke University Press, 1998); Lucy Sussex, *Women Writers in Nineteenth-Century Crime Fiction: The Mothers of the Mystery Genre* (New York: Palgrave Macmillan, 2010).

11. JAT, Diary, 1881; see also book lists in Diaries, 1885 and 1886, TFP.

12. JAT to MMT, December 28, 1887, TFP.

13. Ibid.

14. JAT to MAT, April 1888, TFP.

15. *Prospectus, Hickox's School of Shorthand and Typewriting* (Boston, ca. 1890), in TFP.

16. "Business Directory," in *The Boston Directory* (Boston: Sampson, Murdock, and Company, 1890), 1475.

17. JAT to MAT, undated letter [spring 1891], TFP.

18. "The History of the T," Massachusetts Bay Transportation Authority, accessed November 11, 2023, https://www.mbta.com/history. See also Steven Beaucher, *Boston in Transit: Mapping the History of Public Transportation in The Hub* (Cambridge, MA: MIT Press, 2023); Doug Most, *The Race Underground: Boston, New York, and the Incredible Rivalry That Built America's First Subway* (New York: St. Martin's, 2014); Sam Bass Warner, *Streetcar Suburbs: The Process of Growth in Boston (1870–1900)*, 2nd ed. (Cambridge, MA: Harvard University Press, 1978).

19. JAT to MAT, January 31, 1892, TFP.

20. The phrase is Jane's summary of Bill's criticism in JAT to MAT, ca. January 21, 1892, TFP.

21. Mollie's comments embedded in JAT to MAT, May 24, 1891, TFP.

22. JAT to MAT, May 24, 1891, TFP. On physician Charles P. Thayer, see Alaric Bertrand Start, *History of Tufts College* (Medford, MA: Tufts College, 1896), 186–188. Internet Archive.

23. JAT to MAT, May 1, 1892, TFP.

24. JAT to MAT, November 12, 1892, TFP.

25. Ibid.

26. Ibid.

27. Ibid.

28. JAT to MAT, October 15, 1892, TFP.

29. JAT to MAT, December 18, 1892, TFP.

30. CS, Letter of reference, April 22, 1893, TFP. See also J. L. Smyser, Letter of reference, April 18, 1893, TFP; F. D. Carley, Letter of reference, April 19, 1893, TFP.

31. JAT to MAT, September 20, 1893, TFP.

32. Mark Zachary Taylor, *Presidential Leadership in Feeble Times: Explaining Executive Power in the Gilded Age* (Oxford: Oxford University Press, 2023), 299–319. Accessed March 15, 2024. ProQuest Ebook Central; see also "Panic of 1893," Daily Dose Documentary, July 26, 2023, https://www.youtube.com/watch?v=1xVZoWA4mjc.

33. JAT to Richard H. Tucker, November 8, 1893, TFP.

34. JAT to MAT, and JAT to MMT, November 23, 1893, TFP.

35. "Patience Stapleton Dead," *NYT*, November 26, 1893; "Patience Stapleton Dead," *Daily Inter Ocean* (Chicago), November 26, 1893.

36. Jane Addams coined the term *family claim* in her 1910 autobiographical history of the founding of Hull-House. See Addams, *Twenty Years at*

Hull-House (Champaign: University of Illinois Press, 1989), 10, 71. Accessed November 12, 2023. ProQuest Ebook Central.
37. JAT to MMT, ca. December 1, 1893, TFP.
38. JAT to MMT, December 23, 1893, TFP.
39. JAT to MAT, December 26, 1893, TFP.
40. JAT to MAT, January 4, 1894, TFP.
41. JAT to MAT, November 12 and 20, 1892, TFP.
42. CS to JAT, January 21, 1894, TFP.
43. Ibid.

2. My Dear Mr. Rodes

1. "Madeline's Story," *ES*, March 16, 1894.
2. "The Colonel," *CE*, April 3, 1894.
3. "Madeline's Story," *ES*, March 19, 1894.
4. On women in college, see Lynn Peril, *College Girls: Bluestockings, Sex Kittens, and Coeds, Then and Now* (New York: W. W. Norton and Co., 2006).
5. The contract was later reported lost in the second of two house fires at Nannie Pollard's home. See "The Bridgeport Fire," *Frankfort* (KY) *Roundabout*, May 22, 1880; and "Bridgeport," *Frankfort Roundabout*, January 10, 1885.
6. "Aliases Under which the [*sic*] Madeleine Has Gone," Memorandum, ca. 1893–94, BFP. Joseph Blackburn was a senator from Kentucky. Possible inspirations for Madeleine's recrafted name include Maria Edgeworth's *Vivian* (1814) and Annie S. Swann, *Ursula Vivian: The Sister-Mother* (1884). A rare example of Pollard's schoolgirl writing is her romance story "A Prophecy," reprinted in "Miss Pollard's Story," *ES*, March 16, 1894.
7. "Literary Societies," in *Annual Catalogue Cincinnati Wesleyan College for Young Women, 1883–84* (Cincinnati: Western Methodist Book Concern, 1884), 33.
8. "Wesleyan College. The Lyceum Versus the Cincinnatium," *CE*, March 15, 1884.
9. "Memoranda of Miss Madeleine's Attendance at Sayre Institute Taken from the Books by H. McClellan, Principal," Box 793, BFP. On the history of Sayre School, see J. Winston Coleman, *A Centennial History of Sayre School, 1854–1954* (Lexington, KY, 1954); and William Trent Williams, *All Rise: A History of Sayre School, 1854–1990* (Lexington, KY, ca. 1993).
10. John W. Reps, *Washington on View: The Nation's Capital Since 1790* (Chapel Hill: The University of North Carolina Press, 1991), 202; "Table 12: Population of the 100 Largest Urban Places: 1890," US Bureau of the Census, June 15, 1998, https://www2.census.gov/library/working-papers/1998/demographics/pop-twps0027/tab12.txt.

11. On changes in Washington, see Reps, *Washington on View*, 202–235.

12. *MPvB*, 65–66, 77–78.

13. *MPvB*, 46–47, 78; *RMP*, 261.

14. MP to James Rodes, June 8, 1888, Box 782, BFP.

15. Margery Davies, *Woman's Place Is at the Typewriter: Office Work and Office Workers, 1870–1930* (Philadelphia: Temple University Press, 1982), 28–30, 55, and Table 1, 177–178. See also Cindy S. Aron, "'To Barter Their Souls for Gold': Female Clerks in Federal Government Offices, 1862–1890," *Journal of American History* 67, no. 4 (March 1981): 835–853, https://doi.org/10.2307/1888052.

16. MP to James Rodes, October 18, 1887, Box 782, BFP.

17. See Francis Ellington Leupp, *How to Prepare for a Civil Service Examination* (New York: Hinds and Noble, 1898), 52, 135–136. According to *MPvB*, 193, Madeleine applied to take the civil service exam in Cincinnati in 1887; Breckinridge stated she failed the exam in "More of His Story," *ES*, March 30, 1894.

18. [Madeleine V. B. Pollard], "Application for Appointment in the Census Office," File No. 625, Records of the Office of the Secretary of the Interior, Record Group 48.5.1, Records of the Appointments Division, NARA.

19. WCPB to Robert P. Porter, May 31, 1889, File No. 625, Records of the Office of the Secretary of the Interior, NARA.

20. Breckinridge denied assisting Madeleine in getting her Agriculture Department position. "More of His Story."

21. *Official Register of the United States, Containing a List of Officers and Employés in the Civil, Military, and Naval Service on the First of July 1889.* Vol. 1. (Washington, DC: Government Printing Office, 1889), 675; and MP to James Rodes, January 30, 1889 [*sic*] [1890], Box 783, BFP.

22. WCPB to Robert P. Porter, January 11, 1890, in [Madeleine V. B. Pollard], File No. 625, Records of the Office of the Secretary of the Interior, NARA.

23. Madeleine Pollard, Application and Appointment Record, File No. 625, Records of the Office of the Secretary of the Interior, NARA.

24. MP to James Rodes, January 30, 1889 [*sic*] [1890], Box 783, BFP.

25. Aron, "'To Barter Their Souls for Gold,'" 847.

26. MP to James Rodes, January 30, 1889 [*sic*] [1890], Box 783, BFP; "James C. Rodes," Burial Records, Lexington (KY) Cemetery.

27. Leonard C. Bruno, "Plate, Punch Card and Instructions for Herman Hollerith's Electric Sorting and Tabulating Machine, ca. 1895," Words and Deeds in American History, American Memory, Library of Congress, accessed February 26, 2015, http://memory.loc.gov/cgi-bin/query/r?ammem/mcc:@field (DOCID+@lit(mcc/023)).

28. Madeleine V. B. Pollard, Personal Record, 1889–1897, vol. 2, 509, Record Group 29. Records of the Bureau of the Census, Administrative Records

of the Census Office. Records of the Eleventh Census. Records of the First Division—Appointments, NARA.

29. Acting Superintendent of the Census Bureau to the Secretary of the Interior, June 12, 1891, File No. 625, Records of the Office of the Secretary of the Interior, NARA. A curious story, repeated in several newspapers in the summer 1891, states that Madeleine was fired at the behest of the president when she made a caustic remark on the death of General George Tecumseh Sherman. Given Sherman's February 1891 death and funerals, and the paper trail of her dismissal, months later, one wonders if the story (error-filled in the newspapers) was a face-saving tale.

30. On the Blackburns' courtship and marriage, see Nancy Disher Baird, *Luke Pryor Blackburn: Physician, Governor, Reformer* (Lexington: University Press of Kentucky, 1979). See also Tim Talbott, "Churchill Downs," *ExploreKYHistory*, accessed November 13, 2023, https://explorekyhistory.ky .gov/items/show/318.

31. Madeleine Vinton Dahlgren, *Etiquette of Social Life in Washington*, 5th ed. (Philadelphia: J. B. Lippincott & Co., 1881), 53.

32. Ibid. See also Dahlgren's biography in Ida Hinman, *The Washington Sketch Book: A Society Souvenir* (Washington, DC: Hartman and Cadick, 1895), 97.

33. "Society's Endless Round," *WP*, January 28, 1893; "The Social World," *ES*, January 28, 1893.

34. Madeleine was not a formal student at the Harvard Annex, the precursor to Radcliffe College. With her literary connections, it is possible that Madeleine was a special or nondegree student, requiring only a recommendation letter for admission. Radcliffe College, Office of the Registrar Records, 1874–1966, RG XII, and Admissions Office. Records of the Admissions Office, 1869–1979, RG XI, Radcliffe College Archives, Schlesinger Library, Radcliffe Institute, Harvard University, Cambridge, MA.

35. "Personal Paragraphs," *WP*, June 3, 1891. There is no evidence that Madeleine went on this trip.

36. Clara K. Curtis, "Joseph Battell: An Appreciation," 6. Unpublished typescript, ca. 1915. Document courtesy of David Stameshkin.

37. Mrs. H. L. [Herbert] Bridgeman, "Bread Loaf," *Standard Union*, July 16, 1892.

38. H. B. Cornwall to Desha Breckinridge, March 20, 1894, Box 790, BFP.

39. Curtis, "Joseph Battell," 7.

40. "Another Name of National Note," *CE*, February 22, 1894.

41. "A Smile," *CE*, March 10, 1894.

42. *MPvB*, 27–29, 235–238; "Willie," *CE*, February 19, 1894; "A Smile," *CE*, March 10, 1894.

43. Accounts of this weekend tryst include "Tears," March 21, 1894; "Scenes," March 22, 1894; and "Smoothly," March 31, 1894, *CE*.

44. "Smoothly," *CE*, March 31, 1894.
45. Ibid.
46. Ibid.
47. Moore's testimony appears in "A Smile," *CE*, March 10, 1894.
48. *MPvB*, 78–79; "Madeline," *CE*, March 17, 1894; "Told Her Sad Story," *WP*, March 17, 1894.
49. *MPvB*, 80.

3. A Considerable Surprise

1. "Social Matters," *ES*, June 23, 1893; "Social and Personal Chat," *WP*, June 23, 1893; "W. C. P. Breckinridge to Marry," *NYT*, June 24, 1893; "Breckinridge-Pollard," *Frankfort Roundabout*, July 1, 1893; "Matrimonial Matters," *Interior Journal* (Stanford, KY), June 27, 1893; No Title, *CE*, June 24, 1893; "Under Fire Today," *ES*, April 2, 1894.
2. MP to WCPB, Letter, June 23, 1893, in "Madeline," *CE*, March 17, 1894.
3. WCBP to MP, Letter, June 27, 1893 in "Madeline," *CE*, March 17, 1894.
4. "Under Fire Today."
5. "His Marriage Certificate Filed," *WP*, March 17, 1894; "April Marriage," *ES*, March 17, 1894.
6. "April Marriage."
7. "Under Fire Today"; "Personal Mention," *Brooklyn (NY) Daily Eagle*, July 3, 1893.
8. MP to WCPB, ca. July 3, 1893, BFP.
9. "Madeline's Story," *ES*, March 16, 1894.
10. "His Marriage Certificate Filed"; "April Marriage."
11. [No Title] and "Breckinridge-Wing," *CJ*, July 16, 1893; "The Louisville Lady," *CE*, July 16, 1893; "Congressman Breckinridge," *Semi-Weekly Interior Journal* (Stanford, KY), July 18, 1893.
12. "Col. Breckinridge Wedded," *CJ*, July 19, 1893; "Earlier," *CE*, July 19, 1893; "Mr. Breckinridge's Marriage," [New York] *Sun*, July 19, 1893.
13. "Col. Breckinridge Wedded."
14. "Matrimonial," *Frankfort (KY) Roundabout*, July 22, 1893.
15. "Col. Breckinridge's Marriage a Surprise," *NYT*, July 21, 1893; "A Great Surprise," *CE*, July 17, 1893.
16. LW to Ella Scott Green, [July 26,1893], Green Family Papers, Series III, Box 1, Folder 4, Western Kentucky University, Bowling Green, Kentucky.
17. "The *Minneapolis* Afloat," *New-York Tribune*, August 13, 1893; "Another Big Cruiser," *Times* (Philadelphia), August 13, 1893; "All in Readiness for the Launch," *Philadelphia Inquirer*, August 12, 1893; "Increasing the Navy—Launching of the Battleship Minneapolis," *ES*, August 12, 1893.

18. On Edward Rumsey Wing, see Jonathan Jeffrey, "Serendipity," WKU Libraries Blog, January 16, 2019, https://library.blog.wku.edu/tag/edward -rumsey-wing/; Hinman, "Chapter II: The Etiquette of Society at the National Capital and Phases of Social Life," in *The Washington Sketch Book*, 25–41; and Dahlgren, *Etiquette of Social Life*, passim.

19. "Another Big Cruiser."

20. *MPvB*, 18–19; "Gentle Was Death's Touch and Jeremiah M. Wilson Obeyed Summons," *CE*, September 25, 1901.

21. "Miss Pollard's Petition," in *MPvB*, [9–12]; "The Petition," *CE*, August 13, 1893.

22. Mary Coombs, "Agency and Partnership: A Study of Breach of Promise Plaintiffs," *Yale Journal of Law and Feminism* 2 (1989): 1–24. See also Lawrence M. Friedman, "Crimes of Mobility," *Stanford Law Review* 43 (February 1991): 637–658; Denise Bates, *Breach of Promise to Marry: A History of How Jilted Brides Settled Scores* (Barnsley, UK: Pen and Sword, 2014); Saskia Lettmaier, *Broken Engagements: The Action for Breach of Promise of Marriage and the Feminine Ideal, 1800–1940* (Oxford University Press, 2010); Rebecca Tushnet, "Rules of Engagement," *Yale Law Journal* 107 (June 1998): 2582–2618; and Estelle Freedman, *Redefining Rape: Sexual Violence in the Era of Suffrage and Segregation* (Cambridge, MA: Harvard University Press, 2013), 35.

23. On the gold standard debate, see Wyatt Wells, "Rhetoric of the Standards: The Debate over Gold and Silver in the 1890s," *Journal of the Gilded Age and Progressive Era* 14, no. 1 (2015): 49–68, http://www.jstor.org /stable/43903057.

24. "Vows," *CE*, August 13, 1893.

25. "For Breach of Promise . . . Sensational Charges," *WP*, August 13, 1894; "Miss Pollard's Suit . . . Trifled," *Chicago Tribune*, August 13, 1894; "Romance with Bitter Realities," *CE*, August 14, 1894; "A Congressman in Trouble," *NYT*, August 13, 1893; "Breckinridge Sued," *Times* (Philadelphia), August 13, 1893.

26. E. D. E. N. Southworth to Charlotte Southworth Lawrence, August 15, 1893, Box 1, Emma Dorothy Eliza Nevitte Southworth Papers, MSS 50849, LOC; see Southworth's biography in Hinman, *The Washington Sketch Book*, 97.

27. William Lindsay to Eleanor Holmes Lindsay, August 15, 1893, Lindsay Family Papers, Box 11, Margaret King Library, University of Kentucky, Lexington [hereafter LFP].

28. "Mama" to Eleanor Lindsay, [August 17?], LFP.

29. "Mama" to Eleanor Lindsay, September 6, 1893, LFP.

30. "Mama" to Eleanor Lindsay, September 9, 1893; and William Lindsay to Eleanor Lindsay, September 1893, LFP.

31. "Vows Said to Have Been Broken," *CE*, August 13, 1894.

32. James C. Graves to WCPB, November 20, 1893, Box 788, BFP.

33. This depiction of Madeleine writing her account is summarized from C. E. Sears, "Miss Pollard's Story of Col. Breckinridge," *World* (New York), September 17, 1893.

34. Madeleine Valeria Pollard, "To the New York World," in Sears, "Miss Pollard's Story."

35. *RMP*, 29, 86–87, 241–244. See also "Report of Association for Works of Mercy [House of Mercy]," in *Annual Report of the Commissioners of the District of Columbia* (Washington, DC: Government Printing Office, 1894), 101, 234–235.

36. "Seeking Evidence," *CE*, August 19, 1893.

37. "Testimony for Miss Pollard," *ES*, September 2, 1893; "Outraged," *CE*, September 2, 1893; "Mrs. Blackburn Indignant," *CJ*, September 3, 1893.

38. CS to WCPB, February 8, 1894, Box 789, BFP.

4. No Mistakes

1. "Miss Pollard's Suit . . . Said to Have Been Settled," *CE*, December 24, 1893; "Fooling . . . Settlement Probably False," *CE*, December 26, 1893.

2. CS to Desha Breckinridge, January 8, 1894, Box 788, BFP.

3. Desha Breckinridge to WCPB, January 12, 1894, Bound Volume 463, BFP.

4. CS to WCPB, January 16, 1894, Box 788, BFP.

5. Ibid.; see also CS to WCPB, February 8, 1894, Box 789, BFP.

6. MAT to MMT, January 26, 1894, TFP.

7. Ibid.

8. MMT to MAT, January 25, 1894, TFP.

9. MAT to MMT, January 26, 1894.

10. "Omni Parker House: A Brief History," Omni Parker House, accessed November 13, 2023, https://www.omnihotels.com/-/media/images/hotels/bospar /hotel/pdfs/parker-house-history.pdf?la=en.

11. *RMP*, 12.

12. *RMP*, 10.

13. "Miss Pollard's Whereabouts," *WP*, October 1, 1893; "Revenge Not Her Motive," *WP*, October 2, 1893; *RMP*, 13, 15.

14. *RMP*, 16.

15. CS to WCPB, January 31, 1894, Box 789, BFP.

16. *RMP*, 15.

17. *RMP*, 19–20.

18. Period sources use *detective* and *spy* interchangeably. The *New York Herald* called her a "girl spy"; Stoll later verified that Jane had done "detective" work.

19. JAT to MAT, January 28, 1894, TFP.

20. *RMP*, 22–23.
21. "Revenge Not Her Motive."
22. *RMP*, 23, 24–25.

5. Pitiful Stories

1. Scenes depicting Jane's work in the House of Mercy and her encounters with Madeleine Pollard are drawn from the *RMP* and are cited with inclusive page numbers for the entire scene. See also the author's note on sources for citation conventions used in this work. Jane's first encounter with Sister Dorothea is drawn from *RMP*, 22–27.

2. *Annual Report of the Commissioners of the District of Columbia for the Year Ending June 30, 1894* (Washington, DC: Government Printing Office, 1894), 234.

3. Sister Dorothea uses this phrase in the *Annual Report of the Commissioners of the District of Columbia for the Year Ending June 30, 1896* (Washington, DC: Government Printing Office, 1896), 307.

4. *Annual Report of the Commissioners of the District of Columbia for the Year Ending June 30, 1894*, 234.

5. Jane's daily reports and notes to CS are embedded in the *RMP*, which is constructed as a series of letters from Agnes Parker to "Mr. X." The original reports do not survive.

6. Jane's return to the House of Mercy and first day are described in *RMP*, 28–36.

7. *RMP*, 33. Miss Dudley's first name is never mentioned in the *RMP*.

8. Day two, Wednesday, January 31, is covered in *RMP*, 36–41.

9. *RMP*, 31.

10. Thursday, February 1, is described in *RMP*, 41–49.

11. In 1895, four girls managed an escape. "Over the Garden Wall," *Morning Times* (Washington, DC), July 29, 1895; "Escaped over the Wall," *ES*, July 29, 1895.

12. *The Scarlet Letter* opened on September 12, 1892, at Daly's Theater in New York. See "Amusements: Mr. Mansfield and 'The Scarlet Letter,'" *NYT*, September 13, 1892.

13. Cora Elisabeth Burbank, *Business Correspondence or The Stenographer's Guide* (Boston: Beale Publishing Company, 1893), 54.

14. See Jane's complete letters to the "Doctor" and to "Julia," February 1, 1894, in *RMP*, 50–53.

15. CS to WCPB, February 8, 1894, Box 789, BFP.

16. The early record books of the House of Mercy do not survive. Mary O. Klein, archivist, Episcopal Diocese of Maryland, Baltimore, email message to author, March 28, 2017.

17. *Annual Report of the Commissioners of the District of Columbia for the Year Ending June 30, 1894*, 234.

18. See Priscilla Brewer, "The Chafing Dish and the College Girl: The Evolution and Meaning of the 'Spread' at Northern Women's Colleges, 1870–1910," in *Eating in Eden: Food and American Utopias*, ed. Etta Madden and Martha L. Finch (Lincoln: University of Nebraska Press, 2006), 203–219. See also Martha Cobb Sanford, "The Chafing Dish and the College Girl," *Woman's Home Companion*, April 1904.

19. "Lobster Newberg History and Recipe," What's Cooking America, accessed June 1, 2023, https://whatscookingamerica.net/history /lobsternewberghistory.htm; and Charles Ranhofer, *The Epicurean* (1894), Feeding America: The Historic American Cookbook Project, accessed June 1, 2023, https://d.lib.msu.edu/fa/26.

20. *RMP*, 47.

6. The Stenographer's Guide to Spying

1. February 2, 1894, is described in *RMP*, 53–59.

2. The New York fantasy is found in *RMP*, 53–54.

3. On Bly's race around the world, see Matthew Goodman, *Eighty Days: Nellie Bly and Elizabeth Bisland's History-Making Race Around the World* (New York: Ballantine Books, 2013).

4. Saturday, February 3, 1894, is covered in *RMP*, 60–63.

5. Sunday, February 4, 1894, is described in *RMP*, 63–66.

6. Monday, February 5, 1894, is found in *RMP*, 66–68.

7. Jane's final day as a resident of the House of Mercy is described in *RMP*, 68–71.

8. The Ebbitt House was a well-known boardinghouse and Washington's oldest saloon. https://www.ebbitt.com/about/, accessed August 14, 2023; *RMP*, 69.

9. *RMP*, 79–80.

7. So Darned Clever in My Work

1. Jane's lengthy report to CS: *RMP*, 71–76.

2. Agnes Parker [JAT] to Mr. X [CS], February 7, 1894, in *RMP*, 78–80.

3. JAT to MAT and "Daddy," February 6, 1894, TFP; JAT to MAT, February 11, 1894, TFP.

4. The shopping adventure is recorded in *RMP*, 81–82; Tom Lewis, *Washington: A History of Our National City* (New York: Basic Books, 2015), 211–212; "City and District: A New Palace of Commerce," *ES*, April 1, 1887. Woodward and Lothrop was initially known as the Boston Store or Boston Dry Goods House.

5. *RMP*, 81.

6. *RMP*, 81–82; Purchases also described in WCPB to Desha Breckinridge, February 9, 1894, Box 789, BFP.

7. *RMP*, 82–83.

8. "Railroads: Chesapeake and Ohio Railway [schedule]," *ES*, November 16, 1893.

9. Phyllis O'Daniel, V/P Mission Advancement, Masonic Homes of Kentucky, email to the author, August 10, 2015. Dudley, Horatio, and Rosalie were admitted on December 10, 1877. The boys left on January 31, 1887. Rosalie returned to their mother's care in 1880; consumption claimed her in 1884. See "Frankfort, June 7, 1884," *Frankfort Roundabout*, June 7, 1884.

10. Francis M. Cox, ed. and compiler, *Fifty-Third Congress [First Session], Official Congressional Directory for the Use of the United States Congress*, 2nd ed. (Washington, DC: Government Printing Office, 1894), 219, 322, 323; HathiTrust, accessed August 22, 2024, https://babel.hathitrust.org/cgi/pt?id =mdp.39015022758133&seq=19.

11. Burbank, *The Stenographer's Guide*, 69.

12. Dudley and JAT's afternoon together is described in *RMP*, 82–84; see also "Miss Pollard Again Pays a Visit to Cincinnati," *CE*, February 10, 1894; "Pollard vs. Breckinridge," *WP*, February 10, 1894; "Testimony for Miss Pollard: Examination of Witnesses at Cincinnati Resumed," *WP*, February 12, 1894.

13. See Nancy Baird, *Luke Pryor Blackburn: Physician, Governor, Reformer* (Lexington: University Press of Kentucky, 1979), and "Luke Pryor Blackburn," National Governors Association, accessed November 16, 2023, https://www.nga.org/governor/luke-pryor-blackburn/.

14. "Mrs. Blackburn Aids Miss Pollard," *Chicago Daily Tribune*, February 20, 1894; "Willie," *CE*, February 19, 1894; Desha Breckinridge to WCPB, February 6, 1894, Box 789, BFP.

15. JAT to MAT, February 11, 1894, TFP.

16. Ibid.

17. JAT to MAT and "Daddy," February 6, 1894, TFP.

18. JAT to MAT, February 11, 1894, TFP.

19. Mollie to MMT, February 19, 1894, TFP.

20. *RMP*, 79–80.

21. *RMP*, 125, 264–265; Jeremiah "Jere" Wilson was often referred to as "Judge Wilson." To avoid confusion with the trial judge, Andrew Bradley, I do not use that appellation. "Sarcasm," *CE*, April 13, 1894; "Smoothly," *CE*, March 31, 1894.

22. *RMP*, 89; James C. Klotter, *The Breckinridges of Kentucky* (Lexington: University Press of Kentucky, 1986), 166; "Mrs. Luke Blackburn," *CE*, March 25, 1894.

23. *RMP*, 103–104.

24. *RMP*, 92, 97, 106.

25. *RMP*, 96.

26. *RMP*, 85.

27. *RMP*, 76, 79.

28. *RMP*, 90, 92, 103, 106, and passim.

29. *RMP*, 91.

30. *RMP*, 92.

31. *RMP*, 92, notes Dudley Pollard roomed at 407 Fourth Street, NW. *RMP*, 106, states 407 D Street.

32. *RMP*, 106, 107.

33. *RMP*, 108.

34. *RMP*, 99. Broker S. V. White lost all his customers' money in March 1893. Nonetheless, Madeleine wrote him in June 1893 asking to invest more funds. White refused, writing that he was "deeply disappointed in my own affairs" and how, if he did manage to be reinstated, "he could not then take the management of money which its owners could not afford to lose." This note, he stated, indicated his "final" correspondence. S. V. White to MP, June 20, 1893, BFP.

35. *RMP*, 99–100.

36. *RMP*, 100.

37. *RMP*, 100–101.

38. JAT to CS, February 24, 1894, Box 790, BFP.

39. [Worthington] to JAT, February 28, 1894, Box 790, BFP.

40. Ibid.

41. Ibid.

42. JAT to MAT, March 2, 1894, TFP. See also *RMP*, 112, and [Worthington] to JAT, February 26, 1894, Box 790, BFP.

43. JAT to Mr. W[orthington], ca. early March 1894, TFP.

44. MAT to MMT, April 10, 1894, TFP.

45. MAT to MMT, February 22, 1894, TFP.

46. JAT to MAT, February 20, 1894.

47. JAT to MAT, February 23, 1894, TFP.

48. WCPB to Miss P, March 2, 1894, Box 790, BFP.

49. JAT to MAT, March 2, 1894, TFP. See Paul Kahan, *Amiable Scoundrel: Simon Cameron, Lincoln's Scandalous Secretary of War* (Lincoln: University of Nebraska Press, 2016), https://doi.org/10.2307/j.ctt1d8h8kh.

50. JAT to Worthington, undated, [early March], 1894, TFP.

51. *RMP*, 115.

52. *RMP*, 121.

53. Ibid.

54. Discussion of MP's relationship with Charles Dudley Warner: *RMP*, 122–124.

55. *RMP*, 124.

56. *RMP*, 125.

57. *RMP*, 131.

58. Ibid.

59. WCPB to Sophonisba Breckinridge, March 7, 1894, Box 790, BFP.

60. WCPB to CS, February 21, 1894, Box 790, BFP.

61. JAT to MAT, February 23, 1894, TFP.

8. A Fellow Woman, Ambitious and Smart

1. Scenes depicting the trial are drawn from *MPvB* and synthesized from newspaper coverage. These sources are cited collectively for each entire scene. See also the author's note on sources for citation conventions used in this work. The first day of the trial is recorded in *MPvB*, 17–23; "Started," CE, March 9, 1894; and "A Jury to Try It," ES, March 8, 1894.

2. *Interior Journal* (Stanford, KY), March 2, 1894.

3. Journalist George Alfred Townsend (1841–1914) reported for the *Enquirer* under the byline GATH. "Started." The CE, a morning paper, reported on courtroom events in the following day's paper.

4. JAT to MAT, March 10, 1894, TFP.

5. "Ex-Bailiff Lenard; An Offensive Officer," *Washington Bee*, April 21, 1894.

6. George Alfred Townsend, "A Smile Played the Features," CE, March 10, 1894.

7. JAT to Worthington, March 9, 1894, Box 790, BFP.

8. Trial coverage on day two, March 9, includes "A Smile Played"; "Madeline in Tears," ES, March 9, 1894; and *MPvB*, 23–40.

9. "A Smile Played."

10. The testimony that follows is drawn from "A Smile Played" and "Madeline in Tears."

11. See "Funeral of Mrs. Breckinridge," WP, July 17, 1892.

12. Townsend, "A Smile Played."

13. *MPvB*, 37; see Bertram Wyatt-Brown, *Southern Honor: Ethics and Behavior in the Old South* (New York: Oxford University Press, 2007).

14. *MPvB*, 46; "Madeline in Tears."

15. *RMP*, 132–136, covers Jane's visit to the House of Mercy on March 9 and subsequent report to CS.

16. JAT to MAT, March 10, 1894, TFP.

17. Ibid.

18. Jane's March 11 encounter is *RMP*, 136–140. On beef tea, see Lynne Olver, "Beef Tea," The Food Timeline, accessed November 16, 2023, https://www.foodtimeline.org/foodbeverages.html#beeftea; Fannie Farmer, *Food and Cookery for the Sick and Convalescent* (Boston: Little, Brown, and Company, 1905). Feeding America: The Historic American Cookbook Project, Michigan State University Libraries, accessed August 22, 2024, https://n2t.net/ark:/85335 /m5wh4p; see whiskey, 56, 60; beef teas, 83–84, 86–87.

19. *RMP*, 136; "Whiskey Milk Punch," accessed May 24, 2023, https://mrbostondrinks.com/recipes/whiskey-milk-punch-1935; and Farmer, *Food and Cookery*, 56, 60, 75.

20. *RMP*, 139.

9. The Only Chance a Girl Will Get

1. "Women Excluded," *ES*, March 12, 1894. Trial coverage of Monday, March 12, is also found in "Uppercuts," *CE*, March 13, 1894, and "Gave Way to Emotion," *WP*, March 13, 1894.

2. See Gloria Moldow, *Women Doctors in Gilded Age Washington: Race, Gender, and Professionalization* (Urbana: University of Illinois Press, 1987); and "History," Howard University, accessed August 31, 2024, https://howard.edu/about/history.

3. "Wanted—At Once—A Wet Nurse," *ES*, February 3, 1888; see also *RMP*, 238.

4. *RMP*, 143.

5. "Uppercuts." The bailiff is not named.

6. "They Had No Arms," *ES*, March 13, 1894; "Uppercuts."

7. JAT described March 12 in *RMP*, 140–141.

8. *WP*, March 13, 1894; "Women Excluded."

9. *RMP*, 140–141.

10. JAT described March 13 in *RMP*, 142–147.

11. "Sister Cecelia Proves a Stumbling Block," *CE*, March 14, 1894.

12. *Curtis Journal, 1894*, March 13, 1894, MS 0212, Kiplinger Research Library, DC History Center.

13. JAT likely read "They Had No Arms."

14. JAT and Ellis's conversation appeared in *RMP*, 145–147.

15. *RMP*, 146–147.

16. Day four of the trial, March 14, is reported in "Fighting," *CE*, March 15, 1894, and *MPvB*, 50–56.

17. M. Gertrude Burgoyne, May 29, 1885, St. Joseph Infant and Maternity Home, Admission Record; and Marie Gertrude Burgoyne, June 1, 1885, St. Joseph Infant and Maternity Home, Baptism Record, Archdiocese of Cincinnati Archives.

18. "Fighting."

19. "Counsel Unarmed," *Richmond (Virginia) Dispatch*, March 14, 1894.

20. Kate Perry Cain to Desha Breckinridge, March 5, 1894, Box 790, BFP.

21. See Judith Walzer Leavitt, "Under the Shadow of Maternity: American Women's Responses to Death and Debility Fears in Nineteenth-Century Childbirth," *Feminist Studies* 12, no. 1 (1986): 129–154, https://doi.org/10.2307/3177988.

22. See Nancy Schrom Dye and Daniel Blake Smith, "Mother Love and Infant Death, 1750–1920," *Journal of American History* 73, no. 2 (1986): 329–353, https://doi.org/10.2307/1908225.

23. Nannie Pollard's travel to daughter Mamie Pollard Struve is captured in "Bridgeport," February 7 and May 2, 1885, *Frankfort Roundabout*.

24. *Atchinson (Kansas) Daily Champion*, May 8, 1883; 1884 Columbus, Ohio, City Directory; 1885 Cincinnati, Ohio, City Directory.

25. "Fighting."

26. "Fighting"; "Counsel Unarmed."

27. JAT described March 14 in *RMP*, 147–148.

10. Hems to the Tops of Her Shoes

1. Testimony of March 15, 1894, is described in "Years of Guilt," *ES*, March 15, 1894; "Shifts the Scene to Lexington," *CE*, March 16, 1894," and "Pointed to Madeline," *WP*, March 16, 1894.

2. The surname was variously spelled *Gess, Guess, Gist,* and *Gest. Gist* appears on Sarah's gravestone in the family plot, African Cemetery No. 2, Lexington, Kentucky, and is the spelling of her enslaver/father's surname.

3. "Shifts."

4. "Pointed to Madeline."

5. "Sherriff's Sale," *North Alabamian* (Tuscumbia, AL), January 30, 1841.

6. Sixth Census of the United States, 1840. (NARA microfilm publication M704, Record Group 29). Records of the Bureau of the Census, NARA. On slavery, see Wilma King, *Stolen Childhood: Slave Youth in Nineteenth-Century America* (Bloomington: Indiana University Press, 2011); Deborah Gray White, *Ar'n't I a Woman? Female Slaves in the Plantation South* (New York: W. W. Norton, 1999); Susanna Delfino, *Bonds of Womanhood: Slavery and the Decline of a Kentucky Plantation* (Lexington: University Press of Kentucky, 2021); and Marion B. Lucas, *A History of Blacks in Kentucky: From Slavery to Segregation, 1760–1891*, 2nd ed. (Lexington: University Press of Kentucky, 2003).

7. Seventh Census of the United States, 1850 (NARA microfilm publication M432, Record Group 29). Records of the Bureau of the Census, NARA; Aaron Obid [Obey] and Elizabeth [Gist] Obid, "Declaration of Marriages," Book 1, p. 1, married October 11, 1854, declared May 22, 1866, Fayette County Clerk's Office, Lexington, Kentucky; Deed Book 37, pp. 250–251, April 30, 1862, Fayette County Clerk's Office.

8. Their brother Robert is absent in Lexington records, and his fate is unknown. "Tuner," Dictionary of Old Occupations, accessed August 22, 2024, https://www.familyresearcher.co.uk/glossary/Dictionary-of-Old-Occupations -Index.html.

9. See, for example, Maryjean Wall, *Madam Belle: Sex, Money and Influence in a Southern Brothel* (Lexington: University Press of Kentucky, 2014).

10. The seduction at Gist's home is drawn from "Pointed to Madeline"; "Shifts"; "An Outcast," *CE*, March 20, 1894; *MPvB*, 76, 82, 93–94, 185–187.

11. "Pointed to Madeline."

12. Ibid.

13. Mary Wilson and Mary Scott. The identify of the third Mary is unclear—there are several possibilities among Gist's extended family and circle of friends. CS to WCPB, February 8, 1894, Box 789, BFP.

14. "Shifts." Other accounts indicate the boardinghouse matron was a Mrs. Emory.

15. JAT's March 15th encounter is described in *RMP*, 149–154.

16. *RMP*, 154.

17. Ibid.

18. JAT to MAT, March 17, 1894, TFP.

19. *RMP*, 152.

11. So like a Woman

1. Madeleine's first day of testimony, Friday, March 16, is drawn from "Madeline," *CE*, March 17, 1894; "Madeline's Story," *ES*, March 16, 1894.

2. The 1870 Federal census lists her age as seven and living in Crab Orchard; the 1880 Federal census captures Madeleine living in Pittsburgh with the Cowans at age sixteen, born "about 1864." Ninth Census of the United States, 1870 (Microfilm Publication M593, Record Group 29); and Tenth Census of the United States, 1880 (Microfilm Publication T9, Record Group 29), Records of the Bureau of the Census, NARA.

3. "Madeline's Story."

4. "Madeline."

5. JAT described Friday, March 16, in *RMP*, 154–162. See also W[orthington] to Miss P [JAT], March 16, 1894, Box 790, BFP.

6. "Mr. Breckinridge's Marriage," *ES*, March 16, 1894; "The Cause of Delay," *ES*, March 16, 1894; *RMP*, 155.

7. JAT described Saturday, March 17, in *RMP*, 162–166.

8. "Pollard's Confession," *ES*, March 17, 1894; *RMP*, 162–163.

9. *RMP*, 163–164.

10. JAT to MAT March 17, 1894, TFP.

11. Sunday, March 18, is described in *RMP*, 166–170.

12. [Bridgeman, Mrs. Herbert], "Breadloaf," *Standard Union* (Brooklyn, NY), July 16, 1892; and "Miss Pollard," *Standard Union*, March 17, 1894. Although Madeleine knew the identity of the author, both articles were published anonymously. Breckinridge was desperate to identify the author.

See WCPB to "Editor" [Herbert Bridgeman], March 18, 1894, and WCPB to Mrs. Bridges [*sic*], March 19, 1894, Box 790, BFP.

13. The erroneous attribution, and Madeleine's subsequent correction, is found in "A Talented Girl," *Lexington Herald-Leader*, July 28, 1888, and "Denies the Soft Impeachment," *Lexington Herald-Leader*, August 13, 1888.

14. *RMP*, 170.

15. JAT to MMT, March 10, 1894, TFP.

16. Ibid.

17. JAT to MMT, March 18, 1894, TFP.

18. Monday, March 19, is drawn from "An Outcast," *CE*, March 20, 1894; and "Madeline's Story," *ES*, March 19, 1894.

19. *Washington Bee*, March 24, 1894.

20. "Tears," *CE*, March 21, 1894.

21. Ibid.

22. "An Outcast."

23. JAT at the House of Mercy on March 19: *RMP*, 171–182.

24. *RMP*, 175.

25. *RMP*, 177–178.

26. Madeleine's third day of testimony is drawn from "Deluded Mr. Rodes," *ES*, March 20, 1894; "Tears."

12. Happiest Woman in Washington

1. "Breckinridge-Wing," *Louisville Courier-Journal*, July 16, 1893.

2. Thomas D. Clark, *Footloose in Jacksonian America: Robert W. Scott and His Agrarian World* (Frankfort: Kentucky Historical Society, 1989), 166–167.

3. On Wing's dull guest, see "King, John Floyd," *History, Art and Archives, US House of Representatives*, accessed November 17, 2023, https://history .house.gov/People/Listing/K/KING,-John-Floyd-(K000206)/.

4. LW to WCPB, February 14, 1893, Box 786, BFP.

5. LW to WCPB, February 20, 1893, Box 786, BFP.

6. LW to WCPB, February 23, 1893, Box 786, BFP.

7. LW to WCPB, February 28 [?], 1893, Box 786, BFP.

8. LW to WCPB, March 2, 1893, Box 786, BFP.

9. Ella Scott Green to WCPB, March 3, 1893, Box 786, BFP.

10. LW to WCPB, March 20, 1893, Box 786, BFP.

11. LW to WCPB, March 21, 1893, Box 786, BFP.

12. LW to WCPB, March 24, 1893, Box 786, BFP.

13. Ibid.

14. LW to WCPB, March 28, 1893, Box 786, BFP.

15. LW to WCPB, April 20, 1893, Box 786, BFP.

16. *MPvB*, 232.

17. LW to WCPB, May 18, 1893, Box 786, BFP.

18. LW to WCPB, May 22, 1893, Box 786, BFP.

19. LW to WCPB, May 23, 1893, Box 786, BFP.

20. LW to WCPB, May 26, 1893, Box 786, BFP.

21. LW to WCPB, May 27, 1893, Box 786, BFP.

22. LW to WCPB, May 26, 1893, Box 786, BFP.

23. Ibid.

24. LW to WCPB, May 30, 1893, Box 786, BFP.

25. Physician (name unknown) to WCPB, May 30, 1893, Box 786, BFP.

26. LW to WCPB, June 4, 1893, Box 786, BFP.

27. LW to WCPB, June 5, 1893, Box 786, BFP.

28. "A True Story," *CE*, March 20, 1894; "Said He Had No Wife," *WP*, March 20, 1894.

29. LW to WCPB, June 26, 1893, Box 786, BFP.

30. LW to WCPB, June 27, 1893, Box 786, BFP.

31. LW to WCPB, June 28, 1893, Box 786, BFP.

32. LW to WCPB, June 27, 1893, Box 786, BFP.

33. "The Marriage Record Wanted," *CE*, March 10, 1894; "A Secret Marriage," *CE*, March 14, 1894; "He Was Married," *CE*, March 17, 1894; "Breckinridge Admits the Truth" and "Confirmed," *CE*, March 17, 1894.

34. Tuesday, March 20, is drawn from "Deluded Mr. Rodes," *ES*, March 20, 1894; "An Abrupt Question," *WP*, March 21, 1894; and "Tears," *CE*, March 21, 1894.

35. "A Troublesome Error," *CE*, March 17, 1894.

36. "Tears."

37. Ibid.

38. JAT's encounter with Madeleine on March 20 appears in *RMP*, 189–191.

39. JAT to Worthington, March 20, 1894, Box 790, BFP.

40. Ibid.; see also Worthington to JAT, March 20, 1894, Box 790, BFP.

41. JAT and MP on March 21, 1894: *RMP*, 191–194.

42. Court on March 21 is drawn from "Scenes," *CE*, March 22, 1894; and "The Other Side," *ES*, March 20, 1894.

43. "Scenes."

13. French Dressing

1. L. R. D. [CS] to JAT, March 21, 1894, Box 790, BFP.

2. Ibid.

3. Ibid; JAT to MAT, March 22, 1894, TFP.

4. On the popularity of French cooking, Laura Shapiro, *What She Ate: Six Remarkable Women and the Food That Tells Their Stories* (New York: Viking, 2017), 68–69; Harvey Levenstein, *Revolution at the Table: The Transformation*

of the American Diet (Berkeley: University of California Press, 2003), 14–15, 18. On French dressing (vinaigrette), "French Dressing and Vinaigrette," Food Timeline, accessed August 30, 2021, https://www.foodtimeline.org/foodsalads .html#frenchdressing; Mrs. Emma P. Ewing, *Cookery Manuals No. 3, Salad and Salad Making* (Chicago: Fairbanks, Palmer, and Company, 1884), 13–14. On salad greens, Robert Dirks, *Food in the Gilded Age: What Ordinary Americans Ate* (New York: Rowman and Littlefield, 2016), 74.

5. The evening of March 22 is recorded in *RMP*, 195–198.

6. On the lewd depositions, see "A Point," *CE*, March 26, 1894; "*Scathing*," *CE*, March 27, 1894.

7. WCPB's testimony on March 29 is drawn from "Denials," *CE*, March 30, 1894; *MPvB*, 168–184; "His Story Begun," *ES*, March 29, 1894.

8. JAT's description of March 29 at the House of Mercy is found in *RMP*, 229–230.

9. L. R. D [CS] to JAT, March 29, 1894, Box 790, BFP.

10. JAT to MAT, April 1, 1894, TFP.

11. WCPB's testimony of March 30 is drawn from "Smoothly," *CE*, March 31, 1894; "His Story in Detail," *WP*, March 31, 1894; "More of His Story," *ES*, March 30, 1894; *MPvB*, 184–204.

12. JAT and MP on March 29 and 30, 1894: *RMP*, 229–234.

13. L. R. D. [CS] to JAT, March 29, 1894, Box 790, BFP.

14. *RMP*, 230.

15. *RMP*, 232.

16. "A Poet" to MP, March 19, 1894, in *RMP*, 201.

17. L. R. D. [CS] to JAT, March 29, 1894, Box 790, BFP; JAT to MAT, April 1, 1894, TFP.

18. Jane may have been romantically interested in Max. In a letter to Jane written in 1895, Max apologized for his actions the previous fall (1894): "It is a horrible thing to appear perhaps like a cad in the eyes of a dear, sweet girl who had every right to my love; it is a more horrible thing to sacrifice one's life to duty and unhappiness despite the brightest prospects that had to be set aside for the sake of honor and duty." Max De Lippman to JAT, May 3, 1895, TFP.

19. JAT to MAT, April 1, 1894, TFP.

20. Ibid.

21. *RMP*, 237. On the relatives' testimony: *MPvB*, 243; "Mystery in a Name," *ES*, April 5, 1894.

14. Treacherous Type-Writers, She-Fanatics, and the Short-Haired Women of Boston

1. "Under Fire Today," *ES*, April 2, 1894. The depiction of April 2 is drawn from "Under Fire Today" and "The Colonel," *CE*, April 3, 1894.

2. "The Colonel."

3. WCPB to JAT, February 26, 1894, Box 790, BFP.

4. *MPvB*, 210–212.

5. *RMP*, 239.

6. MP's revelations to JAT: *RMP*, 237–240.

7. MP's note: *RMP*, 238–239.

8. JAT's report to WCPB: *RMP*, 237–240.

9. "Acts of Deception," *ES*, April 4, 1894; "Jere," *CE*, April 5, 1894.

10. *RMP*, 240.

11. Ibid.

12. Testimony of April 3 is drawn from "Letters," *CE*, April 4, 1894; "Letters to Louise," *ES*, April 3, 1894.

13. *RMP*, 246.

14. "Louise Lowell," *Register of Civil, Military, and Naval Service*, 1895, vol. 1, Treasury Department, page 83; "Louise Lowell," RG 56, Entry A1 210, Applications and Recommendations for Positions in the Washington, DC, Offices of the Treasury Department, Box 356, NARA; *MPvB*, 218.

15. "Letters."

16. "Letters to Louise"; "Letters"; *MPvB*, 217.

17. JAT's encounter with Sister Dorothea: *RMP*, 241–244.

18. *RMP*, 244–246.

19. William E. Hickox, *The Correspondent's Manual: A Praxis for Stenographers, Typewriter Operators, and Clerks* (Boston: Lee and Shepard, 1902), 124.

20. Burbank, *The Stenographer's Guide*, 21.

21. *RMP*, 245–246.

22. Depiction of April 4 drawn from *MPvB*, 228–241; "Jere"; "Acts of Deception."

23. "X" [CS] to Miss Parker [JAT], April 5 [4], 1894, in *RMP*, 253–254.

24. Ibid.; "Jere."

25. JAT to MAT, April 12, 1894, TFP.

26. "X to Miss Parker."

27. JAT to MMT, March 28, 1894, TFP.

28. Agnes Parker to X, April 5 [4], 1894, in *RMP*, 254–255. It appears JAT misdated this exchange of letters between her and Stoll in the *RMP*. Breckinridge dropped his bombshell on April 4, not the fifth.

29. JAT and MP's conversation of April 4: *RMP*, 247–252. Judge Bradley's comment, *MPvB*, 228.

30. *RMP*, 254–255.

31. "White Frost," *CE*, March 29, 1894.

32. "Rankin L. Rosselle," *CE*, March 30, 1894; "Rozell's Story Denied," *ES*, March 30, 1894.

33. Day 20 of the trial is drawn from *MPvB*, 241–252; "Mystery in a Name," *ES*, April 5, 1894; "Constant," *CE*, April 6, 1894. Brown was accompanied by activist Sarah Doan LaFetra, see "Mrs. Sarah Doan LaFetra," in Ida Hinman, *The Washington Sketchbook: A Society Souvenir* (Washington, DC: Hartman and Cadick, 1895), 97.

34. Martha McClellan Brown to "Editor," April 1894, MS-147, Martha McClellan Brown and Rev. William Kennedy Brown Papers, Special Collections and Archives, University Libraries, Wright State University, Dayton, Ohio.

35. Ibid.

36. WCPB to M. Layson, April 5, 1894, Box 790, BFP.

37. WCPB to Dr. George Graves, April 24, 1894, Box 790, BFP.

38. John F. Phillips to WCPB, April 16, 1994, Box 790, BFP.

39. The final day of testimony: *MPvB*, 252–257; "Nearing the End," *ES*, April 6, 1894; "Denials," *CE*, April 7, 1894.

40. JAT and MP's conversation, April 7: *RMP*, 255–259. On gender and color, see Clair Bates, "Should We Not Dress Girls in Pink?," *BBC Magazine*, BBC, January 8, 2009, http://news.bbc.co.uk/2/hi/uk_news/magazine/7817496 .stm; Jeanne Maglaty, "When Did Girls Start Wearing Pink?," *Smithsonian Magazine*, April 7, 2011, https://www.smithsonianmag.com/arts-culture/when -did-girls-start-wearing-pink-1370097/?no-ist=; Jo B. Paoletti, *Pink and Blue: Telling the Boys from the Girls in America* (Bloomington: Indiana University Press, 2012), accessed October 7, 2023, ProQuest Ebook Central.

41. *RMP*, 260.

42. *RMP*, 256–257.

43. *RMP*, 251, 258–260.

44. *RMP*, 153.

45. JAT to MAT, March 2, 1894, TFP.

15. The Eve of My Waterloo

1. *ES*, April 9, 1894.

2. "Public Opinion," *Washington Bee*, March 24, 1894.

3. "Small Bees with Large Stingers," *Washington Bee*, March 24, 1894.

4. *RMP*, 264.

5. Ibid.

6. *RMP*, 265.

7. "Snow Five Feet Deep," *ES*, April 9, 1894.

8. "Hard Words Used," *ES*, April 10, 1894; *RMP*, 267.

9. "Scenes," *CE*, April 11, 1894.

10. Ibid.

11. Ibid.

12. Ibid.

13. "Hard Words Used."

14. "Scenes."

15. Ibid.

16. JAT visits MP, April 10: *RMP*, 268–271.

17. "Bold Ben," *CE*, April 12, 1894.

18. Ibid. A century later, neuroscientists explain the "freeze" response. See Victoria Wilson, "Neuroscience Shows Why Sex Assault Victims 'Freeze.' It's Not Consent," Duke Research Blog, July 6, 2023, https://researchblog .duke.edu/2023/07/06/neuroscience-shows-why-sex-assault-victims-freeze-its -not-consent/; Ebani Dhawan and Patrick Haggard, "Neuroscience Evidence Counters a Rape Myth," *Nature Human Behaviour* 7 (2023): 835–838, https://doi.org/10.1038/s41562-023-01598-6.

19. "Bold Ben."

20. *RMP*, 293–294.

21. "Butterworth," *CE*, April 13, 1894.

22. Ibid.

23. Ibid.

24. JAT and MP, April 12: *RMP*, 294–299.

25. *RMP*, 298–299.

26. "Sarcasm," *CE*, April 14, 1894; "For Miss Pollard," *ES*, April 13, 1894.

27. A comic opera made use of Butterworth's allusion to Breckinridge as Mary's lamb. "Madeleine; or, The Magic Kiss" played in Boston and Chicago following the trial. In the opera, "Mary Had a Little Lamb" contained references to Congress, the gold standard debate, the congressman's oratory, and Breckinridge's antipathy toward women's rights activists. Julian Edwards, "Songs and Selections from Madeleine, or, the Magic Kiss," Sheet Music (Cincinnati, OH: John Church Company, 1894), Lester Levy Sheet Music Collection, The Sheridan Libraries, Johns Hopkins University, Baltimore, MD, https://levysheetmusic.mse.jhu.edu/collection/142/040.

28. "For Miss Pollard."

29. JAT's last visit to MP at the House of Mercy, Friday, April 13: *RMP*, 299–305.

30. *RMP*, 305.

16. The Trouble with All Detective Stories

1. *RMP*, 317.

2. "Miss Pollard Wins," *Baltimore Sun*, April 16, 1894.

3. "Miss Pollard," *CE*, April 15, 1894.

4. Ibid.

5. "Flowers for Mr. Wilson," *ES*, April 14, 1894. The flowers were delivered to the courtroom during the noon recess. Marshal Wilson moved them to his private office.

6. The WPL's activities were discussed in "Women," *CE*, April 16, 1894.

7. Ibid.

8. *RMP*, 306.

9. JAT to MAT, ca. April 15, 1894, TFP.

10. JAT's April 19 visit: *RMP*, 313–320.

11. "Madeline's Letter," *Kennebec (Maine) Journal*, April 17, 1894; also printed in the *Atlanta Constitution*. The New York paper indicated as the source of the letter has not been identified.

12. "Miss Pollard and the Stage," *Brooklyn Daily Eagle*, August 13, 1894.

13. "The Elevation of the Stage," *NYT*, September 16, 1894.

14. JAT's last visit with MP concludes the *RMP*, 327–336.

15. *RMP*, 333. Fayette Lexington, *The Celebrated Case of Col. W. C. P. Breckinridge and Madeline Pollard* (Chicago: The Current Events Publishing Company, 1894). The pseudonymous author's name is a play on Fayette County, where Lexington is located.

16. Nevada [McNeill], *A Marriage above Zero* (New York: G. W. Dillingham, 1894), 19, Internet Archive, https://archive.org/details/marriage abovezeroooomcne_t9n4.

17. *RMP*, 331.

18. Mary Coffey, 1303 F Street, NW, Washington, DC, *Business Directory* (1893), 79.

19. *RMP*, 335.

20. JAT to MAT, ca. April 15, 1894.

21. MAT to MMT, April 26, 1894, TFP.

22. JAT to MAT, ca. April 15, 1894.

23. JAT to WCPB, May 28, 1894, Box 791, BFP.

24. Sophonisba Breckinridge to WCPB, June 2, 1894, Box 791, BFP.

25. In the collection of the Lexington (KY) Public Library. Access the digitized, transcribed e-book at https://lexpublib.overdrive.com/media/1719737.

26. Jim Kelly [James F. Kelly] to MMT, June 29, 1894, TFP.

27. "Miss Pollard as She Is," *New York Herald*, June 24, 1894.

28. "Miss Pollard as She Is," *WP*, June 24, 1894.

29. "The New Books," *Times-Picayune* (New Orleans), August 6, 1894.

30. "Current Literature," *Inter Ocean* (Chicago), August 4, 1894.

31. Jim Kelly [James F. Kelly] to MMT, June 29, 1894, TFP.

32. Ibid.

33. Advertisement, "Book Department," D. B. Loveman Co., *Chattanooga Daily Times*, July 22, 1894.

34. Jim Kelly [James F. Kelly] to MMT, ca. July 4, 1894, TFP.

35. JAT to MMT, September 14, 1894, TFP.

36. CS, Certified Statement, November 15, 1894, TFP; JAT to MMT, November 11 and November 19, 1894, TFP.

37. "Under the River," *Portland (Maine) Daily Press*, August 24, 1894.

38. "Lincoln County: Wiscasset," *Lewiston (Maine) Weekly Journal*, October 4, 1894; also in the *Lewiston (Maine) Sun Journal*, September 27, 1894, and the *Bangor Daily Whig and Courier*, September 29, 1894.

39. JAT to MMT, September 14, 1894.

40. Ibid.

Epilogue

1. On women agitating against Breckinridge supporters, see William Patterson to Ella Scott Green, November 10, 1894, Letter 27, Series II, Box 1, Folder 7, Green Family Papers (MSS 49), Western Kentucky University.

2. JAT to MAT, April 1, 1894, TFP; on women's impact on Breckinridge's campaign, see Paul Fuller, "An Early Venture of Kentucky Women in Politics: The Breckinridge Congressional Campaign of 1894," *Filson Club History Quarterly* 63, no. 2 (April 1989): 224–242.

3. On the full scope of W. C. P. Breckinridge's life, see James C. Klotter, *The Breckinridges of Kentucky* (Lexington: University Press of Kentucky, 1986), 137–185.

4. See letters from Wing in October 1918, Series IV, Box 2, Folder 4, Green Family Papers, Western Kentucky University, Bowling Green.

5. "Mrs. Louise Scott Breckinridge Dies," *Lexington Herald*, April 29, 1920.

6. On the life of Sophonisba Breckinridge, see Anya Jabour, *Sophonisba Breckinridge: Championing Women's Activism in Modern America* (Champaign: University of Illinois Press, 2019), accessed November 14, 2023, ProQuest Ebook Central; and Klotter, *The Breckinridges of Kentucky*, 189–207.

7. JAT to MAT, December 11, 1904, TFP.

8. Correspondence between Sophonisba Breckinridge and Herbert Putnam, Librarian of Congress, and Worthington Ford, Chief of the Library of Congress Manuscript Division, is found in the Sophonisba Breckinridge Papers, ca. 1904–1906, within the BFP. Herbert Putnam described the newly received Breckinridge Collection in *Report of the Librarian of Congress and Report of the Superintendent of the Library Building and Grounds* (Washington, DC: Government Printing Office, 1905), 22–25.

9. MAT to MMT, March 8 and March 17, 1896, TFP.

10. JAT to MAT, December 30, 1898, TFP; on Kehew's accomplishments, see "Mrs. Mary Morton Kehew Is Dead," *Boston Globe*, February 13, 1918.

11. JAT to MAT, December 20, 1900, TFP.

12. H. W. Gossard to JAT, April 4, 1903, TFP.

13. JAT to MAT, December 7, 1905, TFP.

14. "Charles H. Stoll," Find a Grave, accessed November 10, 2023, https://www.findagrave.com/memorial/231759880/charles-henry-stoll.

15. Obituary [1899], *Bath (Maine) Independent*, undated clipping, TFP.

16. Jane Armstrong Tucker, comp., *The State of Maine Cook Book* ([Maine]: The Democratic Women of Maine, ca. 1925; facsimile of original, Carlisle, MA: Applewood Books, 2009).

17. "Miss Jane Tucker, Sea Captain's Daughter, Dies," *Portland (Maine) Press Herald*, April 29, 1964.

18. No title, *Interior Journal* (Stanford, KY), July 28, 1899; "Records of Mares of the Past and Present as Speed Producers," *Cincinnati Enquirer*, May 24, 1914; *The Register of the American Saddle-Horse Breeders' Association*, vol. 1 (Chicago: American Saddle-Horse Breeders' Association, 1908), 316; *American Berkshire Record* (Springfield, IL: American Berkshire Association, 1903), 20, 258; *Herd Book of the Maine State Jersey Cattle Association*, vol. VIII (Pub. by the Association, 1898), 41; *Engineering and Mining Journal*, vol. 62 (New York: Scientific Publishing Company, 1896), 206.

19. See, for example, "About New York," *CE*, July 27, 1895.

20. Monica Lewinsky, "Shame and Survival," *Vanity Fair*, June 2014, 146.

21. On how I recovered Madeleine Pollard's post-scandal life, see Elizabeth DeWolfe, "'Not Ruined, but Hindered': Rethinking Scandal, Re-examining Transatlantic Sources, and Recovering Madeleine Pollard," *Legacy: A Journal of American Women Writers* 31 (2014): 300–310.

22. 1901 and 1911 England, Wales and Scotland Census Transcription, accessed November 8, 2014, Findmypast.co.uk.

23. Madeleine Pollard's 1917 passport indicates Lawrence Mansions as her address.

24. Correspondence of Margaret T. Tjader is found in the Papers of Frank N. D. Buchman, Boxes 90–92, Records of Moral Re-Armament, Inc., MSS 56671, LOC; *RMP*, 299.

25. Passenger Lists, Arrivals, New York, 1928, Ancestry.com.

26. Dorothy Scarborough Papers, Baylor University, The Texas Collection.

27. Caprice Woodburn, phone call with the author, August 3, 2015. The interviewee is Dudley Pollard's great-granddaughter. Her grandmother told stories of the scandal but had no knowledge of what happened to Madeleine and never met her. The stories were told to explain how Dudley, a Southern gentleman, ended up in New York City.

28. Madeleine Pollard, Will, September 26, 1938. HM Courts and Tribunals Service, Leeds Probate Registry, Leeds, England.

29. Frances Faviell, *A Chelsea Concerto* (London: Cassell and Company, 1959), 2.

30. "Biggest Air-Raid Test: Chelsea Hides Itself from Enemy in Quick Time," *Manchester Guardian*, June 20, 1939.

31. Josephine May Oakman, Diary, September 14, 1940, Typescript, Local Studies Collection, Kensington and Chelsea Library, London. See also Faviell, *A Chelsea Concerto*, 113–115.

32. "Bomb Incidents in Chelsea. In Street Order," Josephine May Oakman, compiler, June 4, 1949, Local Studies Collection, Kensington and Chelsea Library, London.

33. Faviell, *A Chelsea Concerto*, 179.

34. Oakman, Diary, October 21, 1940.

35. The last entry for Hassard's phone number appears in the spring 1940 phone book. Phone books were published in the spring (February) and fall (November). British Phone Books, February 1940, p. 1052, BT Archives, London.

36. Violet Hassard's 1943 will recorded her address as 6 Madeira Road, Streatham. The Probate Registry referenced her residence as Cliff House and "formerly of Madeira Road, Streatham, London." Probate Register, September 20, 1945, and Violet Emily Hassard, Will, May 22, 1943, HM Courts and Tribunals Service, Leeds Probate Registry, Leeds, England.

37. Violet Emily Hassard, Will, May 22, 1943.

38. Pollard left her entire to estate to her "beloved friend" Violet Emily Hassard. As Hassard had died, Pollard's estate, which at the time of her death included Hassard's estate, went to her second heir, Vida Dopping, Violet's niece. Madeleine Pollard, Will, September 26, 1938, HM Courts and Tribunals Service, Leeds Probate Registry, Leeds, England.

INDEX